Chasing
Chaos

Chasing Chaos

A Foreign Correspondent's Memoir

Sean Kelly

Outskirts Press, Inc.
Denver, Colorado

Chasing Chaos
A Foreign Correspondent's Memoir
All Rights Reserved.
Copyright © 2010 Sean Kelly
v7.0

Cover photo by Brenton Kelly. Mandela photo from Oryx Archive, Capetown South Africa. Author's back cover photo by Paul Rifkin.

Outskirts Press, Inc.
http://www.outskirtspress.com

ISBN: 978-1-4327-4552-3

Outskirts Press and the "OP" logo are trademarks belonging to Outskirts Press, Inc.

PRINTED IN THE UNITED STATES OF AMERICA

To Helen Bodurtha Picard

For once. For now. For all time.

Contents

Foreword

This is a book about chaotic events and journalists who cover them. In particular, it is about myself. I was lucky enough to be a foreign correspondent when the going was still pretty good. I covered chaos in Africa, Asia, and Latin America when instant communication had yet to be invented. Broadcast correspondents often had to book radio circuits 24 hours in advance. Communication with editors was largely by telegraph or telex, a more genteel process than by telephone since the participants were at least separated by the written word. Altogether, the personal risks were about the same, but I think we probably had more fun working through them.

Admittedly, this is written with the benefit of much hindsight. But there is little I would do differently, given the chance to do it again. Except of course to try and do it better.

1.

Ambushed in Zimbabwe, Deathlisted in El Salvador

Zimbabwe, in January 1980, was having trouble being born.

Still called Rhodesia and torn apart by ten years
of liberation struggle, the former British colony was
being ruled temporarily by a London-appointed
caretaker government. Democratic elections were
due to take place in April. In the meantime, a hast-
ily-arranged cease-fire was beginning to fall apart.
I had flown in from Nairobi to cover the crisis for
the Voice of America, an international broadcasting
organization.

Clearly some risks would be involved, but I didn't
think too much about them at the time.

Chasing chaos, which had become a sort of career
choice for me, had frequently involved risks. I first
encountered them in the Congo and Nigeria during

the 1960s. By the time I reached Laos, Cambodia and Vietnam in the 1970s, some degree of risk was virtually assumed.

I had become — mostly by default, it seemed to me — a foreign correspondent who tended to specialize in reporting small wars and revolutions — low intensity events, for the most part, usually in distant places with names difficult to pronounce.

None of this was by design. I was born into a newspaper family, but I fled the family newspaper, as well as the small Southern California community in which it was published. Chasing chaos and conflict became my ticket out of town and I willingly accepted it. Over a period of time I came to view taking personal risks as part of a dues-paying process. It went along with the rest of a foreign correspondent's territory.

What brought me to Zimbabwe in January 1980 was the long struggle to free the former British colony from minority white rule which finally ended in a victory for black nationalism. It was a conflict I had witnessed at its earliest stages, as a young diplomat posted to Africa in the 1950s. Now Britain had finally returned to oversee the transition from white Rhodesia to black Zimbabwe and I had come back to report the story as a journalist. The key to this process was the April 1980 general election that ended up bringing Robert Mugabe to power.

The cease fire negotiated by the British required

Mugabe's guerrilla forces to turn themselves in — with their weapons — at special assembly points being set up around the country by the British army. Many of Mugabe's soldiers were showing up with their weapons, but significant numbers were not.

Foxtrot was the name given by the British to one of these assembly points in Eastern Zimbabwe, near the border with Mozambique — an area that had seen some of the bitterest fighting during the civil war. I drove there on January 16, 1980 with Gregory Jaynes of the New York Times and Michael Farr of the London Daily Telegraph.

We wanted to look Foxtrot over. We hoped to talk to the British who were supervising the cease-fire, and, if possible, we wanted to meet with the guerrillas themselves. Our trip had been approved, by military and civil authorities in Salisbury (since renamed Harare) who asked us to stop in Umtali (since renamed Mutare) to get the latest security up-date from the local British commander. He used his wall map to show us how to reach Assembly Point Foxtrot by road and he assured us that the way had been cleared of land mines.

"We are sending food convoys down that road in heavy lorries nearly every day," he said. "There has been no sign of any terrorist activity, but," he stressed, "you proceed at your own risk, of course."

"Of course," we agreed as we headed off to Foxtrot in the New York Times Alfa Romeo sedan.

The car was at least ten years old, but it still had a bright blue paint job. Its four-speed transmission was rather worn and the shift from first gear to second often involved some searching around. After unintionally ending up in fourth gear and stalling the car several times, Jaynes asked me to drive. Farr sat in the back seat and gave us the benefit of his accumulated experience in Zimbabwe. He had actually been in the country several weeks longer than ourselves — a fact he was not reluctant to point out to us from time to time.

We turned off the main east-west highway at the town of Rusape and headed south on a dirt road through a farming area the Rhodesians called the Sabi Tribal Trust Land. We had driven for about twenty minutes when we crossed over a hilltop and down into a small village. Several men were standing by the side of the road, flagging us down. I noticed they were not wearing uniforms and they were carrying AK-47 assault rifles which they were pointing at us.

We stopped and quickly identified ourselves, but remained in the car. One of the men then became very agitated, particularly when Farr tried to speak to him in the Shona language. He flicked the AK-47's bayonet into position and ordered us out of the vehicle.

"If we leave the car, we are dead," Farr whispered, "Let's move the hell out of here!"

I agreed with him, but I was also concerned

there could be more AK-47s trained on us from the farm buildings near the road. Suddenly, there was a shot — very close by. Discussion time had run out. I quickly started up the Alfa and gunned the engine hard. Jaynes and Farr threw themselves to the floor. I spun the wheels to churn up as much of the dirt road as I could.

We roared out of the village sideways in a thick cloud of dust. I prayed the gearshift lever would find its way from first to second without straying into fourth — as it had been doing all morning.

Six AK-47 shots passed over the Alpha in rapid fire. I braced for the next bullets to hit the vehicle, but none did. We drove at considerable speed for several miles before pulling over to the side of the road to catch our collective breaths. My heart was racing as I got out and checked the car for possible damage. It was then that I saw an armed convoy heading up the road towards us from the opposite direction.

It was led by a Rhodesian armored vehicle which I noticed had its hatches closed and its main gun trained on us. I raised both hands in the air and urgently suggested to Jaynes and Farr that they do the same.

The turret popped open and a white Rhodesian Sergeant appeared. "What the fuck are you guys doing on this road in that silly fucking car?," he shouted.

"We are journalists on our way to Assembly Point Foxtrot," I shouted back. "We've been cleared through by the British in Umtali who told us the road was safe."

"Safe maybe for military vehicles in convoy," he replied, "but that is the first bright blue Alfa Romeo sedan that's been down this road in in a very long time. You three present an incredibly soft target for the terrorists."

"Let us tell you something about that," said I, smiling. We then proceeded to detail the circumstances of our encounter with the guerrillas. The Sergeant took it all down and then radioed his headquarters. Two Rhodesian helicopter gunships shortly appeared overhead, circled briefly and then headed in the direction of the village.

We took our leave of the Rhodesian military convoy after being assured that there were no further villages between us and Foxtrot and that we should have no problems getting to the assembly point. This time, the information proved accurate.

When we pulled into Foxtrot, we discovered it was a vast tented camp accommodating several thousand guerrillas under the nominal supervision of no more than a dozen armed British soldiers. The guerrillas were also armed with personal weapons — ranging from AK-47s to RPG anti-tank rockets. No rebel soldier seemed particularly eager to turn in his weapon and the British were not pressing the issue.

Farr quickly found a helicopter ride back to Salisbury while Jaynes and I stayed behind to talk to some of the guerrillas and the British soldiers guarding them. We were both impressed with the disparity between the large number of armed guerrillas and the small British guard force. Everybody seemed to be on friendly terms, however.

The British had rigged up a public address system to get word out to the guerrillas. It seemed to be in fairly constant use. We heard it announce, in crisply British tones: "Will Comrade George please come to the headquarters tent?"

"Who is Comrade George?," we asked.

We were told he was the Foxtrot guerrilla commander.

When we interviewed Comrade George we couldn't help notice that he didn't wear any military rank. We asked the British about this and were told that none of the guerrillas seemed to have any rank, but everyone knew who was in charge.

"We hope you are in charge," said Jaynes.

"We are," said the British commander, "but only because they let us be."

Assembly Point Foxtrot turned out to have plenty of amenities for visitors: food, shelter, even Scotch whiskey, but no facilities for journalists to file stories. The British soldiers told Jaynes that word of our safe arrival had been passed back to headquarters, so we settled down and prepared to spend the night in the bush — happily, among friends.

But then I flipped on my portable shortwave radio

and discovered we were leading the news on both the Voice of America and the BBC. Farr had filed his story to the Daily Telegraph from Salisbury.

"A shot from a Kalashnikov assault rifle," wrote Farr, "aimed at my head from three feet persuaded me of the fragile nature of the Rhodesian ceasefire."

Farr had also passed the story along to several wire service colleagues, thus assuring that it would get even wider play. This meant of course that editors at both the Voice of America and the New York Times had by now received news accounts about their own reporters being ambushed in Zimbabwe, but had not heard directly from the correspondents themselves. It was not an ideal situation and Greg and I decided we had best cut short our stay at Foxtrot and head for the nearest telephone.

We drove back to Salisbury very early the next morning and spent the day on the telephone and telex bringing our respective news organizations up to date. By that time, the Rhodesian Department of Information had issued its own version of the incident: "Just after midday yesterday (January 16) in the Sabi Tribal Trust Land, a civilian vehicle carrying three overseas journalists was stopped by two armed and uniformed ZANLA (Zimbabwe African National Liberation Army — Mugabe's guerrillas) elements."

Identifying us and our employers, the government press release went on to describe how we were harassed at gun and bayonet point and told to identify ourselves. "After they had done this," continued the press release, "one of the ZANLA men fired a shot and Mr. Kelly drove the vehicle away. More shots were fired at the vehicle, but it was not hit. All three journalists were on an authorized journey to an assembly point at the time of the incident."

Once I had cleared up loose ends with the VOA newsroom, I stopped by Mugabe's ZANU-PF office to see how they were reacting to the government version of events. Their spokesman at the time was Edison Zvogbo, who later became a senior minister in Mugabe's government.

I asked him if he had any idea who had shot at us.

"No," he said, "but it wasn't any of our people."

"How can you be so sure?", I asked. "We were clearly in your part of the country."

"Well," he said, with a slight smile, "if it had been our soldiers, we certainly would not have missed."

I decided not to pursue the subject further.

꩜꩜꩜

A year later, I was in El Salvador trying to make sense out of the chaos of another civil war. There were some similarities with Zimbabwe, but we were a lot closer geographically to the United States and many more American journalists were on the scene. That made a noticeable difference. Quite a few had banded together to form an organization they called the Salvadoran Press Corps Association, or SPCA — like the Society for the Prevention of Cruelty to Animals. The similarity was not unintended.

Unfortunately, the Salvadoran Press Corps Association was unable to do very much towards the prevention of cruelty to either animals or journalists in El Salvador. Its real function seemed to be issuing colorful press cards and t-shirts — both of which had practical value.

The SPCA press card helped establish a foreign correspondent's professional credentials in El Salvador. The t-shirts had the SPCA logo on the front, but large letters on the back carried the important message: *"Periodista!* (Journalist!) *No Dispare* (Don't Shoot!)"

Access to both the guerrillas and the government side was fairly easy for foreign journalists in El Salvador. However, there could be some serious risks involved in the process.

On El Salvador's election day in 1982, Juan Tomayo of the Miami Herald and I were heading down the Pan American Highway in a rented car with several other journalists. We had left San Salvador before dawn, too early to have caught the rebel *Radio Venceremos* broadcast which warned journalists covering the voting to be sure to hang white strips of cloth on their vehicles.

We rounded a bend in the mostly unpaved

highway and suddenly found ourselves facing a small group of rebel soldiers. Their weapons were pointed directly at our car. Like Zimbabwe, it was AK-47s again, but this time they were backed up by several of the ubiquitous RPGs — Soviet anti-tank rockets which could rip a car apart.

The guerrilla soldiers yelled for us to halt and I hit the brakes very hard. As we slid to a stop, I stuck my head out the window and shouted *"Periodistas! La Prensa! Television!."* Juan Tomayo, meanwhile, ducked out the other side of the car, camera in hand, clearly intent on filming our guerrilla encounter for posterity.

This time there were no shots. The guerrillas motioned for us to come forward. As we did, they began taking us to task for having failed to follow the *Radio Venceremos* warning to hang white strips of cloth from our car. When we explained that we had left town too early to catch the broadcast, they told us to be sure and stop in the next town to get some white sheeting for the car.

"We will be everywhere today," they said. "We will be on all the roads and our next group may not be so forgiving."

We followed their advice, but not before getting a few interviews. We took pictures of them — and we took pictures of ourselves with them.

Later in the afternoon — after a day of visiting polling stations all over El Salvador — we passed the same group of rebel soldiers, at the same location on the side of the highway. They were being interviewed by an American television network. Apparently the government forces were all out voting that day. The civil war in El Salvador had seemingly taken an electoral recess.

Getting into the field with Salvadoran government soldiers proved to be somewhat more difficult. We pestered the military briefing officers for access to the territory they claimed to have taken back from from the guerrillas. Some of us ventured into these areas on our own, without permission. We found evidence of deliberate massacres by government forces and when these received worldwide attention, the Defense Ministry became all the more sensitive about the foreign press.

But on one memorable occasion, we were flown in government helicopters (American Hueys with the doors open — very reminiscent of Vietnam) to a recently contested area in eastern *Las Cabanas* province. We were met by Colonel Salvador Ochoa, a very fit-looking officer in his mid-forties, who took us on a long hike up mountain sides and through canyons to an empty village that he said had recently been held by guerrillas.

It was very hot and I was wearing police body armor under my shirt — protection against rebel mortar fire that happily never came. The pace was fairly intense, broken only by television crews stopping

Colonel Ochoa for on-camera interviews. Unlike the military flak vests that I had worn in Vietnam and Cambodia the police vests — *chalecos*, as they were called by the Salvadorans — did not open in the front and the heat build up inside was both uncomfortable and debilitating.

As we climbed back up out of the valley, I was trying to keep up with Colonel Ochoa, but found myself falling further and further behind. At one point, I was resting beside the trail when a long-haired Salvadoran youngster appeared, carrying an AK-47. He was clearly a rebel soldier, and I thought to myself, "Dear God, I've fallen so far behind the government forces, I have joined the guerrilla side!"

I smiled at him and said weakly that I was a foreign journalist who had become separated from the main group. He laughed and said he was one of Colonel Ochoa's special forces. The Colonel had sent him back to look after me and see if I needed help. Some of the other — older — reporters had also dropped by the wayside, particularly the television cameramen with their heavy equipment.

When I met up with Colonel Ochoa, he seemed pleased with himself for having led the foreign press on such a merry chase through the mountains. I interviewed him in Spanish (*"Por favor, Coronel. Donde estamos, exactamente?"*) and later that day fed the tape over the telephone to VOA in Washington. It was broadcast back to Latin America the following morning on VOA's popular *"Buenos Dias, America"* breakfast show. This somehow made the whole experience seem worthwhile, except we didn't really learn very much for all the hiking we did — apart from the certain knowledge that age imposes its own limitations on a journalist.

I later discussed this at some length with Dial Torgerson of the Los Angeles Times. We were in Buenos Aires together, during the Falklands War. We both agreed that, after fifty years of age, generally speaking, the war reporting process should be turned over to younger men and women.

Except — we agreed — if you had survived to the age of fifty as a war correspondent — you might conceivably have acquired that special sort of wisdom that gave you hunches you could use to a competitive advantage over a younger colleague.

Nonetheless, there were limits. Dial, who had already covered civil wars in Africa and the Middle East, said he had told the Los Angeles Times he wanted to retire after his current Latin American assignment.

As it turned out, Dial didn't make it. He was killed the following year in a land mine explosion along the Honduras-Nicaragua border. Would a younger journalist have spotted that the road had been mined? Maybe. Maybe not.

Apart from the rebels and the government, there was a further side to the war in El Salvador. It was a shadowy behind-the-scenes force that carried out the dirty work for the Far Right — the big landowners and senior armed forces officers. It engaged in political assassinations, set off bombs in front of judges' houses, and it published death lists of journalists.

One such list was issued on March 10, 1982. I first heard about it when a Salvadoran colleague asked me if I knew that I had been deathlisted. "By whom?" I asked, "Who has the list and how do we get a copy of it?"

We drove together to a local radio station where the list had been slid under the front door during the night. This had happened before and the station took it very seriously. After reading our names over the air, they made us a copy of the list which read was signed by the "General Maximiliano Hernandez Martinez Anti-Communist Alliance of El Salvador." It contained the names of 35 reporters and photographers of various nationalities, most of whom worked for U.S. news organizations.

The document accused us of being "at the service of international subversion" and condemned us all to death. I was number 29, about two-thirds of the way down the list. My name had been spelled phonetically in Spanish as "Jhon Kelly" but it was clear whom they had in mind when they described me as being from the United States and working for the Voice of America.

When I reported the story of the list — and my appearance on it — to the VOA newsroom in

Washington, I was asked about staying on in El Salvador. Did I want to be pulled off the story? Should someone else be sent in? I said I thought I should stay on and would certainly let them know if the time ever came when I felt I should leave.

Later that day, I was interviewed on Swedish television by a young reporter I had known the year before in Zimbabwe.

"Have you ever been condemned to death before, Mr. Kelly?"

She was smiling as she asked the question. I thought to keep the interview light-hearted.

"Not to the very best of my knowledge," I smiled back.

"But surely you take the death list seriously?," she asked.

"I take all death lists seriously," I replied, "particularly when my name is on them. This one contains many other good names as well and I am pleased to find myself in their company. But I can tell you frankly that, on the whole, the experience is a bit unsettling."

Actually, I was rather proud to be listed with such distinguished colleagues. The list included foreign correspondents from some of the finest news organizations in the world. Many of the reporters had spent years covering Latin America. I was a newcomer to the scene and yet there I was — condemned to death along with the best in the business.

I told VOA I wanted to stay on the story and I promised to get the best advice I could on how to avoid encountering any representatives of the General Maximiliano Hernandez Martinez Anti-Communist Alliance of El Salvador.

The Salvadoran Press Corps Association (SPCA) quickly organized a meeting with security officers from the U.S. Embassy in El Salvador. We were briefed on the significance of the death list: "Best take it seriously. Keep an eye out for any suspicious-looking characters around the hotel. Look to see if any one is following you down the highway. Change your driving patterns from one day to the next."

Then came some unusual, but very practical advice: "Keep your cars dirty. Stop paying those kids in the hotel parking lot to wash your cars every day. It's very difficult for anyone to put a bomb under the hood of a dusty car without giving the whole thing away. The more dust, the better. Also check your cars every morning for any wires leading out from underneath them. Again, let them get dusty as hell. Think of dust as your automobile insurance."

At the end of the briefing, the SPCA handed me its latest t-shirt. On the front was printed my number on the deathlist. On the back was a large bull's-eye.

I struggled to slip the shirt over my large frame.

It was marked King-Size.

But it didn't fit.

Of course, there was a time when it might have.

2.

Enter Nixon, Briefly.

Halfway through the summer of 1967, while I was covering a rebellion in the Congo, the Voice of America suddenly shifted me to report on rioting in Nigeria. It was there, in Lagos, that I came face-to-face with, of all people, Richard Nixon. An unexpected encounter, particularly since he and I turned out to have shared a common history.

Nigeria was in serious trouble. Its government had been overthrown twice the year before. The entire eastern third of the West African nation had since broken away, proclaiming itself the Republic of Biafra. Senior military officers in Lagos, the Nigerian capital, were trying to hold the rest of the country together, amid growing confusion and disorder.

"To keep Nigeria one is the task that must be done!" declared the Lagos military government resolutely, on television and radio, in newspaper headlines and on giant billboards throughout much of the country — nearly everywhere, except, of course, within the former Eastern Region which had already seceeded.

Civil war was in the air, but Lagos, despite its heat and malaria, had become host to an influx of world statesmen, arms dealers, mercenaries, journalists and foreign adventurers of one sort or another. One such visitor was Richard M. Nixon, not yet the disgraced 37th president of the United States.

As a VOA correspondent still on my first foreign assignment, I had spent the past year in the Congo, covering the final phases of a rebellion in which Cuban revolutionary hero Che Guevara had been an active, but covert participant. Heavily disguised, he had gone virtually undetected — not only by me, but all the other reporters, as well. In spite of his presence, the rebellion had mostly been defeated with U.S. help, covert and otherwise.

Nixon in the meantime was touring world trouble spots to update his foreign policy credentials. He was planning to enter the 1968 presidential election, hoping to become the Republican party's most knowledgeable candidate on foreign affairs. He had come out the loser in the 1960 presidential debates with John F. Kennedy and he intended to do better this time around — whoever might be his opponent.

A handful of other journalists and I went out to

meet him at Lagos airport. He held an on the spot news conference and we quickly ran through the questions about his political plans before the subject shifted to Nigeria, itself. Nixon, to our surprise, seemed genuinely interested in our views and began asking us questions. Was war inevitable in Nigeria? Could the Lagos government win it? At what cost in human life? He pressed hard for answers.

Several of us had just returned from Biafra and we told him what we had seen there. I mentioned I had been reporting the effects of civil war in the Congo and I was concerned that the food situation could reach a similar crisis in Biafra. He listened with what seemed to be thoughtful attention.

As we walked out to his waiting airliner (Lagos airport security was virtually non-existent in those days), he turned to me and asked where I was from in the United States.

"Whittier," I said, fully aware that it was also his home town. "Whittier, California." Then I added that I was Rex Kennedy's grandson.

Nixon's hand shot forward to grasp mine. "Whittier! Rex Kennedy! Why didn't you say so before?"

Then his voiced dropped to an almost reverent tone. "Rex Kennedy," he exclaimed, "was my mentor!"

At that point, I would like to think that my grandfather may have whirled at least once in his grave.

Despite his life-long devotion to the Republican Party, Rex Kennedy, editor and publisher of the Whittier *News*, was not too impressed with the way Nixon had turned out as a politician.

It is possible that he may have had serious second thoughts about his own role in helping to launch Nixon's political career. He might even have been proud to learn that his grandson went on to cover the Watergate scandal that ultimately forced Nixon to retire from politics.

All of this, of course, was a long way from Nigeria in 1967, but Whittier and Rex Kennedy had been very much a part of my life and, more particularly, my decision to become an overseas journalist.

Newspapering had already occupied several generations in my family by the time I came along. Rex's father, C.K.Kennedy, moved west across the United States with the railway in the 1870s, editing and publishing several small town newspapers before reaching the Pacific coast at the turn of the century.

Like the Whittier *News*, these were very much family enterprises. We all pitched in. I had learned to help out at the *News* at an early age, pasting up copy even before I could read it.

Rex grew up on the Villisca, Iowa *Review*, a weekly his father had bought in 1875 at the age of 26, using a team of horses as a down payment. Rex and his brothers learned to set type and sell advertising while their mother, Luella Green Kennedy, wrote a regular column of family advice to other Iowa women. She often began it: "Dear Sisters".

Many years later, while covering a Senate race in Iowa. I stopped by Villisca to see what had become of the *Review*. It was still there, but I couldn't help but notice that the staff seemed to consist entirely of women. I asked the editor about this. She laughed and said, "No, we haven't had a male around here since the cat died."

From all accounts, my great-grandmother would probably have seen some irony in this. Her "Dear Sisters" column and its tentative efforts to reach out to other pioneering women in Iowa had prevailed in Villisca to an extent she could never have imagined.

Her son Rex, who was six foot four inches tall and weighed nearly two hundred pounds, went on from Villisca to the University of Chicago where he and his older brother Walter played football for Coach Amos Alonzo Stagg. After graduation, the two Kennedy brothers borrowed some money and bought the Albion, Michigan *Recorder* which they published together for several years until Rex, having married a banker's daughter, decided he would move west and run his own newspaper.

He sold his half-interest in the Albion *Recorder* in 1911 and headed for California, taking with him his wife Edith and their two small daughters, Mary Frances, aged four, and Anne, my mother, who was two at the time. After looking at several small

California newspapers, Rex bought the Whittier *News*. Over the next forty years, he turned it into a successful enterprise that brought its influence to bear on Whittier and all of us, in one way or another.

As the paper and the family prospered, Rex and Edith bought property south of Whittier on Painter Avenue and raised four children and eventually a grandson there. The Ranch, as we called it, consisted of about fifteen acres of orange trees surrounding a big white house at the end of a long driveway leading in from Painter Avenue. There were several other buildings — a large barn, a cook's house, a guest cottage and eventually a horse corral.

When my parents' marriage ended in divorce after three years, my visits to the Kennedy Ranch tended to become more frequent and of longer duration. My mother and I went to live in San Francisco where she worked in a number of jobs, including writing advice to the love-lorn in a local newspaper. She had some financial help from Edith and Rex, but being a single parent would not have been easy during the Depression years of the 1930s. My father, Ted Kelly, provided only occasional support. He had little interest in me when I was young and later, when he discovered some curiosity, it was far too late.

I remember being looked after by a series of nannies, one of whom — I learned much later — boasted that she had opened the first brothel in the Panama Canal Zone. Her name was Healy and she used to take me to the afternoon horse races in South San Francisco. It may have been Healy and the horse races that caused Edith and Rex to decide in November 1939 that Whittier would be a more healthy environment for me than San Francisco. They drove north and brought me back to the Ranch.

I was six years old and not interested in learning how to read. A child psychologist suggested that I was afraid my mother would stop reading to me, once I learned how to do it myself. My grandmother Edith easily overcame this anxiety, if that is what it was, by teaching me to read aloud to her at the Ranch. She was a wonderfully warm and loving person who hugged me a lot and introduced me to a whole new world of books and libraries. I soon forgot about Healy and the horse races.

My grandfather Rex did not hug me very much, but I remember being tremendously impressed by his sheer size. When he strode through the house, the whole building seemed to tremble. He became my role model at an early age. I learned to mimic the sound of his footsteps so closely even Edith could not tell the difference (or so I thought) as I stomped my way onto the back porch and through the kitchen.

Radio first became a daily part of my life in those days. War was beginning to break out in Europe. Edith and Rex had both visited there in the 1930s and followed the news closely from that part of the world. We listened nightly for the sonorous tones of

Edward R. Murrow broadcasting from London. His name would eventually come to mean much more to me. What was perhaps more important at that stage of my life was the 6 p.m. frost report carried by radio station KFI in Los Angeles. It would forecast pre-dawn temperatures in the Southern California citrus areas and let us know whether we had to light fires in our smudge pots during the night. Otherwise, Rex could stand to lose his orange crop.

The Ranch had been built many years before the Kennedys bought it. Earlier occupants had planted fir trees which had grown to a great height in the front yard and along the gravel driveway leading in from Painter avenue. I would walk out to the end of the driveway every morning and wait for the bright yellow bus that would take me to the East Whittier Elementary School. I was one of the last children to be dropped off at day's end. I remember being able to see the tall fir trees in the front yard from the school bus at least a mile down Painter Avenue.

The Kennedy children all grew up playing among those trees, as I did twenty years later. We all took the bus from the Ranch to East Whittier Elementary School, but most of us went away from Whittier for high school and college. We came back on vacations to be with Rex and Edith, particularly at Christmas, but none of us ever developed much enthusiasm for remaining permanently in Whittier, let alone taking over the family newspaper.

Mary Frances, the eldest daughter, had been the first to leave. She went to Europe, establishing herself as a writer on her own, under the name M.F.K. Fisher. My mother, Anne Kennedy, had headed for San Francisco with me in tow. The third daughter, Norah, studied in Chicago to become a psychiatric social worker. My Uncle David, for reasons that have never been clear to me, killed himself at the age of 23.

Whittier eventually became more of a home to me than any of the many places I lived over the years with my mother or father. After David's death, and the departure of my mother and her sisters, Rex may have felt I might one day want to follow in his footsteps, settle in Whittier and take over running the *News*. He helped out financially with my education, both in high school and in college. Later, he made a very deliberate point of showing me how his days were spent as a small town editor and publisher.

The two of us went to the Rotary Club luncheons and the Whittier civic functions that had become so much a part of his life. In time, I think he came to understand that I did not want to make them part of mine. Not at that point, at any rate, and maybe never.

The Korean War broke out the week I graduated from high school, but I managed to complete a couple of years of university before my draft board gave me the choice of being drafted into the Army or volunteering for one of the other armed services. The Air Force recruiting office in Whittier told me there was a chance I might get assigned as a military journalist if I voluntarily enlisted — instead of waiting for the Army to draft me. So I signed up for the Air Force at the age of 19, putting Whittier behind me for the first time in my life.

My military career got off to a very shaky start. I managed to be absent without leave on my first day in the Air Force. My last 12 hours as a civilian had been spent with a girl friend. Much wine had been consumed by both of us. I woke up the next morning in her apartment terribly aware that I had not only missed my first military roll call, but also the bus that was to take me and my fellow recruits to the Los Angeles airport.

She drove me there at high speed and we managed to arrive ahead of the Air Force bus, but barely. I was met by two armed military policemen who said they intended to arrest me for being absent without leave. I apologized for having missed the roll call, but pointed out that I was reporting for duty ahead of the bus and, anyway, couldn't they give me a break on my first day in the United States Air Force?

One of the military policemen winked at the lady behind the wheel and the other let me off with the advice that this was probably not the best way to begin a military career.

Remarkably, my luck with the Air Force continued. A shortage of recruits with newspaper experience resulted in my basic training being cut short and I was flown to Houston, Texas to work on an Air Force base newspaper. In short time, I was made editor as a brand-new Private First Class — with several Corporals and a Sergeant working for me as reporters.

One of them had just returned from Korea where he told me there were opportunities to cover the war for military publications, get discharged overseas, and go to work for a wire service, such as the Associated Press. I promptly volunteered through official channels for an immediate transfer to Korea. But the Air Force, in its wisdom, decided to send me to Alaska, instead — quite possibly to cool off.

It turned out to be not such a bad move. Houston was already beginning to wear. Editing a weekly newspaper staffed by military reporters who outranked me had its downside in terms of personal friendships. There was also, by this time, another lady in my life. The new relationship, however, seemed to have more to do with my settling down in Texas than anything else and I wasn't ready for that — not anymore than I had been in Whittier.

This time, I didn't miss the bus to the airport. I drove straight from Houston to Whittier, California — determined never to drink another Lone Star beer, eat another black-eyed pea, or see another Texas sunset.

When I pulled bleary-eyed into the driveway at the Whittier Ranch some two days later, Rex was just heading off to the *News*. He asked me if I had driven all night. "Which night?," I replied. He laughed and put the account in his daily editor's column "Heard at the Barbershop". It was one of the few times any of us made it into the column. As a rule, Rex kept the family out of the paper.

On my last night in Whittier, I drove Rex into Los Angeles to attend a testimonial dinner for his University of Chicago football coach — Amos Alonzo Stagg — then in his nineties and still coaching. Rex was 76, dying of lung disease, but still smoking at least two packs of Parliaments a day. He greeted Stagg warmly, but his old coach took one look at him and said sternly: "Kennedy, put out that cigarette!"

I drove Rex home, said good bye to him the next morning and headed for Alaska. It was my last view of him, or the Ranch. He died three months later. The family newspaper was sold while I was away and the Ranch subdivided into middle income tract houses. The few acres surrounding the main house were given to the City of Whittier by my mother and her sisters so that children moving into the new residential area might have a park with tall trees to play in.

It was more than twenty-five years before I got back to Whittier. I drove up South Painter Avenue, stopping off where the Ranch used to be. The main house was gone, as was the long driveway leading in from the road. It was not easy trying to determine where the Ranch buildings had actually been. A few of the tall fir trees remained and a wooden sign hung from one of them. It read simply "Kennedy Park". Most people probably thought it was named in honor of President John F. Kennedy.

Nixon would have known better.

3.

Coming of Age Along the Yukon.

I made the voyage from Whittier, California to Whittier, Alaska in January 1953 — most of it in a crowded troopship. We left San Francisco at dusk, sailing through the Golden Gate and out into a magnificent sunset that lit up the city behind us until we were well out to sea. Then we abruptly turned north and soon found ourselves in a howling gale. January, I was to learn at first hand, is not the best of times for an ocean cruise through the North Pacific.

We plowed our way north to Alaska through terrible seas. The troopship rolled and pitched every nautical mile of the way. Waves broke over the bow and the rear of the ship rose out of the sea, causing the propellers to spin wildly as they clawed the air. The below deck troop compartments were cramped. Most of my fellow passengers were seasick. The latrines were awash in vomit. I survived the ten day voyage largely on soda crackers and occasional sips of Cognac from a large bottle I smuggled on deck in my military overcoat.

To my great relief, the seas finally calmed as we entered Prince William Sound. The troopship headed down a long inlet and we docked at the military seaport of Whittier. We gathered up our gear, hoisted our barracks bags on our shoulders and made our way down the gang plank directly from the ship to a waiting Army train. Somewhere along the way, I managed to jettison the empty Cognac bottle, unnoticed.

The train pulled out of the Whittier station shortly after we had boarded and the sense of movement continued. The high seas rocking motion that had been with us since San Francisco was replaced by the easy but persistent roll of the railway.

We stopped at the airbase outside Anchorage. With great pent-up enthusiasm, we all piled out, not immediately aware that the ground was frozen and the pavement icy. This was our first contact with *terra firma* in ten days. Feet suddenly went sliding and several hundred of us were soon on the ground, flat on our backs in our overcoats, laughing and clutching our barracks bags.

We were greeted with great roars of laughter from those who had come to meet us. I later learned it was a rite of passage to Alaska — one of many. Seasoned Alaskan veterans made a point of coming down to the train station to watch new arrivals slip and slide around in the snow, particularly when the weather had been severe — as it was much of the time.

My orders had assigned me to work on the weekly newspaper at Elmendorf Air Force Base in Anchorage, but I had hoped to get out into the interior of Alaska and see something of the backwoods. An opportunity came up to join the Alaskan Network of the Armed Forces Radio Service (AFRS, which more recently has become Armed Forces Radio and Television Service, or AFRTS). This was a loose collection of small military-operated radio stations broadcasting throughout Alaska, many of them in remote areas of the territory. It would be several years before Alaska became a state and the military provided many services that later would be taken over by private enterprise. AFRS was one of them.

We were trained in all aspects of small radio station operations at AFRS Alaskan network headquarters in Anchorage. By the time the course was finished, we could read and write the news, edit tape, do live interviews, even change the tubes in the transmitter. It was great training and it gave me skills I would depend upon when I went back to college and, much later, at the Voice of America.

We ran typical small town American radio stations in the remote Alaskan bush. Many of us were housed and fed at Distant Early Warning radar sites, out along the fringes of what became known as the

DEW Line. Basically, our mission was to broadcast to American military personnel, but the bulk of our listeners were Alaskan natives and they took us into their hearts.

The townspeople of Nome, Alaska thought so much of the AFRS station, they chipped in and bought it a piano. Then they brought in a huge pink bathtub, with matching sink and toilet. Paint and lumber followed to build private bedrooms for the station's staff. Finally, the whole building had to be put off limits to the rest of the air base, but word did get around Alaska about the pink bathroom set. High-ranking visitors dropped in to use it while the rest of the Nome air base put up with communal facilities flushed uncomfortably by freezing water.

Galena was different. Its small airstrip on the banks of the Yukon River had been built for the Soviet Air Force during World War II. Located about halfway between Nome and Fairbanks, Galena was intended to serve as an alternate refueling stop for Lend Lease fighter aircraft being ferried by the Soviets across the Bering Sea to Siberia.

When I arrived in 1953, there were still Russian-language signs in the Galena hangar, a primitive wooden structure which also served as austere living quarters for people stationed there. Nobody stayed very long. Conditions were too severe. Aircrews and fighter aircraft were rotated in and out on short-term assignment. Even then, Galena One was miserable duty.

The rest of us lived on a nearby hilltop, where both AFRS and the radar station was located. Galena Two was a very modern series of inter-connecting buildings and passageways, many of which were covered over by snow during the winter. From the air, it looked like a station at the South Pole. We even had our own unpaved uphill airstrip which was served by commercial bush pilots as well as the elderly Air Force DC-3 transports widely in use throughout Alaska at the time.

I had been scheduled to fly out to Galena from Fairbanks with an Air Force Chaplain who was planning to conduct Easter services at the radar site's small make-shift chapel. But an earlier DC-3 flight became available and I was able to get a seat on it, instead. As it turned out, the Chaplain's flight never made it. The pilot was unable to lower the DC-3's landing gear and the Fairbanks tower ordered him to turn around and come back. The Fairbanks runway was longer and more suitable for an emergency wheels-up landing. There was also more crash equipment available, plus the services of a large Air Force hospital.

We had no such amenities at Galena. In fact, the AFRS radio station was housed in what was intended to be the hospital. This had its advantages for the broadcast staff. Sadly, there were no female nurses, but there was a small kitchen fridge stocked with seemingly unlimited supplies of pineapple juice and grain alcohol. The combination helped ease the chill out of many an Arctic evening.

My first broadcast at AFRS Galena included reading the news item that Easter services had been canceled, but that the Chaplain's aircraft and its passengers had survived the controlled crash landing in Fairbanks. The plane had been damaged, but the crew and passengers were safe, including the Chaplain. Having originally been scheduled to join them for the flight, I was particularly pleased to announce its happy outcome.

My luck with the Air Force was holding up.

AFRS Galena was on the air every day for 18 hours, from six in the morning to midnight. We broadcast what was in those days a typical program schedule for an American radio station: disc-jockey music shows, interspersed with news and local announcements, backed up by network-supplied comedy and adventure programs. The objective was to sound like the sort of radio station one might hear anywhere across the broad reaches of middle America in the 1950s — not too ethnic, rarely controversial.

We prided ourselves on our self-sufficiency. The stations were run by enlisted men serving on detached duty from Alaskan Network headquarters in Anchorage. No officers were involved. Claude Turner, head of the network, was a civilian professional who had spent a lifetime in commercial radio.

He had a small administrative and technical staff at network headquarters in Anchorage. The rest of us were in the field, all over Alaska. Turner would often pick up our stations while flying around the territory. He would then send us detailed critiques. We always assumed he was listening. somewhere. It kept us on our toes.

Each station team was led by a Sergeant or a Corporal who was responsible directly to Turner in Anchorage. The rest of the team included a program manager, who looked after the day to day broadcast operations, and a broadcast technician who kept the station on the air. We usually had one or two staff announcers pulling six-hour shifts, plus several volunteers. Everybody got on the air at one time or another during the station's 18-hour broadcast day.

The early 1950s were the last, great days of American commercial radio. Television was on the way, but radio still drew the audiences. We had comedy by Jack Benny, drama by "Gunsmoke", and police action by "Dragnet". Bob Hope and Big Crosby did special broadcasts. AFRS headquarters in Hollywood recorded them all off the air, took out the commercials, and shipped them out on long-playing discs to AFRS stations around the world.

Each shipment of recordings would include a week's programming, plus the latest popular and classical music recordings from the United States. We normally stockpiled several weeks in advance to cover emergencies, or the Alaskan weather that often delayed incoming shipments.

Other AFRS stations in remote areas had the same problems. Late shipments must have been particularly difficult for the mobile AFRS stations operating near the front lines in Korea. Lacking a fixed address, they had names like AFRS Vagabond, Troubadour and Gypsy. Their programming logistics were infinitely more complex than our own — no one had yet discovered a way to parachute a box of broadcast recordings successfully.

News, of course, could not be pre-recorded and shipped out to the stations. It had to be put together on the scene and read live on the air. AFRS headquarters experimented with news broadcast at dictation speed on special shortwave service transmissions. Fortunately at Galena, we were able to pick up the Associated Press wire service by radio teletype which we would edit down to newscast length and add in whatever items of local interest we could find. It was not the CBS Evening News Roundup with Edward R. Murrow, but we tried to come as close as we could — under the circumstances.

For young men (we had no ladies among us, unfortunately) with no broadcast experience, AFRS was a superb training ground. We were free to experiment, within reason, and each of us got as much on-the-air time as the audience would allow without complaining. Although our primary obligation was to meet the listening demands of an American military audience, we received a lot of fan mail from Alaskans. Country music programs were especially popular with our local listeners.

At one point, so much mail came into the station we had to appeal to listeners to send us post cards instead of letters. We had no staff at Galena to open all of the envelopes. To make it easier for listeners along the Yukon, we put up our own mail box at a nearby river landing. We told our listeners it wasn't even necessary to put postage stamps on the post cards — just drop them off at our Yukon River mail box.

Some of the fan mail was personal. To our very pleasant surprise, we discovered we had lady listeners out along the Yukon. Many of them seemed fairly attractive, judging from the photos they sent in with their letters. Quite a few offered hospitality if we could ever manage to visit their villages. I set about in earnest to find out how that might be possible.

Most of our mail at Galena was delivered from Fairbanks by commercial bush pilots flying small, single-engined airplanes. They made their way up the river, stopping at villages along the way. In the summer months they landed on make-shift airstrips. During the winter, when the Yukon was frozen over, they put down on the ice itself, using skis instead of wheels.

I got to know the most of the bush pilots who landed at Galena because I was frequently on the

outlook for program shipments from AFRS headquarters and therefore had to meet many of the flights.
We got even better acquainted when, as a service to
the community, we began broadcasting the expected
arrival times at the villages served by the bush mail
planes. This gave each community a chance to get
their outgoing mail together and haul it out to the
river landing spot or the airstrip, depending on the
season.

As the pilot landed at the Galena airstrip, he
would hand me a list of his estimated arrival times
further down the Yukon. These varied from day to
day, depending on weather and cargo. We would then
broadcast the list, notifying villagers along the river
when to expect the mail plane. The system became
very popular with both the pilots and the villagers
because it cut down on the amount of ground time
at each landing, making it more likely that the pilots
would be able to get back to Fairbanks before darkness set in.

In return, the bush pilots offered us free rides up
and down the Yukon when they had space available.
Since we took a portable radio along to keep track of
what was happening back at the station, we called the
trips "extended audience surveys." Everyone at the
station must have availed themselves of at least one
such flight. I managed to take several.

The longest, and most memorable, was from
December 5, 1953 to January 2, 1954. The Yukon

was frozen over solidly and the ancient, single-engined Norseman bush plane was equipped with landing skis. We look off around noon and headed leisurely to Koyukuk, a small fishing village about fifty miles down river. The aircraft flew on its own mostly, cruising along about 800 feet over the frozen river while the pilot busied himself filling out postal forms.

Occasionally, he would peer out the side window, make a minor course correction, and then go back to his paperwork. As we approached Koyukuk, we could see a group of villagers out on the Yukon ice with a dog team pulling several sacks of mail in a sled. The pilot eased the Norseman down to the river, but the impact with the ice seemed harsh, because of the screeching noise made by the skis.

I was not staying in Koyukuk, having visited there several times already. But I jumped out to help with the mail. Standing on the icy Yukon, the temperature seemed much colder to me than it had been when we left Galena less than a half hour before. When I mentioned this to the pilot and he said he was glad that Nulato, our next stop, would be his last mail delivery of the day. He was concerned about getting back to Fairbanks in daylight before the weather worsened.

Nulato was a Yukon riverfront town with an onion-domed Russian church that must have dated back to the 1800s. It was a further fifty miles or so down the Yukon from Koyukuk and I had planned to spend my 21st birthday there with friends, including some female listeners who had written particularly inviting fanmail.

My birthday came and went and I was made quite warm and comfortable while the weather went from bad to worse. In those days in Alaska, bush pilots stopped flying at about twenty below zero. The temperature in Nulato stayed at about thirty below through most of December. There were no flights at all. No mail. No direct contact with the outside world.

A sense of guilt settled in around Christmas. I had managed to send a radio message back to Galena that I was stuck in Nulato without any way out, short of a dog sled up the river. I was still hoping for a break in the weather so that I could catch a ride back with a bush pilot.

None came. My sense of guilt worsened. I had been passing the long days and nights in Nulato with a number of local ladies, several of them — as it turned out — serious beer-drinkers. There seemed no end to the supply of canned Miller's High Life Beer in Nulato and it went down quite well with smoked salmon jerky, a locally-made delicacy. At night, we would tune in AFRS Galena to hear "Land of the Midnight Sean," but without Sean. It was a late-hour music show I usually hosted and I could hear my colleagues filling in for me. "Come back, Sean," they would say, "All is forgiven. Come back, we need you here! Please come back to Galena!!"

These nightly pleas added to my growing sense of guilt over the extended audience survey in Nulato. Although the outside temperature hit sixty below zero on New Years Day 1954, I began making arrangements to hire a dog team for my overdue return back up the frozen Yukon to Galena. My task was made easier by the large number of visitors to the village attracted by the organized New Years celebrations which had included fireworks and dancing.

Friends introduced me to a young man named Sebastian who had traveled down river with his dog team from Galena. A regular listener to AFRS Galena. Sebastian had learned of my plight and he agreed to take me back to Galena for a reasonable price. If the weather held, he said we could make the trip in two days — spending the night halfway at Vernetti's trading post in Koyukuk where I had already been a guest on several previous occasions.

We left early the next morning. It was still sixty below zero, but there was no wind on the river and the sky was bright and clear. I wore long winter underwear under a layer of woolen trousers and a heavy shirt. Over these hung a pair of quilted Army survival pants so thick and heavy they had to be kept in place by suspenders. On top of it all was a thick parka with a wolverine-trimmed hood that could be zipped up to form a breathing funnel in front on my face. My hands were kept warm by a pair of giant mittens I picked up at an Eskimo trading post near

Nome. Sebastian got by with wearing much less, but then he ran behind the dog sled most of the way.

We followed the course of the frozen Yukon, mushing along a fairly well-marked trail. We made good time where the surface was smooth and hard, but had to detour occasionally around places in the river where the ice had jammed up into piles. Sebastian stopped periodically to rotate the dogs, resting one of them in the sled with me. This provided a most welcome added source of warmth. For several of the stretches, I jogged along with Sebastian, but found it difficult to sustain his pace over any distance. We both agreed it would be better for me to remain in the sled with the spare dog.

The lights at Koyukuk came up a day's end and could not have been more welcome. In spite of the heavy clothing, the occasional jog alongside the sled, and the warmth of the extra dog, I was beginning to feel that Alaska was gaining ground on me. It was quite cold and the night was already upon us.

A roaring fire at Vernetti's Koyukuk trading post and a double whiskey brought me back to life, partially. A hot rabbit stew and a bottle of good red wine did the rest. Good companionship around the table brought to mind my aunt Mary Frances' widely-quoted observation: "There is a communion of more than our bodies when bread is broken and wine drunk".

The trip further up river to Galena went smoothly the next day. Sebastian dropped me off near the

AFRS mail box at the river landing and I walked the rest of the way to the station in time to take over my regular shift on "The Land of the Midnight Sean." Special thanks went out that night to all those along the way who had made the long trip possible, particularly my return home.

A week or so later, the realities of military life caught up with me. It was just past midnight and I had signed the radio station off the air and shut down the transmitter. We were sitting in the station, talking about nothing in particular when the phone rang.

"Do not acknowledge this transmission," said the operator, "An alert exercise is underway. all personnel will take up alert positions immediately. I repeat, an alert exercise is underway. Take up alert positions immediately."

My own special alert position was a machine gun post out on a hilltop overlooking the Yukon. I was to gather up my team, collect weapons and ammunition, and proceed to the position as quickly as possible. A clock was running somewhere. We were being timed on how long it would take for us to get into place, set up the machine gun and report in by radio.

We managed it in good time and when I radioed the command post to report our status. I was told to be on guard against infiltrators. This meant that the Army had brought in helicopter teams from Fairbanks, supposedly far enough from us so that we would not hear them landing on the frozen Yukon. But sound carries a long way on a cold Alaskan night and helicopters make a lot of noise landing on ice in the dark. We could hear them and so did our perimeter patrols who set up ambushes on the approaches to the base. From then on, it was a matter of waiting them out.

All the Army infiltration teams were easily rounded up. Most of their men were freezing, several were actually suffering from frostbite. Our victory over the invaders was complete. We had defended Galena against an outside force. It had been child's play compared with a hundred mile dog sled run up the frozen Yukon.

I had come of age. Whittier was far behind me. I felt ready to take on the world.

4.

Remembering Anti-Dote, also known as M.F.K. Fisher.

It was in Alaska that I discovered M.F.K. Fisher, the writer. She had, of course, discovered me much earlier — not very long after I was born in fact.

She was my mother's older sister and I had known her as Mary Frances, or Dote — sometimes even Anti-Dote, but that came later. Her books — "Serve It Forth," "Consider the Oyster", and "The Gastronomical Me," which had been dedicated to my mother, were a part of my growing up. But I did not begin to appreciate her writing until I was far away from her.

"M.F.K. Fisher writes about food," one critic had observed, "as others write about love, but rather better." Indeed, said W.H. Auden, "I do not know of anyone in the United States today who writes better prose."

After her death in 1992, when an extensive volume of her correspondence was published, it became clear that some of her best writing was to be found in the letters she wrote to other people.

I was fortunate enough to have been one of them.

While I was in Alaska, we began a long distance communication that was to last more than thirty years — until shortly before her death. Throughout this lengthy correspondence, there were also many occasions when we met in person. Either way, she was always ready to give counsel and she did so at many of the more important crossroads in my life.

She was very much more to me than my mother's older sister. In many respects she was closer to me than either of my parents. There was even a time, she told me, when she and her husband, Dillwyn Parrish, had wanted to adopt me as their own child, except my mother's pride and Dillwyn's worsening health made this impossible.

They were living in the desert, near Hemet, California, on ninety acres of rocky hillside they named Bareacres. I was seven years old and attending a military academy near Glendora, California where I had been placed because neither of my divorced parents had room for me in their own lives. I would have quite willingly made the move to Bareacres. Dillwyn, whom I called Timmy, had already become a close friend and Mary Frances, whom the rest of the family called Dote, was fast becoming a special sort of Anti-Dote to me.

On week-ends, my mother would sometimes collect me from the military academy and we would drive the fifty or sixty miles to Bareacres together. Those were great adventures for me and I always dreaded the moment when they came to an end. Often I would contrive to leave a jacket or some other article of clothing behind at Bareacres, thus establishing, in my own mind at least, some faint assurance that I would return. My mother usually saw through this maneuver, and made certain that nothing got left behind.

Bareacres was also home to several dogs and cats. Timmy made special little doors for them to come in and out of the main house. Then he put leather fringed curtains over the doors to discourage scorpions and other wildlife from gaining entrance as well. My favorite cat was named Blackberry. Mary Francis later wrote about his many ways of survival in her book entitled "A Cordiall Water". She and Timmy were convinced that the presence of the cats at Bareacres tended to keep rattlesnakes and other unwelcome desert creatures away from the house.

There were also two dogs to whom I became devoted. Butch was Dote's special Pekingese who had amazing dignity for a dog his size. His close companion was a miniature Doberman I always knew as "Colonel". Many years later, I learned his full name.

Mary Frances had christened him Colonel Timothy Arrow-Ass because of the arrow-shaped marking underneath his tail.

In the last year of Timmy's life, he, Mary Frances, my mother, the two dogs and I, generally accompanied by several cats, would often hike up the road above the main house at Bareacres. Our trip would end at a large corrugated metal storage tank. It supplied water to the main house and also occasionally served as a target for nearby hunters whose marksmanship would leave small streams spouting from its sides. Timmy would stuff these with intricately carved pegs that he turned out at his carpenter's bench where he also made frames for his paintings. The sides of the Bareacres water tank eventually bristled with Timmy's handiwork.

By that time, Timmy was on crutches with one leg amputated and a creeping illness in the other. He managed to get about very gracefully, but once — with all the innocence of young childhood — I called out his arrival to Mary Frances: "Here comes Timmy, hippity-hop!" They both laughed, and Dote recalled the incident with amusement many years later.

Timmy's suicide in 1941 was my first experience with death and I took it badly. The precise circumstances were not explained to me at the time, wisely as it turned out since I would not have understood them. He had a rare blood disease that was gradually killing him. When he and Dote were living in

Switzerland, they were able to obtain a drug that slowed the progress of the disease. When they fled Europe in 1939, the drug was no longer available to them. Timmy must have seen himself becoming an increasing burden on Dote, so he took his life to spare her having to care for him.

She had just published her second book, "Consider the Oyster," which she had written as a sort of light-hearted gift to him. Sadly, he never lived to see it in published form. I was not aware of any of this at the time, but I wept at the loss of my friend Timmy who, in my constant search for a parent, had clearly filled an important gap in my own life.

Later in 1941, after Tim's death, my mother and I were living in Beverly Hills. She had found a small apartment on Elm Drive, just off Wilshire Boulevard. We had no car, but my elementary school was near-by and her job as an assistant to George Hurrell, the Hollywood portrait photographer, was an easy stroll up Wilshire to Rodeo Drive.

Dote, meanwhile, was working as a writer at Paramount Studios, but trying to keep Bareacres going in spite of the one hundred miles of driving involved in getting there and back. She had kept the large Oldsmobile convertible she and Timmy had driven across the country the previous year. It had one of the first automatic transmissions — no clutch, no gear shift — making it possible for Timmy to drive on his own. The Oldsmobile, beige with green leather seats, was to play a significant role in our lives that year.

My ninth birthday fell on Monday, a school day, so I had made plans to celebrate it the day before, on Sunday, December 7, 1941. The news from Pearl Harbor reached the West Coast about mid-morning, as I recall, and it swept aside whatever birthday celebrations may have been planned. Mary Frances came over and we all listened to the radio, hearing for the first time a phrase we would never really become used to: "We interrupt this program to bring you a special news bulletin…"

The war hysteria on the West Coast affected all our lives. There were frequent blackouts and on more than one occasion they caught us on the road between Beverly Hills and Bareacres. We would have to pull to the side of the highway, turn off the headlights, and wait until there was an all clear signal. I remember spending one night in an orange grove near Azusa, California. Dote's Oldsmobile convertible, with its tufted green leather upholstery, had a back seat that was comfortable for me to curl up on. I had no trouble getting to sleep and my subsequent account of the experience made a considerable impression on my fourth grade classmates at Beverly Vista Elementary School.

My first awareness of restaurant food and menus came during those wartime excursions across Southern California. Mary Frances was always quite insistent that I choose my dinner carefully from the menu, but we often stopped at a small restaurant named Jarupa's — just beyond Riverside. The menu at Jarupa's was not extensive and I usually ended up with a milk shake, a cheeseburger, some potato chips, and a pickle — all chosen by me with great care. This choosing process seemed particularly important to Mary Frances.

She liked to see people making decisions and standing by them. If I read something and liked it, she would want me to tell her why. She disliked what she called wishy-washy explanations. She expected you to make a case for your likes and dislikes, otherwise — in her view — they weren't worth having. This point comes up again and again in her writing. An early example is in "The Gastronomical Me" where she describes a restaurant dinner with a favorite uncle "a quietly worldly man, professorial at times but always enjoyably so, who knew more about the pleasures of the table than anyone I had yet been with."

She was nineteen and learning "for the first time that a menu is not something to be looked at with hasty and often completely phony nonchalance." But she nearly fails the test. Asked what she would like to eat, she mumbles stiffly, "Oh, anything … anything, thank you."

Her uncle reacts with a cold almost disgusted look in his eyes. "It was as if he were saying," she writes, 'You stupid uncouth young ninny, how dare you say such a thoughtless thing, when I bother to bring you to a good place to eat…'."

She snaps out of it, calmly informing her uncle that she would like iced consomme, sweetbreads sous cloche and a watercress salad. "He sat back in his chair a little", she wrote, "clearly impressed." She never again would let herself say, or even think, "Oh, anything," about a meal, even if she were dining alone, perhaps especially then.

Years later, she would order a drink with me before a luncheon at Fisherman's Wharf in San Francisco with equal precision: "A double Gibson, please, straight up, and preferably made with Beefeater's." Then we would proceed to the menu.

You were careful what you said around Mary Frances, as well as how you said it. If she thought you were on weak ground, she would challenge you, boring in wherever she found you were most vulnerable. In the end, she would usually emerge the victor, rarely gloatingly so, nor was she particularly magnanimous. She would simply move on to another subject.

Journalists generally found her to be a challenging interview. Small children, myself included, often found her perplexing, even a little frightening.

When I was eight, she offered me a set of roller-skates if I would memorize Abraham Lincoln's Gettysburg Address. I had no idea what the speech was about, what, for instance, "four score and seven years ago" really meant, or what "the last full measure of their devotion" entailed. In retrospect, I think she may have been trying to get me to develop an early appreciation for Lincoln's use of language, the fine rhythm of his syntax, but his words themselves had no real meaning to me, even though I managed eventually to deliver them in the order he had put them down.

I wrote letters to her from Alaska and later from various other parts of the world, often on borrowed typewriters with differing keyboards and type faces. Her replies always began brightly, sometimes amusingly: "I do like your new typewriter…much more easily read, at least by this poor old lady who in actuality is neither poor, nor very old, and often suspiciously not a real lady."

It became a sort of given that love of language would be a common link between us and that I would probably make it a central feature of my own life. She had, through our correspondence and in the example she had set, pointed the way for me to do so. I felt very proud when she wrote "For Sean K. Kelly, my colleague, friend and even nephew!" on my copy of "The Art of Eating" which she gave me for Christmas in Aix-en-Provence in 1954.

I had flown up from Casablanca, Morocco, where I was editing a weekly newspaper and beginning to feel as though I wanted to make a life's work out of journalism, providing I could continue to do it in places like Casablanca — as opposed to, say, Whittier, California.

She of course drew on Whittier memories throughout much of her writing, most particularly in "Among Friends" which was about growing up there as a non-Quaker. When she was invited back to help celebrate Whittier's centennial, she found the place quite changed. She wrote me:

"About going down to Whittier: I think I told you that I meant to smile sweetly and be very gracious, but I really felt rather peeved, mostly because of the really low-down reaction of some of the old Quakers after Cleveland Amory broadcast over NBC that M.F.K. Fisher had written that Quakers were bastards. What I did say in "Among Friends" is that some Quakers are saints and some are bastards...but take that out of context and may God help us all!"

Once there, she found she was so moved by the general decency and kindness of people, one to another, during Whittier's recent earthquakes that, as she later wrote in a letter to me, "I completely forgot my very unadmirable emotions."

In later years, she was faced with a progressively worsening succession of health problems. This did not stop her from finding occasional humor in the aging process, and she even poked fun at it in "Sister Age" as well as in some of her published journals and correspondence. She would sometimes shock close friends and relatives by telling them she hoped they might never grow old. By this, of course, she meant having to confront the problems of growing old, as opposed to dying before these occurred, but it was a startling statement, nonetheless — which is why she took such pleasure in making it. Typically Dote, as we would say.

Confined to a wheel chair. she was once strapped to a freight pallet and hoisted into an awaiting airplane by fork-lift. Describing this experience in a letter to me, she wrote: "I left in somewhat of a burst of glory. There was a pouring rainfall. I was casually put on a fork-lift, after the baggage had been loaded and I sat there in the downpour for almost a half-hour. I could see the plane with its door open and waiting and in the distance was the terminal with white hankies waving at me from the windows... and finally the fork-lift moved very majestically toward the plane, and I rose some forty feet up to the cabin door. While my chair was unstrapped, I gave a queenly wave...first the right hand and then the left hand...to the waving white hankies in the far-off windows, Then the door swung shut, and they started wringing me out. It was one of the funniest exits I've ever made."

In her final letter to me, written a year or so before her death, she said: "I've just announced to Marsha (Moran, her assistant) that I plan to write a real letter to you finally. Your last two were very good ones and I have thought often of a proper answer to the Valentine one … and now there is another one that came today."

"I'll start out by telling you that I find it very hard to write at all. Unfortunately for me, I've always been a real chatterbox, and now I can't talk at all. I find it a hard situation to cope with, but I have a feeling that I'll outgrow this, given the time of course, which is something I cannot be too nonchalant about at the age of 82. Today Marsha and I are trying out a new system and I am sitting across the room from her, whispering into a microphone, which she can understand."

Mary France's new system of communication worked for a while, but not long enough for her to complete the publication of "Stay Me, Oh Comfort Me", a collection of stories and early journals. Her younger sister, Norah Kennedy Barr, helped with the editing — as well as with the household. She wrote me from her home in Jenner, California that she was sharing my letters to her with Mary Frances. "MF loves to hear from you, but the process of answering is up to Marsha entirely; and the two of them are also hard at work on her journals, which have already been bought."

"MF is very, very frail," Norah wrote. "Her mind is whizzing along as ever, although she says she feels increasingly dull. I wonder from week to week how she can continue as she does, usually with good humor but an occasional dull day. I am spending two days a week over there filling in some gaps in her intricate schedule of nurses. As you can imagine, that is a juggling game. Kennedy (MF's daughter, who lived near Oakland) comes up on Wednesday evenings and we console one another. MF has absolutely no voice, but if I get my ear next to her lips, I can usually make out something essential. Anything intricate is out of the question, however."

As it happened, I was visiting California that year and planned to see Norah, but I wasn't sure about dropping in on Mary Frances. I wrote Norah that I much preferred to remember Dote as I had known her over the years — witty, articulate, and full of interest in the world around her. The thought of seeing her in ill health, bedridden, and unable to communicate directly, if at all, left me with little enthusiasm — nor was I even certain that the visit would mean that much to her.

Norah wrote back: "Sean, I think if you are in Berkeley and she is alive, you should make the drive up (to Dote's home near Sonoma), if just for a short squeeze of the hand. I do know how hard it is for you, though — but she is your Anti-Dote."

I made the drive up to Sonoma — for a short, final squeeze of the hand. A few days later, while I was catching a flight to Paris, I heard from Norah that Mary Frances had died. There were plans for a memorial service and I would be invited, but I was halfway to South Africa by then. So I held my own small service in Paris. It took place at *Le Recamier* on tiny *rue Recamier*, deep in the Left Bank — a neighborhood Mary Frances knew very well. A superb meal was served, among very close friends, and more than one glass was raised to the memory of M.F.K.Fisher.

After I had returned to Africa, I received a long letter from Kennedy, Dote's daughter, about my final visit with Mary Frances: "That day was, for me," she wrote, "the beginning of the realization that Dote was dying. I did not know it then, but she had suddenly become much more distant. I sensed that she was interested in us and in our interaction in a different way that day, and learned the following day from the hospice worker, that what I had sensed was indeed a change often made in the last stages of life. There is a part of me that wonders if she was waiting for you to come. You were the last of the family members whom she had not seen in awhile, and I think she may have held on to know that you were OK, and for you to know that she was, although dying, OK, too. I think we will never understand, but I am grateful to you for coming, and I believe that she really did enjoy having us all together."

Mary Frances loathed good-byes, particularly in the last years of her life. *A bientot*, or even *au revoir* were more preferable. I cannot remember what sort of farewell I summoned up on that last visit, but I am very glad today that I was there to say it myself.

5.

Casablanca: Early Chaos.

"What about Casablanca, French Morocco?," asked my friend in Personnel.

Memories of Humphrey Bogart and Ingrid Bergman quickly came to mind. I replied that I had seen the film several times and was definitely ready to go there.

It was mid-1954, I had been back from the Alaskan bush just long enough to learn that I could not afford to live in the United States on a Corporal's pay. I was working in television, but still wearing a uniform. My new stateside life style vastly exceeded my income and I began seriously looking for a way back overseas, fast.

This time I knew better than to apply through Air Force channels, simply volunteering to be sent any-where as I had before. I had a friend who worked in

Personnel and I had left word with her to keep an eye open for a good overseas vacancy in my field.

"It could be risky," she said. Moroccans had been rioting against French colonial rule. The French had responded with force — which had led to more rioting. "Are you still interested?," she asked.

"All the more so," I replied. "How soon can I leave?"

I packed my bags, sold my car, and caught a plane to New York. An old friend from high school days had become a struggling writer and was living in a modest apartment near Greenwich Village. He and his wife offered to put me up until my troopship sailed.

To help prepare me for my Moroccan adventure, we all went to see "The Desert Song," a Sigmund Romberg operetta set in French Morocco that proved to have little relation to Moroccan reality, but turned out to be amusing, nonetheless.

More serious research at a New York public library revealed that 1954 had not been a very good year for French colonialism, particularly in Indochina where France had just suffered a decisive defeat at Dien Bien Phu. Many soldiers on the French side had been taken prisoner — including colonial troops imported from North Africa to help fight the Vietnamese.

Moroccans and Algerians were among these prisoners. Bernard Fall, writing years later about the battle of Dien Bien Phu, recalls the interrogation of the North Africans. "Since you are such good soldiers," asked their Vietnamese captors, "why do you fight for the colonialists? Why don't you fight for yourselves and get a country of your own?"

Many of them decided to do just that.

At the time of the French surrender in Indochina, the United States was paying nearly eighty percent of the war's cost. This was in support of the Eisenhower domino theory that if one Indochinese territory fell to Communist forces, all would soon suffer the same fate. In partial return for the American assistance, the French had reluctantly allowed the U.S. Air Force to build three strategic bomber bases in Morocco, including the one near Casablanca where I was headed.

When our troopship docked in the Casablanca port, we were taken under armed convoy to the recently-constructed air base at Nouasseur (now the Mohammed V International Airport), twenty miles or so south of the city. The lumbering armored vehicles leading our convoy through downtown Casablanca underscored the reality of the worsening political situation.

I learned much later that the American diplomats in Morocco were reporting to Washington "a sharp increase in terrorism…with last week witnessing approximately 50 armed attacks (bombings and shootings) identified by French sources as politically motivated. Casablanca has been the main trouble spot…"

Nouasseur was on the main highway and railway line to Marrakech, 100 miles further south towards the Sahara. Initially, I lived on base, sharing a Dallas hut with six other men. These were wooden prefabricated structures, designed by Texas oil exploration companies for use in the Middle East. The Air Force preferred to refer to them officially as "hutments", possibly because it sounded more military to do so.

Each Dallas Hut came supplied with a Moroccan male civilian employee who swept and mopped the floors and also kept the oil heater working properly in winter. Ali, who worked in my hut, had been a soldier in the French colonial army and I practiced speaking very bad French with him which he good-naturedly encouraged. It helped that I kept him supplied with my empty American cigarette packs which he cleverly used to disguise the fact that he actually smoked Casa-Sports, a local brand boycotted by the Moroccan liberation movement.

In Casablanca's mild climate, the Dallas Huts were reasonably comfortable, with wooden shutters that could be let down for shade when it got very warm. On cold nights, we were grateful for Ali's oil-fired space heater. The weather reminded me of the amusing exchange in the film "Casablanca" when Claude Rains asks Humphrey Bogart what first brought him to Morocco.

"I came here for the waters," Bogart replies. But, says Rains, "We're in the middle of a desert."

"I was misinformed," says Bogart.

Both were misinformed. Casablanca has a moderate coastal climate not unlike that of Southern California where the film "Casablanca" was actually made. There was very little desert landscape around — a few camels, but no sand dunes. Nonetheless, the Air Force felt obliged to issue us with pith helmets. These had a tendency to blow off when caught in a prop wash or a heavy wind. Once they started rolling down a runway, they were very difficult to recover.

As it happened, I didn't spend much time in either my hutment, or my pith helmet. I was made editor of the Minaret, an Air Force weekly newspaper printed in Casablanca by *Maroc-Presse*, one of the country's leading daily newspapers, and a liberal voice in Morocco's struggle for independence. Most of my days were spent at *Maroc-Presse*, where, because of security, the Air Force reasoned I was better off wearing civilian clothes. Our uniforms were very similar in color to those of the French Air Force at the time. Since the French airmen were being regularly targeted in grenade attacks by the Moroccans, I was grateful to the U.S. Air Force for this consideration.

I very much enjoyed working in Casablanca and wearing civilian clothes. Eventually I was even given a small expense account to cover my taxis and my meals at downtown restaurants. I didn't mind that, either. The occasional bomb blast, as the struggle for independence increased its pace, didn't deter me.

I was 21, living abroad, and having the time of my life.

Casablanca in 1954 was still a very French city. The main city square was the *Place de France*. There were broad boulevards heading out from it in all directions, including the *Boulevard de la Gare* which led to *Maroc-Presse.* There were innumerable French restaurants, large and small, some spectacular, some modest, many of them with sidewalk tables. They had names like *Le Petit Poucet* and *La Poule au Pot*. Living and working in Casablanca in those days was how I imagined living and working in Paris might be and I came to enjoy every minute of it.

Although the Minaret was a military newspaper, published primarily for a military readership, it tried to sustain itself financially through commercial advertising. The U.S. Air Force, prohibited by law from being seen as endorsing the products and services advertised in the Minaret, preferred not to overstate the newspaper's official connection. That was fine with me, too.

I tried to increase the Minaret's advertising to help cover printing costs, but soon discovered a more reliable source of funding for the newspaper. As an official publication, the Minaret was permitted to draw on beer profits that poured into the air base's Non-Appropriated Consolidated Welfare Fund. This creative accounting literally kept the newspaper afloat on Pabst Blue Ribbon and Miller's High Life at no direct cost to the Air Force, or the American taxpayer.

Getting the Minaret out on time was even more challenging than getting it paid for. The *Maroc-Presse* printing staff neither spoke nor read English. All copy had to be submitted to the lino-typists days in advance and then checked and double-checked. Each time a correction was made, more errors would inevitably crop up on the composing table.

My high school French quickly proved unequal to the task and I had to plunge myself into intensive language training. A French girl friend helped, initially. Then I enrolled in night classes at the air base and lost the girl friend because most of my evenings were taken up in class studying French.

It was in one such class that I first met Anne, who happened to be the daughter of my Commanding General. She was very attractive, in a quietly regal sort of way. She dressed well and her hair was an intriguing reddish gold — not unlike, I thought, a Turner sunset. She was about my age, and I began making a point of sitting next to her. I had been in the Air Force long enough to know that general's daughters do not normally date enlisted men, but I considered myself at heart a civilian obliged by the draft laws of my country to become a temporary soldier. So I asked her out to dinner.

I thought she would probably turn me down, but to my considerable surprise, she accepted and even asked me to walk her back to the Women Officer's Quarters where she was living at the time.

One date led to another, most of them in Casablanca where we were well away from official observers. Anne's father's headquarters was a two hour drive north in Rabat, but many of his staff officers passed through the air base at Casablanca and would keep him up to date on his daughter. She made a point of occasionally showing up at the Officer's Club, putting in an appearance she knew would be reported back to her father. Our secret romance remained undetected for several months.

We spent most week-ends off base, exploring Casablanca, Marrakech, and the Atlas Mountains. Occasionally, we stayed at a friend's beach house near Pont Blondin, just north of Casablanca. Sometimes we drove all the way to Tangier, racing to get through Spanish Morocco before the border at the old Tangier International Zone closed at midnight.

We discovered we could often pay for the whole trip up to Tangier and back with the difference in the dollar-franc exchange rate. This was particularly true if we managed to schedule the visit just as the French government was falling — which it seemed to do fairly frequently those days.

Marrakech remained our favorite week-end expedition. We often took the train down from Casablanca, renting bicycles once we got there. We enjoyed the gardens and the bar at the Mamounia Hotel, but we usually stayed at a smaller, less public hotel over-looking the main marketplace. It was shortly after one of these getaway week-ends that Anne told me she was pregnant.

I was stunned. It seemed to me I had always taken precautions against such an event. Certainly I had meant to. By the accepted rules of the game, I should not even have been dating Anne. The Air Force in the 1950s may have been more forward-looking than either the Army and the Navy, but Corporals did not socialize with general officers, or their daughters. Anne and I had shattered some rather serious military protocol. We now had to face up to the consequences.

We didn't panic. We reasoned that we had some time to work things out. Eloping was a possibility, but where? And how to get married unnoticed abroad? Her father was my Commanding General. With a simple phone call, he could order my immediate transfer to the farthest reaches of his command — which happened, in those days, to be thousands of miles from Casablanca.

I decided I needed some legal advice and went to see the Air Force lawyer who handled the Minaret's legal affairs. He seemed a reasonable man and I was able to establish that our attorney-client relationship would keep my problem going any further than his office. Even then, he could not resist making light of the situation.

"Holy Christ," he whispered, looking furtively over his shoulder as he did so. "You're telling me you have knocked up the General's daughter? That is very much against Air Force regulations! The fact that you are an enlisted man, makes it even worse! Speaking as your attorney, I would say that you have put yourself in one hell of a spot. Do you want to marry her?"

"I don't feel I have much choice," I replied. "Besides, it does seem the proper thing to do, under the circumstances — don't you think?"

"Maybe not," he confided. "This is French territory. They have doctors here who are willing to take care of these things without a fuss. My best advice would be to go and find one — quickly."

Anne and I sat down that night and discussed the matter in some detail. We were both legally of age. We both intended to go back to college. Neither one of us wanted to bring a child into the world at that stage in our lives, nor did we have any religious objections to abortion. There seemed every reason in the world to terminate the pregnancy as quickly as possible — which we then proceeded to do.

With the help of colleagues at *Maroc-Presse*, I located a French doctor who — when we told him we were married and could not afford a child — agreed to perform the operation in a nearby private clinic. There would be no risk, he said, and the entire procedure could be done over a week-end.

So we slipped away for another rendezvous at

a small hotel we had come to know in Casablanca. This time, of course, there was no need to take any of the precautions against pregnancy we had followed in the past. They hadn't worked, anyway. We had a great Friday and Saturday night and Anne checked into the clinic Sunday morning.

Sadly, it seemed more designed as a place to have babies than to get rid of them. Each room was done in pink and blue pastels and each had a flower painted on the door over a printed French nursery rhyme. The operation went quickly without any complications and we drove back to the air base Monday.

We then talked about what to do next.

Having been through the experience of the pregnancy and then having to decide what to do about it, we were drawn even more closely together than before. Though the immediate problem had been resolved, we could not somehow just walk away from it. We had become too much a part of each other's lives. Furthermore, I found I had begun to fall in love with Anne, the General's daughter.

As she had with me, or so it seemed. We decided to get married, after all. It helped that the Air Force had just raised my salary, promoting me to Sergeant. Anne would keep her civilian job on the air base and we would begin looking for an apartment in Casablanca. Meanwhile, we would bring my Commanding General into the picture. She telephoned him at his headquarters in Rabat.

"Dad," she announced, "I am going to get married."

"Who is the young man?," he asked.

"You wouldn't know him, Dad. He is a Sergeant."

"We need to talk this over. I'll fly down tomorrow morning. Meet me at the Officer's Club at noon. We'll have lunch."

He first asked if she were pregnant. When she assured him she was not, he asked whether she would bring me up to Rabat to meet the family the following week-end. We had prepared for that, and she yes.

I liked her parents and have often since wondered what they really thought of me. The General had broken up several of his daughter's previous relationships, including an engagement, by simply arranging to have the gentlemen concerned transferred out of the country. We eliminated this possibility by insisting the ceremony take place immediately — in Rabat.

The other men in her life had all been young officers who said they intended making a career in the Air Force. When her parents asked me how I felt about the military, I told them I wanted to become a civilian again and get back to college as quickly as possible.

This took them by surprise. I doubt they had ever met anyone who disliked being in uniform as much as I did. I told them I enjoyed my work and was very happy to be in Casablanca, but I would leave the military as soon as I had completed my enlistment. Fortunately, they did not feel it necessary to try and convince me otherwise.

There were obvious differences in our backgrounds, but it certainly helped that the General's daughter wanted to get out of the Air Force almost as much as I did. She was eager to be away from home, well beyond her father's influence. Marriage to me happened to fit in very neatly with her own plans.

So we went ahead with the various steps required by the Air Force before the wedding could take place in Rabat. These were mostly designed to discourage Air Force enlisted men from marrying Moroccan girls. They did not apply, in any realistic way, to two American citizens marrying abroad. We nonetheless had to go through with them. The most time consuming involved a series of counseling sessions for each of us with an Air Force chaplain who was then required to draw up a report recommending for or against the marriage.

We first met with him separately and then together. He was a likable man in his late fifties with large bushy eyebrows that moved up and down without any apparent relationship to what he was saying at a given moment. He told us his church was the Disciples of Christ, a Protestant denomination neither of us knew. Since we did not belong to any church ourselves, it didn't matter particularly who conducted the ceremony. So we asked him if he would marry us and he said he would be delighted to do so.

But first, he had to finish his report on whether or not he thought we should marry. Obviously, he was in favor of our going ahead, or he would not have agreed to perform the ceremony. But he raised a cautionary note.

"About your cultural backgrounds," he said, "they are quite different. You may be drawn to each other now, but this could change over the years. You may find that you both have to work hard at keeping your marriage intact. Do you understand what I mean?," he asked.

We said we did. But in retrospect I am not sure we had any real notion of what he was hinting at. Anne, the General's daughter, was taking on a whole new world and leaving behind the only one she had ever known. She was turning her back on a close and secure family life, supported by her beloved brothers and sister, and a style of living that she had come to accept as routine — much as she might have wanted to escape it at the time.

Her willingness to join me — wherever it might lead her — and her eagerness to make a success of our marriage is a memory I will always treasure — regardless of what has happened since.

In any event, in Morocco in May 1955, our minds were made up and we proceeded to get married.

The General and his wife wanted a much more

elaborate wedding for their daughter than either she or I intended. We were able to scale it down to some extent, but it was still developing into much more of a social event than we would have preferred. There were, for instance, 250 invitations sent out to all of the top French and American military officials in Morocco. I had expressed the wish that there be neither singing nor military uniforms at either the wedding or the reception that followed.

We managed to prevail on the singing, but the commander of the small U.S. Naval facility at Port Lyautey (now Kenitra) showed up in full military uniform accompanied by a Marine honor guard, similarly attired — military decorations, sabers, and all. This upstaged several high-ranking French and American officers who were clearly unhappy at being asked to forego their colorful dress uniforms in favor of dark business suits.

After the ceremony, we moved into a fifth floor pent house apartment — no elevator — in downtown Casablanca. The city was fast becoming a center point in the Moroccan struggle for independence. There were frequent nearby *manifestations* for and against continued French rule. Some of them were directed at *Maroc-Presse*, which was seen by many as advancing the Moroccan movement towards independence.

My office was located at the front of the *Maroc-Presse* building on the ground floor. Several bricks came flying through the front window one afternoon as I was trying to put the Minaret to bed. I took cover under a steel composing table while the Casablanca police used water cannons on the demonstrators outside. Much of the water came through the broken windows, dousing me and the printing staff in the process.

It was my first introduction to street violence and I found myself on the receiving end, insufficiently detached from the two contesting sides. I quickly developed a preference for the role of a more neutral observer.

Our apartment at 16 *rue de Cabris* didn't have much much in the way of a cooking facilities, although it had a lovely veranda overlooking the city. We ate out frequently, mostly at neighborhood restaurants. We were on our way to one of them on July 14, 1955 — Bastille Day — when a tremendous explosion took place just a few blocks away.

A young Moroccan street peddler had left an innocent-appearing ice cream vendor's tricycle in front of a sidewalk cafe. It contained a large quantity of plastic explosive and the blast destroyed the glass partitions between several cafes, as well as their front windows. Shards of shattered glass were sent flying in all directions. We saw some patrons being carried out to ambulances impaled to the chairs they had been sitting in.

Seven people were killed in that Bastille Day

bombing and many others were injured. The over-all security situation worsened in the downtown area and the Air Force began evacuating American families out to the air base at Nouasseur. We wanted to stay at 16 *rue de Cabris*, but under pressure from Anne's father, we moved to the suburban Hotel *Anfa*, site of the historic 1943 Casablanca summit between Roosevelt and Churchill.

The *Anfa* advertised in the Minaret and I was able to get the room at a substantial discount. Bob Tabor, a free-lance journalist who had become a good friend, took up the balance of our lease and bought our few items of furniture at 16 *rue de Cabris*. Life at the *Hotel Anfa* was fun, but we soon missed the excitement of being downtown.

Anne's father, however, had a way of livening up our days. He was determined, for instance, to take his new son-in-law for a ride in his jet fighter. This was not easy to arrange because of his busy schedule in Rabat, and I did not go out of my way to encourage him. He was, nonetheless, insistent.

One morning, he showed up early at the air base in his two-seater Lockheed F-80 Shooting Star with an empty rear seat. We had been out late the night before in Casablanca and I was painfully hung over. I assumed — correctly, as it turned out — that he would probably make me airsick and I had no change of uniform at the air base. Also, at six foot six and 200 or so pounds, I was not ideally designed physically to fit into the cramped cockpit of a jet fighter air-craft. There was no real basis for discussion. I was a Sergeant. He was a Major General and he wanted to take me up for a ride in his airplane.

I was strapped tightly into the ejection seat, my head and face encased in a crash helmet and an oxy-gen mask. The mask contained a live microphone and the helmet had radio earphones built into it. The General and I were in instant and total communica-tion. I could hear every breath he took and I felt he could probably sense my growing anxiety with each breath I took.

"We'll do a little sight-seeing first to empty the wing tanks," he announced, "then we can shoot some aerobatics."

"Never mind any of that," was very much my in-tention at the time, but I doubt that I expressed it in those precise terms. He was, in any case, quite deaf when he chose to be — the result of many years spent flying in open cockpit aircraft. So we went sightsee-ing. We buzzed a few Moroccan villages and spent some time chasing herds of camels through the arid landscape.

"OK", his voice crackled abruptly through my earphones, "here we go!"

He pulled the jet up into an inside loop and all of a sudden the canopy was filled with fast-moving Moroccan countryside. We were upside down and headed into a very steep roller-coaster dive. Between my feet was a metal box that alternately churned out hot air and icy air conditioning. It tried very hard to keep up with what the airplane was doing — producing warm air at chilly high altitudes and then turning comfortably cool when we were down on the deck, which was frequently the case because the General liked flying low. But the automatic system lagged behind: hot air gushed forth while were at low altitudes which then switched to freezing at 30,000 feet.

I very quickly began feeling the effect of gravity and so did my innards. I vomited noisily into my oxygen mask and the General thoughtfully passed me back his white linen handkerchief.

"Lost your cookies, hey? Sorry about that. We'll head back to the base now. No more aerobatics."

I returned his handkerchief several weeks later. Anne had meanwhile stitched in the drawing of an upside down fighter aircraft and the inscription: "Merci, mon beau pere!"

Alfred Hitchcock was filming "The Man Who Knew Too Much," with Jimmy Stewart and Doris Day in Marrakech. I drove down to do a radio interview and a story for "Stars and Stripes." Stewart had been an Air Force Colonel in World War II and had just completed a film about the Strategic Air Command. We spoke of his experiences as a real-life bomber pilot — in comparison to the role he played in the motion picture. I don't remember much about the Doris Day interview, except asking her if she thought rock and roll music had much of a future. She said it did not.

The interviews took place in the lobby of the Hotel Mamounia where most of the cast, including Alfred Hitchcock, were staying. Afterwards, I asked one of the Hollywood production staff at the bar if he had heard of the Moroccan Hand of Fatima charm which had the power to ward off the influence of the Evil Eye and thus bring protection to its wearer. I showed him the silver one Anne had given me, suggesting that, with all of the back-stabbing in Hollywood, he might do well to get one of his own.

Whereupon he pulled open his shirt to reveal the golden Hand of Fatima he had already purchased in Marrakech.

"Thanks," he said, "but I have already become protected."

That night, I snuck back into the Women Officer's Quarters at the air base. Anne had decided to remain there, waiting my return from Marrakesh. It was still off limits for me to be spending the night there, but at least now we were married.

We left Casablanca in January 1956, two months before France granted independence to Morocco. Several friends at the Minaret had assured us we would come back to Africa. It was too much in our lives, they said, to stay away for long.

We had no idea how right they were.

6.

Different Kinds of Africa.

In the summer of 1958, I was finishing my graduate studies at Berkeley and looking for a job that would eventually take me back overseas. More than anything else, I wanted to work as a reporter abroad. This meant making my way up through the professional ladder of a news agency, like the Associated Press, or a newspaper big enough to maintain an overseas staff, or a broadcasting network, such as CBS whose news team I had admired for years, particularly when it was headed by Edward R. Murrow.

There was an economic crisis in 1958. It was being called a recession by the Eisenhower administration. Not many news organizations were hiring young men — or women — fresh out of college, but the U.S. Government was. Thanks to recent Soviet advances in space research — notably, the Sputnik satellite — Washington was looking for potential Cold Warriors — and looking hard.

Several possibilities presented themselves. One of them was the Central Intelligence Agency (CIA) — about which I knew very little. Another was the National Security Agency (NSA) — about which I knew even less. Both of them were offering employment in 1958 to people with journalistic backgrounds and overseas experience. I applied to both.

There was also the possibility of being hired as a reporter at the Voice of America (VOA) in Washington, DC. I was told there were no immediate openings at VOA, but I could apply to its parent organization — the U.S. Information Agency (USIA) — for an appointment as a junior officer trainee. Later, I was assured, I could cross over to VOA. In the meantime, I would be sent overseas as a foreign service officer — which sounded good to me. I mailed in an application to USIA.

The CIA came through first and interviewed me in San Francisco and later at a clandestine site I was told not to say anything about. NSA then congratulated me on passing their qualifying test and asked me to meet their representative who was visiting the Berkeley campus. When I did, his salary offer and terms of employment struck me as being too low and I told him so. The CIA had been talking more money and better terms — so had USIA. He said he would get back to me, but never did.

Not long after that, I got a ticket in the mail inviting me to come to Washington for a USIA panel interview. Since I was going to be in the neighborhood anyway, CIA asked me to stop by for a further session with their recruiters. They proposed I undergo a "polygraph examination". When I learned it was a lie detector test, I declined. The said they would go ahead with a background security check — but there might still be a polygraph requirement, later. Happily, USIA's own security investigation came through first and I was invited back to Washington once more. This time to be sworn in as a junior officer trainee and, after a brief training period, assigned to Addis Ababa, Ethiopia.

The CIA caught up with me later in Ethiopia. Their letter bore the organization's name and address in bold print on the envelope. I was away from my office and this suspicious-looking communication lay on my desk for several days, attracting considerable attention from both the American and Ethiopian staff. I explained to all that I had never really been interested in espionage as a career. My USIA boss passed my thoughts along to the CIA Station Chief at the American Embassy and the next letter I got from the CIA informed me, somewhat tartly, that the position for which I was being considered "had been filled from within the Agency".

I have never regretted making the choice I did. The two professional fields, espionage and journalism, do not mix very well — in spite of their apparent similarities. Reporters and spies both get paid for seeking out information under frequently difficult and hazardous circumstances, but any resemblance between the two jobs ends at about that point. Journalists are occasionally accused of being spies — sometimes with unfortunate results. It doesn't help that CIA and other intelligence agencies have used the news business as a cover from time to time.

Anne and I moved back to Africa with considerable enthusiasm, although Addis Ababa turned out to have no comparison whatsoever to Casablanca. In 1958, the Ethiopian capital seemed mostly composed of tin shacks, apart from a few permanent structures left over from the Italian occupation of 1935-40. My office was located in one of these, overlooking what was then called Haile Selassie I Star Square, but was better known then — and now — as the *"piazza"*.

Italian influences remained everywhere, nearly twenty years after the last fascist soldier had fled the country. The Italian-built opera house was still the best theater in town. *Castelli's* was the finest restaurant. On week-ends, we drove to Mussolini Pass for picnics on the edge of the Rift Valley escarpment. There were, nonetheless, some very specific Ethiopian cultural realities.

Not the least of these was Haile Selassie I, Emperor of Ethiopia, King of Kings, Elect of God, and Conquering Lion of the Tribe of Judah. We junior diplomats were instructed to bow in his presence. If we happened to encounter his Rolls Royce in traffic, we were obliged to pull over to the side of the road, get out of the car as quickly as possible, and then bow.

On one occasion, I was a bit slow extricating myself from my Volkswagen and was sharply reprimanded by the Imperial Bodyguard for not moving quickly enough.

This did not keep me from being invited to an official dinner at the Emperor's old palace, which could then easily seat several hundred guests. The menu was classically Ethiopian including vast platters of raw meat, served at room temperature. Seated next to me was an Ethiopian Army Major. I watched him cut a large slice of raw meat and dip it into a bowl of fiery red pepper sauce. I asked him why he ate raw meat.

"I have to," he said.

"Why?", I persisted.

"Because," he said, "I am a lion."

There was no further explanation and I thought it prudent not to pursue the matter.

One morning, while gazing out at the crowded piazza from my office window, I saw a completely naked black man strolling along the sidewalk. He wore a small beaded bracelet on his left arm and absolutely nothing else, anywhere. Not a head turned as he walked by. The reaction along the *Place de*

France in Casablanca would certainly have been much different.

1958 marked a particularly intense period of Cold War competition between the United States and the Soviet Union. Addis Ababa's diplomatic community was certainly not left untouched by this rivalry. The Soviet Embassy challenged the American Embassy to a sports duel. We were offered the choice between chess, table tennis, or volleyball. We wisely, we thought, chose volleyball.

As a reasonably fit and patriotic 26 year old, I was immediately swept up in the preparations for the Big Match. There were daily afternoon practice sessions at the newly-completed American embassy volley-ball court. Having spent summers on the beaches of Southern California, I was not unfamiliar with volleyball. But Addis Ababa's seven thousand foot altitude proved much more challenging than than the level of play at, say, Laguna Beach. Nonetheless, I made the embassy team.

On the day of the Big Match, the Soviet side was accompanied into the U.S. Embassy compound by a fairly large number of fans, most of them carrying cameras. Then I noticed that our rooting section had its own share of photographers, as well. Even before the game got underway, the clicking of camera shutters and the popping of flash bulbs seemed distracting. The degree of spectator interest on both sides was intense, but it did not seem particularly directed at the game. Diplomats on one side of the court were furiously taking photographs of diplomats on the other side. Not many spectators seemed interested in the game itself.

To this day, I am not certain who won, but the details are very likely contained in a classified file somewhere in either Moscow or Washington, or perhaps both.

My work in Addis Ababa was mostly centered on learning USIA's administrative procedures, particularly the techniques involved in trying to get more money out of Washington. As the most junior member of the staff, I was the one usually sent out to visit Ethiopian schools in outlying areas. This was fine with me and I often took Anne along. She enjoyed the opportunity to break away from the embassy wives' social activities. We traveled all over Ethiopia visiting rural high schools, meeting with students, talking about life in the United States and showing films to people who had rarely seen a movie before — or met an American, for that matter.

I'm not sure how effective these visits were in winning friends for America. I even ended up in jail during one of them. An overly conscientious Ethiopian police officer in the remote village of Debra Marcos locked me up on general principles, but allowed me one phone call to Addis Ababa.

It took a while for the call to get through to the USIA office on Haile Selassie I Square. When an

Ethiopian secretary finally came on the line, I yelled: "Help! This is Mr. Kelly and I have been arrested in Debra Marcos!"

"Mr. Kelly is not here," she replied with maddening self-assurance. "He is away on tour."

Then she hung up.

The Debra Marcos policeman sensed trouble, But after considerable pleading on my part, he let me phone Addis Ababa again. This time, I called my boss on a direct line. He promptly established my identity to the policeman through an Amharic interpreter and I was released from captivity. Debra Marcos was not a town I would have cared to spend much more than an afternoon in.

Gondar would have been much more preferable. I landed there one misty April morning in a venerable DC-3 operated by Ethiopian Airlines. It was on a domestic run to the north and had stopped to pick up a load of animal hides and skins on their way to Eritrea. These were being accompanied to the market place by several Ethiopian herdsmen who proceeded to make themselves comfortable in the back of the airplane. I was invited to the flight deck, happily out of sight and smell of the animal skins.

We soon began to smell something else, however. It was smoke and it was starting to fill the cockpit. The co-pilot quickly grabbed a fire extinguisher and headed through the door to the rear of the plane. I followed closely behind. We discovered several

Ethiopian herdsmen making coffee over an open fire they had built on the metal floor of the airplane. The co-pilot ended the coffee hour abruptly, delivering an animated lecture on flight safety in Amharic as he did so.

Those were the days before the Peace Corps was created and USIA in Africa was making the sort of contact with rural schools and outlying communities that would eventually be taken over by the Peace Corps — which was far better equipped to do it. In the meantime, I was happy to fill in. My trips to the field got me out of the office and gave me a chance to see a part of Africa I never would have known, otherwise.

I began taking a tape recorder with me on some of these expeditions and I put together several feature stories which I sent to VOA in Washington. These were well received and when a major United Nations conference took place on Addis Ababa, VOA set up a direct broadcast circuit to Washington for me to transmit several stories and interviews from the conference hall. It was the first time I had broadcast live on an international circuit and I found the experience an exciting foretaste of things to come.

This marked the beginning of what would develop into a long relationship. VOA was in the process of increasing its daily broadcasts to Africa. Henry Loomis, then Director of VOA, wrote me that he enjoyed listening to my reports and was coming to Africa on a visit. He urged that we get together.

When he arrived in Addis Ababa, he offered me a job in Washington. I thanked him, but said I wasn't sure I could afford to live in the United States on what USIA was paying me. He said he would try to rehire me at a better salary if USIA would let me go. This proved to be impossible and we ultimately agreed to hold off the Washington assignment, for the time being. He made it clear, however, that he wanted me to spend at least a year at VOA headquarters, learning how the organization worked. We would then consider my returning overseas as a broadcast journalist.

I was in no rush to leave Africa. It was a great time to be there. 1960 had already seen the emergence of several newly independent African states. Change was in the air. It looked as though John F. Kennedy would be the next president of the United States and he had already signaled a totally new outlook towards Africa. My apprenticeship tour as a foreign service officer in Ethiopia was coming to an end and I had been offered the opportunity to open a new USIA post in what was then Northern Rhodesia, now Zambia. It seemed a particularly auspicious time.

I tried to learn as much as I could about my new assignment, but very little information seemed available on Northern Rhodesia. John Gunther's recently-published "Inside Africa" was not reassuring. He described Lusaka, the capital city, as a Wild West town with an open sewer running down the middle of it. He also noted that the British colony shared a long northern border with the former Belgian Congo. The post-independence problems of the Congo were dominating world headlines and I wondered what sort of impact they were having on its neighbor to the south.

The British Embassy in Addis Ababa gave me a political briefing on Northern Rhodesia, which was a British colony at the time. I was also brought up to date on the bordering Congolese province of Katanga which had broken away from the rest of the Congo and declared itself an independent state. Katanga's copper mines were linked with those of Northern Rhodesia through interlocking management arrangements, as well as power and railway connections. There were extensive British and American interests involved in the mining activity on both sides of the border. The Congo, with all its chaos, was about to become part of my life.

Lusaka proved to be yet another totally different Africa than either Casablanca or Addis Ababa. Times had been good in recent years. Copper revenues had been high and John Gunther's open sewer had been covered over and landscaped. Northern Rhodesia's capital city was a tidy collection of shops, banks and business offices flanking the main north-south rail line that ran from the Zambezi River to the Congo border. Government House, the colonial legislature, and Lusaka's best hotel were located up along the

Ridgeway (since renamed Independence Avenue) overlooking the town.

It was all fairly new. In the mid-1930s, when Britain decided to create a new capital for its Northern Rhodesian colony, Lusaka was chosen for its central location and not much else. It was little more than a farming community with a crossroads and a railroad siding. When the railway had been pushed up from South Africa in the early 1900s, sidings were built every twenty miles or so. This allowed the single track to be used by trains traveling both north and south. These sidings were often named after local leaders, such as Chief Lusakas.

It was a good place to raise young children, which was fortunate because we now had two sons, Kenyon born in Nairobi in 1960 and Brenton, born in Lusaka two years later.

There was, as yet, no American diplomatic establishment in Lusaka, not even a consulate. The U.S. official presence in Northern Rhodesia consisted of a State Department officer, Charles Pletcher, and myself. We were sent up on loan from the American Consulate General in Salisbury, Southern Rhodesia (now Harare, Zimbabwe) several hundred miles away, across the Zambezi River.

This unusual arrangement was made necessary by the fact that Northern Rhodesia was then part of the Federation of Rhodesia and Nyasaland, a white-ruled political entity pulled together by Britain in the

1950s without much regard for the wishes of the local black population. Southern Rhodesia had quickly succeeded in dominating the federal government structure, although the federal Prime Minister was Sir Roy Welensky, a white Northern Rhodesian former railwayman.

When Sir Roy was approached by the U.S. State Department for permission to open a consulate in Lusaka, he complained it might indicate a "lack of faith in the Federation. Go ahead and open an office", he said, "but don't give it a formal diplomatic or consular title, just call it an office".

Washington bowed to Sir Roy's request and we moved into an office building on Cairo Road, Lusaka's main thoroughfare (named because it was once claimed you would end up in Cairo if you stayed on it long enough) and hung an American flag out the window. We hired a small staff, issued visas, opened a library, and started sending African students to the United States for university education. However, out of consideration to Welensky, we did not call it the American Consulate in Lusaka.

This level of Washington concern over the sensitivities of the white ruling regimes in southern Africa was by no means limited to Northern Rhodesia. Earlier in 1960, the State Department press spokesman in Washington had set off a small crisis by formally expressing U.S. regret over the massacre at Sharpeville, South Africa where 69 people were killed and 180 injured when police opened fire on a crowd of unarmed demonstrators.

Not everybody in the Eisenhower administration took the same view on Sharpeville, least of all the President himself. He called in Secretary of State Christian Herter who — according to the White House account of their meeting — told Eisenhower there had been an internal failure within the State Department whereby a mid-level bureaucrat proposed a statement and the press office released it without checking at the top policy level. The Secretary added that he was furious about it, regarding it as a breach of courtesy between nations.

President Eisenhower told Herter that, if it were his decision, he would find another post for the bureaucrat involved. All he could see to do now, he said, would be to call in the South African ambassador and tell him that, although we are much distressed by events in South Africa, we do not regard it as our business to make public statements about this, and officially regret having done so.

Eventually the matter was taken up between the U.S. Ambassador to South Africa and the South African foreign ministry in Pretoria — with the Ambassador assuring the South Africans there was no change in U.S. policy towards their country.

Happily, the political atmosphere in Lusaka was far less tense, but we could not help but be aware of the growing political turmoil in South Africa. A new South African black leader had already begun making a name for himself. Nelson Mandela was demonstrating the ability to stay one step ahead of the South African police and yet appear, and reappear, at public events all over Africa — from Ghana to Ethiopia. The local press was calling him the "Black Pimpernel" for the way he managed to avoid capture. His luck eventually ran out, however, and he was brought to trial in South Africa and subsequently imprisoned.

Charlie Pletcher and I were in frequent contact with Northern Rhodesia's leading African nationalists, including Kenneth Kaunda of the United National Independence Party and Harry Nkumbula of the African National Congress. British colonial officials encouraged these links, but Welensky's federal government worried we were getting too close to the black African politicians. They feared we were trying to break up their Federation by putting the notion of "independence" in the minds of the Africans. In fact, the Federation, as such, had less than three years to live before it dissolved into the three independent states of Malawi, Zambia, and (ultimately) Zimbabwe.

We tried to ease white settler anxieties by doing good deeds in the local community. Charlie became a member of the local Rotary Club. His wife conducted the church choir, and my wife went to work for the African-American Institute. arranging scholarships for Africans to study at American universities. I joined the Lusaka Junior Chamber of Commerce, ultimately becoming its President. We pitched in and helped raise funds for local charities. I even managed to have USIA in Washington provide sheet music for the King's African Rifles military band, thus introducing John Phillip Sousa to their Saturday morning marches down Cairo Road.

Our small American Library made a more enduring contribution to Lusaka's political and social progress. It was the town's first free public lending library and it quickly became a meeting place for young people of all races. The first constitution for an independent Zambia was drafted on its reading tables and its librarian, Simon Katilungu, became Zambia's first ambassador to London.

By mid-1961, however, we were devoting an increasing amount of attention to events along Northern Rhodesia's border with the Congo. Welensky's Federal Government was getting more closely involved in Moise Tshombe's breakaway province of Katanga.

At one stage, Welensky even began moving military aircraft to the airstrip at Kipushi which actually straddled the border with Katanga. Our trips to the North became more and more frequent.

Tshombe's Katanga was an outlaw state, unrecognized diplomatically by any other country. However, its continued existence presented a special problem for us in Lusaka. European map makers had created a topographical nightmare called the Congolese Pedicle which extended Katanga into Northern Rhodesia, virtually splitting the northern part of the British colony in half. Charlie Pletcher and I found we had to drive across the Pedicle in order to visit the Northern Province.

Technically, we needed Katangese visas to enter the Pedicle, but Washington feared the acceptance of such a visa in an official U.S. passport would somehow constitute diplomatic recognition of Katanga's secessionist regime. As it happened, we did not bother obtaining the colorful and unusual Katanga visas — much as I might have liked having one in my passport as a souvenir.

Washington's hands off attitude towards Katanga may not have extended to arms sales and deliveries. In February 1961, a private American air charter company, Seven Seas Airlines, used a U.S.-registered C-97 cargo aircraft to deliver three disassembled Fouga Magister jet fighters to Elisabethville airport in Katanga. The French-built aircraft were later assembled and equipped with machine guns, rockets, and light bombs. They gave the Katanga air force an advantage that would eventually prove tragic for the UN.

Seven Seas Airlines, based in Europe and using U.S. registered aircraft flown by American crews, was viewed with considerable skepticism by journalists on the scene who suspected that CIA had a hand in the delivery of the Fougas. When their stories were reported in the U.S. press, they caught the attention of President Kennedy who asked the CIA for an explanation. The agency's reply, now on file at the JFK Library in Boston, remains classified to this day — in spite of my repeated attempts to have it made public.

The CIA still asserts that their report on Seven Seas Airlines contains information involving sources and methods that, nearly fifty years later, could affect U.S. national security. My own suspicion is that the CIA's reluctance to release their report has more to do with the fact that at least one of the Fougas delivered by Seven Seas was indirectly involved in the crash of UN Secretary General Dag Hammarskjold in Northern Rhodesia, later in 1961.

The Secretary General's aircraft had been on a flight from Leopoldville (now Kinshasa) to Ndola, Northern Rhodesia when it crashed just short of the Ndola runway. Eyewitnesses said it was forced down by another aircraft, but this was later discounted in the official investigations. The real reason for the crash appears to have been crew fatigue complicated by the fact that the aircraft's pilot had filed false flight plans for security reasons and had flown thousands of miles out of the way to avoid the Katangese Fougas. Any CIA connection with the delivery of the Fougas would clearly be embarrassing to the agency, which is very likely why it has fought to keep the matter secret all these years.

As an American diplomat in Northern Rhodesia, I was precluded from doing any broadcast reporting to VOA from along the Katanga border. I found this increasingly frustrating when Katanga developed into a major international story and journalists came to Northern Rhodesia from all over the world to cover it. Among the many whom I encountered along the border was George Clay, a South African reporter for American radio and television, who became a good friend.

By this time, the street fighting in Katanga had centered around the Elisabethville (now Lubumbashi) post office where Katangese gendarmes were in a pitched battle against the UN's Ghurka soldiers. One of the first victims was the post office itself, forcing George Clay and other foreign journalists to cross the border into Northern Rhodesia to file their stories. It was a two hundred mile round trip involving several Katangese and UN roadblocks, but it was the only way to reach a functioning telegraph line or meet a broadcast circuit.

As a South African, George had an easier time getting through the Katangese roadblocks on the way to the Northern Rhodesian border. South Africa had proven itself friendly to the Katanga secessionists, while Britain and the United States were seen by the Katangans as backing the UN. This made it difficult for British and American journalists, but George generously offered to carry their copy through to the Northern Rhodesian telegraph office.

He did this on several occasions, including the last time we met. It was during the rainy season and he had just pushed through from Elisabethville in his four-wheel-drive Land Rover which, while useful for the rain and the mud, had one important disadvantage.

As George put it: "From the air, the Land Rover looks like a military vehicle and the bloody Indian Air Force has been chasing me all the way from Elisabethville!"

The Indian army and air force had taken over much of the fighting for the UN in Katanga. They had brought in British-built Canberra jet bombers which they were using to patrol roads leading in and out of Elisabethville, including the one George was using to reach the Northern Rhodesian border.

George complained he had been buzzed repeatedly by the Canberras. Each time, he said he had slammed on the brakes and jumped from the vehicle, taking cover in muddy ditches along the side of the road. He said he thought he heard the sound of machine gun fire, but he wasn't sure and he was taking no chances with the Indian Air Force.

In the meantime, he was desperately looking for another — more civilian-looking — vehicle to make the trip back and forth from Katanga. There were no rental cars to be found on the Northern Rhodesian border. Journalists had grabbed them all up for use in Katanga. I had been driving an ancient Vauxhall which I had managed to rent a week earlier and I offered it to George, providing he could clear it with the rental agent. He managed to do so and I swapped keys with him, taking the mud-spattered Land Rover which I promised to leave behind for him in the hotel parking lot.

He was very grateful. Two years later, I was able to be helpful once again to George Clay. It would turn out to be in Stanleyville (now called Kisangani), but that was in 1965 and neither of us had gotten there yet.

In the meantime, my brief career in diplomacy was fast coming to an end. There was an altogether new job waiting for me in Washington. My new boss was going to be Edward R. Murrow, whom I had idolized since I first started broadcasting in Alaska. President Kennedy had appointed Murrow to be the new director of USIA, which included VOA where I was headed, finally, as a broadcast journalist.

7.

The Congo, Che Guevara, and a Gravestone for George.

The altogether new job waiting for me in Washington kept me away from Africa at a busy time. More chaos had burst forth, particularly in the Congo. It helped that my new job put me in fairly close touch with events on the continent. VOA was in the midst of expanding its broadcasts to Africa and had recently opened news bureaus in Lagos and Nairobi.

After a brief training period consisting largely of learning to find my way around the cavernous VOA building at 330 Independence Avenue, I began covering Africa by long distance telephone — or at least I tried to.

VOA in those days was like fifty radio stations broadcasting at the same time in as many languages. They were linked, it seemed, by innumerable staff meetings and, in reality, several miles of teletype circuits. At the center of it all was the Newsroom which was located in a windowless basement that also lacked any doors. Since it was staffed around the clock by three shifts of writers and editors, someone was always on duty. Thus there was never any need to lock the place up. The teletype circuits led out from the Newsroom carrying news and feature copy to the fifty radio stations, or language services, that made up the Voice of America.

It was an invigorating, challenging place to work. My days were consumed with pulling together an evening (Africa time) news broadcast about events in Africa, as well as the rest of the world — but the emphasis was on Africa. The big problem was that timely, accurate coverage of what was actually taking place in Africa was hard to come by. VOA was just beginning to build a network of reporters across the continent and lines of communication to and from Africa were primitive and unreliable, at best. Ed Murrow and Henry Loomis had planned a network of news correspondent bureaus linking major African cities to an elaborate studio center in Monrovia, Liberia which, in turn, had its own circuits with VOA in Washington. Sadly, it was all many years ahead of its time.

The telecommunications infrastructure between African cities had yet to be built. Telephone calls from Nairobi to Dakar, for example, had to pass through London and Paris. It was far easier to call Akron, Ohio from Monrovia — because of the Firestone connection —than Lagos, Nigeria which was, of course, much nearer.

Satellite phones and the Internet had yet to be invented. We relied instead on expensive radio circuits through Europe that had to be booked 24 hours in advance. For the reporter in Africa, this meant filing a story by telex and then spending hours sitting in a radio station trying to get through to VOA in Washington on a transatlantic broadcast circuit. I would usually be waiting at the Washington end of the connection, working against broadcast deadlines to pull the reports in and revoiced when, as was often the case, the broadcast quality of the transatlantic circuits was bad

It was a frustrating and frequently unrewarding process, but it kept me very much aware of what was happening on the scene. This was especially true of events in the Congo where by mid-July 1964, a full scale civil war had broken out. This story led our newscasts for weeks and I was on the phone daily with Leopoldville, Nairobi, Kampala, and other African listening posts where VOA had correspondents reporting the news in and around the Congo.

The rebel Congolese forces, who called themselves *simbas* (Swahili for lion), had begun their offensive in May 1964 along the western shores of Lake Tanganyika. They quickly pushed westward into the interior and seized the provincial center of

Kindu after meeting little resistance from government forces. By the end of July, they threatened to split off the entire eastern portion of the country.

On August 5, our news headlines in Washington were dominated by an incident in the Tonkin Gulf where two U.S. ships were reportedly attacked off the Vietnamese coast. At the same time, the VOA newsroom began receiving reports that the American Consulate in Stanleyville (since renamed Kisangani) had been occupied by Congolese rebel soldiers. Consulate staffmembers were reported to have been physically mistreated and locked up as hostages by the *simbas*.

Like the reports from the Tonkin Gulf, the initial details from Stanleyville were sketchy. We later learned that Michael Hoyt, the American Consul, had managed to avoid capture by hiding in the Consulate security vault with his CIA colleague and two code clerks. The *simbas* tried to shoot their way through the heavy steel door, but gave up when it proved too much for them. By that time, they had found several bottles of cold beer in the Consulate's kitchen.

Hoyt later wrote that he was able to sneak out of the vault unobserved by the rebels and remain under cover for several days. He was also able to use his emergency radio to reach the American embassy in Leopoldville. He was worried, however, that details from his reports were being picked up by VOA and broadcast back to the Congo.

"VOA is broadcasting information about Stanleyville," he radioed the American embassy. "They cite reports from the Consulate saying the city is calm. They should stop", he said, "making reference to us."

As Hoyt later explained in his account of this incident. "I knew the rebels could hear VOA broadcasts in French, English, or Swahili and would realize that the American Consulate was sending out messages. I noticed, " he said, "VOA thereafter stopped commenting on the situation in Stanleyville."

Hoyt and his colleagues were subsequently rescued by Operation *Dragon Rouge*, a complex military raid that dropped 320 Belgian paratroopers on Stanleyville from U.S. Air Force C-130 transports in November 1964. The assault was supported by Cuban exiles, many of them veterans of CIA's 1961 Bay of Pigs invasion. The Cubans, recruited by the CIA for service in the Congo, led the C-130s to the target in World War II-era B-26 bombers, backed up by T-28 fighters which strafed and rocketed rebel positions.

Other Cuban exiles were on the ground. They spearheaded a five-mile-long military column led by South African and Rhodesian mercenaries under the command of the legendary Mike Hoare. The column was fighting its way north to Stanleyville, intending to arrive at dawn November 24, just as the *Dragon Rouge* paradrop was timed to take place on the golf course adjacent to the old Stanleyville airport. As in the air attack, the Cuban exiles were in the lead on the ground. Recruited and trained by the CIA, they formed a special rescue team for Hoyt and the other Consulate staffmembers. For this reason, Hoare placed them at the head of his column.

Delayed by rains and frequent rebel attacks, Hoare had been forced to push through during the night, but eventually ran into a particularly severe *simba* ambush. George Clay, my old friend from Katanga, was riding in Hoare's communications van, recording radio chatter for NBC television. Hit by a sudden burst of rebel machine gun fire, he died instantly.

David Halberstam of the New York Times, who also knew George in Katanga, later wrote that his death "took away one of the great present-day correspondents, a man whose work was marked by bravery, wit, urbanity, tolerance and intellect."

There were other casualties that night, as well. By the time Hoare's delayed column reached Stanleyville, *Dragon Rouge* was well underway and many of the hostages held by the rebels were being executed by them. Still others were killed as the *simbas* retreated to the northeast Congo. *Dragon Rouge* was a costly rescue operation, but it chased the rebels out of Stanleyville and ultimately broke the back of their rebellion.

Not all the *simbas* managed to get away. They abandoned their chief sorceress, Mama Onema, who promptly proclaimed, in revenge, that she was giving all her powers to the central government. This message was widely distributed in a Congolese propaganda poster which quickly became a collector's item.

Michael Hoyt and his American Consulate colleagues returned safely to the United States. They were welcomed as heroes in Washington where they were given special awards. The reaction elsewhere was less enthusiastic. The objections over the Stanleyvile rescue operation were particularly harsh in Africa and at the United Nations in New York.

American Ambassador to Kenya William Attwood summed up the African reaction from his vantage point in Nairobi: "The weakness and impotence of newly independent Africa had been harshly and dramatically revealed to the whole world (by the Stanleyville raid) and the educated African felt deeply humiliated: the white man with a gun, the old plunderer who had enslaved his ancestor, was back again. And there wasn't a damn thing Africa could do about it except yell rape."

And the Africans did just that. The uproar was still underway when I arrived in New York late in 1964 to cover African debate at the United Nations General Assembly. Among the many speakers attacking the U.S. and Belgium was Cuban revolutionary hero Ernesto "Che" Guevara. I watched him vow dramatically "to avenge the crime committed in the Congo."

I should have paid more attention to Che
Guevara. As it turned out, we were both headed for
the Congo — under totally different circumstances.
He slipped in through neighboring Tanzania in May
1965, elaborately disguised, leading a group of 200
Cuban special forces in a last-minute effort to get the
Congolese rebellion started up again.

My own arrival three months later was on an
overnight flight from Paris. I had thought to prepare myself on the way down by rereading Joseph
Conrad's "Heart of Darkness". As we descended
through heavy clouds over the Congo river, Conrad's
1910 description seemed to me to be particularly apt:
"The long stretches of the waterway ran on, deserted,
into the gloom of over-shadowed distances…an empty stream, a great silence, an impenetrable forest."

The sense of gloom, of inherent menace had
stayed with the Congo more than half a century later.
The river looked to me much as it must have seemed
to Conrad, but a city had grown up along side it during the intervening years. The Belgians named it
Leopoldville — for their king. The Congolese later
changed it back to Kinshasa — the name of the small
riverside village Conrad had known.

Leopoldville, when I saw it for the first time in
1965, seemed much like the great river itself: grey,
gloomy, unaccountably ominous. The city was a
disorderly collection of concrete business and residential structures, many of them dating back to the

Congo Belge. Most seemed faded and worn — a few were unfinished. The Belgians had left, precipitously, five years earlier — after a chaotic transfer of power marked by rioting, rape and murder.

The Belgian departure linked two words — Congo and chaos — irrevocably. The subsequent events in Stanleyville and the worldwide reaction to them only served to intensify the Congo's reputation for confusion and disorder — or so it seemed to me at the time. I looked forward to the opportunity of reporting the Congo story firsthand.

It was against this background that Che Guevara had moved his small band of black (at Congolese rebel insistence, Guevara being the primary exception to this rule) Cuban special forces across Lake Tanganyika into the eastern Congo. He hoped to establish a training base for African revolutionaries, not just Congolese, but all Africans living under colonial or minority white regimes: Angolans, Mozambicans, Rhodesians — eventually South Africans themselves. Guevara had met with their exile organizations in route to the Congo and had received what he thought was their encouragement and support — as well as that of China and the Soviet Union.

But before he had a chance to launch his African training project, Che was quickly pushed into combat on behalf of the Congolese rebellion. Laurent Kabila, a Congolese revolutionary leader who — many years later — would become President of the

Congo, insisted that Guevara commit fifty of his Cuban soldiers to an attack on government forces. The target was the well-fortified power station at Bendera, located in the hilly escarpment north of Albertville (now called Kalemie).

Bendera supplied electricity to Albertville, a major port on Lake Tanganyika. Knocking the power plant out of commission would have an obvious psychological effect on the city's civilian and military population. Guevara later wrote that he thought the attack on Bendera was overly ambitious, but he reluctantly agreed to it. He asked Kabila to be allowed to accompany his troops to Bendera. Failing to receive an answer, he remained in camp.

The Bendera attack proved to be a disaster. Not only did Guevara's Cubans fail to take out the power plant, four of them were killed and fourteen were wounded. Worse yet, they left passports and a diary behind. These were subsequently put on display for the international press in Leopoldville, establishing clearly that Cuban soldiers were in the Congo although Guevara's actual presence remained a secret.

In the noisy aftermath of the 1964 Stanleyville raid, several African states — most of the Congo's immediate neighbors, in fact — had come out in support of the rebels. Tanzania had already agreed to channel military aid across Lake Tanganyika to Che Guevara in the eastern Congo. Algerian and Egyptian military aircraft began operating a tenuous arms supply line, using airstrips in the southern Sudan where the weapons could be picked up and trucked to the Congolese border.

After securing Stanleyville, Hoare's mercenaries had moved north and were chasing the rebel soldiers up into the far northeastern corner of the Congo. Eventually they would seal off the border with Sudan and Uganda, but some of the arms were getting through to the rebels from the southern Sudan.

Some, but not all.

To the vast amusement of the Congolese Prime Minister, who briefed the press about it in Leopoldville, rebels in the southern Sudan were ambushing the arms convoys meant for the rebels in the Congo. Thus the weapons destined for the Congolese *simbas* were ending up, instead, in the hands of soldiers trying to overthrow the Sudanese government. The Prime Minister saw the irony in this and wanted to make certain the foreign press saw it, too.

I filed the story, one of my first from the Congo, and I was pleased to hear it come back on the nightly VOA English broadcast to Africa. Instant gratification was one of the benefits of broadcast journalism: unlike your newspaper colleagues, you didn't have to wait for the press clipping to arrive in the mail.

It made me want all the more to get out of Leopoldville and see the northeast Congo for myself. I particularly wanted to visit Stanleyville first hand. My friend from Katanga, George Clay, had been buried there — somewhat hastily, I had heard — after the ambush that took his life the year before.

My flight in a well-worn Air Congo DC-4 followed the course of the Congo River as it made its vast sweep northwards from Leopoldville. The scenery changed along the way from rolling savanna to dense jungle as we approached the equator and turned northeast towards Stanleyville. We landed at the old airport in town — next door to the golf course where the Belgian paratroopers had landed the year before in *Dragon Rouge*.

It still bore the scars of combat. The twisted remnants of another DC-4 airliner could be seen off the end of the main runway. The control tower and terminal building showed evidence of having been hit repeatedly by heavy machine gun fire. Empty fuel drums were scattered everywhere. It was clear, moreover, that military operations were still taking place nearby.

Two T-28s were parked near the partially-destroyed hangar that now served as a passenger terminal. One was being refueled while mechanics worked on the engine of the other. Two more flew low over the field, banked, and descended for a landing.

An ancient and battered taxi was parked under a tree at the Sabena Guest House across the road from the airport. I persuaded the Congolese driver to show me around town in return for several American dollars I had brought along. He had been less interested in accepting Congolese currency. I asked him to take me first to the Stanleyville cemetery.

George's grave was not easy to find. He had been buried in a far corner of the graveyard alongside two South African soldiers who had also been killed on the road to Stanleyville. The graves were marked with simple wooden crosses. Their names and their nationalities had been painted across the front, but in George's case there was nothing to indicate he was a journalist. The cross read "George Clay - South Africa". Anyone reading it might well assume he had been a mercenary soldier — like the two men buried next to him. I felt he should have a proper gravestone and decided to see about getting him one.

Meanwhile, it was obvious from what I had witnessed at the airport that Stanleyville was still being used as a base for ongoing military operations. I checked into a local hotel and found that its bar was a favorite hang-out for mercenary soldiers, including the Cuban exile pilots who were flying the T-28s.

Many of the Cubans were veterans of the failed 1961 Bay of Pigs invasion. CIA had brought them to the Congo soon afterwards, using them as contract pilots in armed training aircraft, such as the T-28s, as well as B-26 bombers left over from World War II. As it turned out, many of the pilots had flown similar aircraft for the Cuban Air Force in the days before Fidel Castro. CIA found it convenient to use them in the Congo. Unlike American contract pilots, their sponsorship by Washington could be more plausibily denied.

One such pilot was Fausto Gomez, who had arrived in the Congo in August 1964, after telling his friends: "If I can't fight against communism in Cuba, I'll fight it wherever I can." He flew close air support missions during *Dragon Rouge* and the subsequent northeast Congo cleanup campaign.

On December 17, his T-28 was hit by rebel ground fire and he crash landed near Lake Albert. South African mercenaries rushed to his rescue. Gomez, who used the radio call sign "El Toro" was popular with the South Africans for the risky flying he undertook to support them. When they reached his aircraft, Gomez was dead and the rebels had mutilated his body.

Ritualistic murder had become an essential characteristic of the *simba* rebellion. In Stanleyville, I found the remnants of the Patrice Lumumba monument used by the rebels as a sacrificial altar during their occupation of the city. Michael Hoyt and members of his American Consulate staff had been driven there to be exhibited to crowds of Congolese who screamed wildly for their execution. They were then inexplicably whisked away by the rebel leaders.

Hoyt called it one of his most harrowing experiences in the three months he was held captive by the rebels. "We were told by members of the mob," he later wrote, "that certain parts of our bodies were to be eaten."

Others had been subjected to torture and ritual dismemberment at the monument. When Hoare's mercenaries arrived there during *Dragon Rouge*, the blood stains on the monument's pedestal were so thick, only dynamite could remove them — which also had the effect of totally destroying the monument.

When I got there less than a year later, the small park had been tidied up and renamed *"Place de Martyrs"*. A simple metal sign had been erected in place of the monument. "Here," it proclaimed, "soldiers of the Congolese National Army, Congolese civilians and foreigners were savagely assassinated".

Stanleyville had seen so much horror in recent times, the atmosphere of the riverfront town seemed heavy with leftover fear and tension. The Cuban pilots I met looked forward to moving their operation south to Albertville, along the shores of Lake Tanganyika. Now that the northeast Congo was being sealed off against the flow of arms to the rebels, Lake Tanganyika itself was the next objective. Of course, the Cubans had no way of knowing that their compatriot Che Guevara was already there.

He had established his African training operation in the high mountains overlooking the western shore of the lake, but he was not having an easy time getting it started. The *simbas* seemed more interested in having Che's special forces carry out the serious work of the rebellion than they were in learning how to do it themselves.

Having assessed the Congolese rebel forces at close range, Che later wrote: "The basic feature of the People's Liberation Army was that it was a parasitic army, it did not work, did not train, did not fight, and it demanded provisions and labor from the population, sometimes with extreme harshness." He noted that *simbas* would often object to carrying heavy weapons or ammunition, exclaiming in Swahili *"Mimi hapana motocari!"* (I'm not a truck!)." Once the Cubans had established themselves at the training camp, this soon became *"Mimi hapana Cubano!"*.

Leopoldville, with its modest claim to civilized amenities, was a welcome change after Stanleyville. My wife Anne, ever the resourceful General's daughter, had found us a house in Djelo Binza, high enough in the hills above the city to see the lights of Brazzaville across the Congo river. My two young sons were finding new companions at the International School and I was welcomed to a meeting of the *Association de la Presse Etrangere*, fondly known as APE among the English-speaking journalists.

There were many members present who recalled George Clay. I mentioned that I had recently seen his grave in Stanleyville and suggested that we might raise a small fund to replace the wooden cross with a decent gravestone. I even volunteered to oversee the project. Several journalists immediately contributed. They included Lloyd Garrison of the New York Times, Angus McDermid of the BBC, Arnold Amber of Reuters and Dietrich Mummendey of United Press International.

It would take me nearly two years before I could complete the assignment, but at least I got it launched the following day. Jim Farber, newly-assigned American Consul in Stanleyville, agreed to place a small advertisement for a *fundi* in the local newspaper. In Swahili, a *fundi* is a known expert in a particular field. Given Stanleyville's recent history, we figured it ought not to be too difficult to locate a gravestone *fundi*.

Meanwhile, in spite of Che Guevara and his Cuban special forces, the Congolese rebellion was not doing well. Mike Hoare and his mercenary commandos had established themselves in Albertville where they were planning a final offensive aimed at sealing off Lake Tanganyika. Guevara was already having difficulties in receiving supplies across the lake. Hoare intended shutting down his supply lines altogether.

By the end of September 1965, Hoare had assembled a small flotilla that included the old Belgian lake steamer *Ermans*, newly outfitted with 75 mm cannon and radar. There were also two barges capable of carrying 200 troops and armored vehicles, plus six of the Seacraft fiber-glass patrol boats flown to Albertville by U.S. Air Force C-130s. Overhead, Hoare could count on six T-28s and two B-26 bombers modified to carry rockets and machine guns for close air support to his amphibious landing force.

The one major piece of equipment that failed to arrive in time for the Lake Tanganyika battle was the now-legendary Swift boat (PCF - Patrol Craft, Fast)) — a fifty-foot, aluminum, twin-diesel patrol craft being introduced at that time in Vietnam. Senator John Kerry of Massachusetts was to emerge a war hero as a result of his Swift boat command in the Mekong delta — an experience that became a major element in his failed 2004 bid for the U.S. presidency.

In 1965, the CIA ordered three Swift boats for Lake Tanganyika, but found there was no easy way of getting them there in a hurry. The U.S. had been sending heavily loaded C-130s — its largest air transport at the time — across the Atlantic to Ascension Island for refueling and then on to the Congo. But the Swift boat was too big to fit in a C-130. Larry Devlin, CIA Station Chief in Leopoldville then borrowed a page from 19th century explorer-journalist Henry Morton Stanley and had the Swift boat — like Stanley's Lady Alice — cut up into pieces to make it more portable. The aluminum pieces were flown by C-130 to Lake Tanganyika where they were put back together, in jig-saw puzzle form, by the Belgian-run Chanic boatyards in Albertville.

Even without the Swift boats, Mike Hoare's *Force Navale* flotilla was a fairly impressive expeditionary group. He had virtually everything he needed on board, except a reliable weather forecaster.

He was thus unprepared for the sudden storm that hit him just as his landing force approached the beach at Baraka. He had been forced by heavy seas to reduce speed and this put him two hours behind the scheduled predawn landing hour. Hoare later wrote that most of his landing party members were so sea-sick they were ready to disembark in broad daylight, in spite of the increasingly accurate machine gun fire from the shore.

Meanwhile, the Cubans flying overhead could no longer see the beach clearly enough to give Hoare covering machine-gun and rocket fire. Concerned that the worsening visibility might cause them to hit the wrong side, they stopped flying altogether. Thus when Hoare most urgently needed the combined fire-power of the T-28s and the B-26s, it was no longer available to him.

A further problem was that Hoare had very little military intelligence about the enemy he was facing at Baraka. He certainly had no idea he was up against 200 Cuban regular soldiers, let alone highly-trained Special Forces under the command of Che Guevara, an experienced guerrilla warfare expert and a hero of the Cuban revolution. The Cubans were well pre-pared for Hoare's landing party and they quickly put up a level of resistance that threatened to imperil the entire operation.

Bob Rogers, an NBC television reporter, was with Hoare. He told me later in Leopoldville that the situation on the beach was very dicey — to use his term — and that there was much incoming small arms fire. He and Hoare were pinned down on the beach during a rebel counter-attack that threatened to cut Hoare's landing party off from their source of ammunition on board the *Ermans* .

Rogers suggested to Hoare that the *Ermans* provide covering fire with its 75 mm cannon. "It was the answer," Hoare later wrote, "Bob Rogers had been an infantry officer in the U.S.Army and had forgotten nothing. I radioed *Ermans* and…with a spout of flame fifteen feet long, she loosed off an armor-piercing 75 mm shell…" It saved the day.

Bob later recalled, with some modesty, that "the reason neither Mike nor his officers thought of the (75 mm cannon) was that the *Ermans* had previously been used exclusively to interdict the rebel's seaborne traffic across the lake."

Che Guevara, for reasons best known to himself, chose to downplay the level of fighting at Baraka. In a rambling October 5, 1965 letter to Fidel Castro, he wrote: "Recently, a group from the (Congolese) army landed in the Baraka area where a (rebel) Major General has no fewer than 1,000 armed men, and captured that strategically important place *almost without a fight* (author's italics)"

Why Guevara chose this particular approach in describing his situation to his leader is not clear, except that his diary is filled with similarly negative comments about the Congolese rebels and what he clearly regarded as their lack of revolutionary spirit. Eventually, he was forced to abandon his mission in the Congo and flee under cover of darkness across Lake Tanganyika November 20. "During those last hours of our time in the Congo," he later wrote, "I felt more alone than I had ever been in Cuba or on any of my wanderings around the globe."

In retrospect, Che's mission seems to have been doomed from the start. He admits this in his personal account of his experience in the Congo. His diary, suppressed for decades by the Cuban government, begins dismally: "This is the history of a failure."

His departure, like his arrival, passed unnoticed in Leopoldville where political developments of a totally different sort were about to get underway. In the early morning hours of November 25, Radio Leopoldville announced that the army high command, led by General Joseph Mobutu, had taken over the government.

It was a coup by communique — the second time in five years that Mobutu had overthrown the government by radio announcement. No shot was fired on either occasion. In September 1960, Mobutu announced he was temporarily "neutralizing" the politicians, not taking over the government. In November 1965, he made it clear he intended to rule by decree for at least five years. It turned out to be much more, but of course none of us knew that at the time.

After the dust settled in Leopoldville, I did some traveling around the Congo, including a trip back to Stanleyville where I discovered that George Clay's gravestone had been completed. The local *fundi* who had constructed it did not speak English and a couple of the words were misspelled. I felt no journalist should suffer the indignity of a typographical error on his tombstone and we made the necessary corrections in the backyard of the American Consulate.

But what I had envisioned as a simple headstone had developed into something much more monumental in size. It weighed over seven hundred pounds and would take twenty Congolese to carry it out of the American Consulate's back yard and put it on George's grave. Twenty otherwise unemployed men were not hard to find in Stanleyville, but locating a vehicle strong enough to move George's massive gravestone to the cemetery was another matter. All functioning trucks in Stanleyville had been seized and driven out of town in a recent army mutiny. I had to wait until a new one was flown from Leopoldville in a C-130. Finally, I succeeded in getting men and truck together and we made our way to the Stanleyville cemetery with George's gravestone.

Twenty years later, it was still there when I last visited Stanleyville, now renamed Kisangani. A large palm tree had grown up around it, but I could still make out the *fundi's* inscription, with corrections: "George Clay, South African Journalist, Killed near

Stanleyville, November 24, 1964. Remembered by His Fellow Journalists."

Mission accomplished, I caught a river boat back to Leopoldville. It turned out to be a five-day journey back in time to a period described by Conrad as "a voyage to the earth's earliest beginnings when trees were kings and vegetation rioted on the face of the earth." What made it all the more bizarre was that the Congolese boat captain stayed drunk on Primus beer for much of the voyage and so, apparently, did most of his crew. Everyone I talked to reeked of the local brew and few made much sense in either French or English.

The ancient steamer nonetheless pushed forward day and night down the steamy Congo, never running aground, rarely slowing, its twin searchlights constantly picking out steering points along both sides of the river. It seemed to me not unlike a floating village with a vast marketplace that constantly replenished itself with fish, meat, and other local products obtained on the move from passing dugout canoes.

Beer seemed to be the preferred currency. Canoes would skillfully intercept the moving riverboat, tie up alongside, and the bargaining would begin. Inside the canoes would be live river fish and other local fauna, including crocodiles, still thrashing about. On board the steamer, Congolese market women competed with each other in throwing wet rags down upon the fresh cargo, in an effort to signify their preferred choice. Bottles of beer were passed back and forth.

One huge canoe, paddled by several men and filled with cases of empty beer bottles, approached the riverboat at a wrong angle, got caught in its bow-wake and quickly overturned. I ran back to the rear of the steamer in time to see the men, cheerfully waving, surrounded by hundreds of empty beer bottles, floating off into the distance.

It must have seemed cooler in the river itself. The heat on board the river boat was unrelenting, particularly as we approached the Equator at Coquilhatville (since renamed Mbandaka). The deck temperature was relieved only by the slight breeze from the boat's down river movement and the astonishingly cold beer from the galley refrigerators.

When I finally reached Leopoldville, there was a message from the VOA newsroom waiting for me: "Proceed Nigeria soonest. Plan spending couple weeks."

Like Mobutu's proposed term in office, my stay in Nigeria turned out to be much longer. As for the Congo, in the view of one senior U.S. diplomat in Kinshasa, "I think this country may finally have reached what could be called a tolerable level of mayhem."

Time indeed to move on.

8.

Nigeria: When Things Fell Apart.

Flying up the West Coast of Africa from the Congo to Nigeria in 1966 was like taking a journey to another planet. The passage itself was made effortless by Pam Am flight attendants deftly pouring champagne and passing canapés thirty thousand feet above the equatorial jungle. It was the difference on arrival that took me by surprise.

Lagos was no less chaotic than Kinshasa, but the Nigerians seemed to accomplish their disorder with more warmth and color — style, even. There appeared to be less outright menace than in the Congo, and what did exist was not necessarily directed towards the visitor. The atmosphere on arrival was almost welcoming. That, at least, was my first impression.

The Nigerians, as it turned out, were often

inclined to be warmer and more generous towards foreigners than to themselves.

The violence taking place between Northern Nigerians and Eastern Nigerians followed its own course without much reference to outside influences. Foreign journalists, for instance, were neither encouraged to involve themselves as witnesses, nor were any real barriers placed in their way — not, at any rate, in the early days of the disorders.

Unlike the chaos in the Congo, there seemed to be more purpose to the Nigerian rioting. In later years, it would come to be known as ethnic cleansing — or even genocide. But when I first arrived in Lagos, in early October 1966, it was simply termed "the rioting in the North." It had been going on for several days with no sign of letting up.

The year had started badly for democracy in Nigeria. A particularly bloody coup d'etat had taken place in January, just as the former British colony had completed hosting its first Commonwealth summit conference. Young soldiers, mostly Christian Ibos from Nigeria's Eastern Region, struck hard and without warning at Nigeria's elected government, particularly its Moslem northern leaders.

The ethnic dimensions of the coup continue to be disputed, particularly by Eastern Nigerians and their supporters, but when the January dust had settled, two of Nigeria's most prominent northern officials — Federal Prime Minister Alhaji Sir Abubakar Tafawa

Balewa and Northern Region Premier Sir Ahmadou Bello, the Sardauna of Sokoto. had been brutally struck down in a precisely planned military operation led by Ibo officers.

The man who ended up in as the new head of government turned out to be the most prominent Easterner in the army, its Army commanding officer: Major General Johnson Thomas Umunakwe Aguiyi-Ironsi, formerly chief of United Nations peacekeeping forces in the Congo.

To an outsider, it looked very much as though Nigeria's Ibos had taken over the rest of the country and now seemed intent on ruling it themselves. In a classic Christian vs. Moslem, North vs. South confrontation, the Christian Southerners appeared to have won the day. However, as Nigerians were fond of saying when times got bad, "No condition is permanent."

Six months later, the Northerners struck back. General Ironsi was among the first to be killed. The shooting quickly spread from one military compound to another — throughout Nigeria. Mainly carried out by Northern troops, the attacks seemed particularly directed at Ibos. When they stopped, nearly 300 officers and men from the Eastern Region were either dead or missing. The young Colonels who formed the new Federal Military Government were virtually all Northerners, including their leader: Lieutenant Colonel Yakubu Gowon.

Gowon was something of an outsider and nobody seemed to know very much about him. He had been away from Nigeria for months, attending Sandhurst and other British military training institutions. General Ironsi obviously had thought fairly highly of him. He had advanced Gowon over several other senior officers to make him Army Chief of Staff, just after the January coup. Although clearly a Northerner, Gowon was also a Christian, not a Moslem — a fact that would certainly not have escaped the politically-minded Ironsi.

As the new head of Nigeria's Federal Military Government. Gowon immediately set about on a course aimed at returning the nation to civilian rule. In a nationwide radio address in August, he made it clear he considered Nigeria's unity under a federal structure to be his first priority. He convened a constitutional conference in September to bring together what he called "leaders of thought" from all regions of Nigeria. He asked the conference to consider a federal Nigeria with a strong central government, or possibly one with a weaker government at the center and more power given to the regions.

"On the other hand," said the 31-year-old acting head of state, "it may be that through your deliberations, we may be able to devise a form of association with an entirely new name yet to be found in any political dictionary in the world, but peculiar to Nigeria."

Gowon's statement reminded me of an earlier attempt by the Congolese to apply what they called *"une solution Bantou"* to the creation of a new government in the Congo. Politically, it would be *"ni de la gauche, ni de la droite, ni meme de la centre."* The search for a bantu solution, unique to Africa, didn't work very well in the Congo and it never got off to a real start in Nigeria.

A new round of rioting broke out in the North while Gowon's constitutional conference was barely underway. As word reached Lagos of widespread anti-Ibo attacks in the North, the delegation from the Eastern Region fled home and the conference broke down altogether. It turned out to be the last such meeting to take place on Nigerian soil before the final rupture between the Eastern Region and the rest of the county in 1967.

In the meantime, the Northerners were making it clear they wanted no Ibos living among them, even in the "sabon garis" — stranger's quarters — on the outskirts of the major towns in the North. It was in these ethnic shantytowns that some of the worst atrocities took place, often carried out by civilians and military alike, in plain view of the police and the international press.

Alan Grossman, whom I had known as a colleague in the Congo, reported in Time Magazine's October 7 edition: "The soldiers did not have to do all the killing. They were soon joined by hundreds of Hausa civilians, who rampaged through the city (Kano) armed with stones, cutlasses, machetes, and home-made weapons of metal and broken glass. Crying 'Heathen' and 'Allah' the mobs and troops invaded the Sabon Gari ransacking, looting and burning Ibo homes and stores and murdering their owners."

Another reporter who had earlier witnessed similar mayhem in the Congo was Colin Legum. He wrote in the Observer newspaper in London on October 16: "While the Hausas in each town and village in the North know what happened in their own localities, only the Ibos know the whole terrible story from the 600,000 or so refugees who have fled to the safety of the Eastern Region — hacked, slashed, mangled, stripped naked and robbed of all their possessions; the orphans, the widows, the traumatized. A woman, mute and dazed, arrived back in her village after traveling for five days with only a bowl in her lap. It held her child's head, which was severed before her eyes."

Many Ibos in the North sought the help of local American residents, particularly Peace Corps volunteers in the Kaduna and Kano areas. A young American foreign service officer — Helen Bodurtha of Cleveland, Ohio — heard a knock at her front door in Kaduna late one evening and opened it to find Lieutenant Colonel Phillip Effiong, accompanied by two other soldiers, all armed and in uniform. They asked the young diplomat to help them escape to their homes in the Eastern Region. Shaken, but concerned for their safety, as well as her own, she invited the three men into her living room and then telephoned an American Consulate colleague.

"I couldn't go into details on the phone," she later told me, "but I managed to convey the urgency of the situation to the Consulate official who agreed to come to my house — in spite of the fact that it was well past midnight. He came and we all sat around trying to figure out what to do next. Eventually, we were able to get Effiong out of the Northern Region disguised as a Catholic priest."

When I arrived in Lagos in October of that year, a massive population shift was taking place throughout Nigeria. Like Phillip Effiong, Ibos were fleeing home to the East from all over the Northern Region. Northerners living in the East, on the other hand, were being ordered in the opposite direction — on the grounds that their safety could no longer be assured in the Eastern Region. The nation was in turmoil with Lagos at the center point and Lieutenant Colonel Yakubu Gowon clearly the key to whatever immediate future was left to Nigeria.

Gowon had yet to meet with foreign journalists. I asked his official spokesman, Mr. A. K. Disu, to try and set up an interview for me. Disu met frequently with the foreign press and had made himself something of a legend when he announced at a news briefing that Nigeria was lifting press censorship. In the commotion that followed, one reporter was heard to shout: "Can we report that?"

"Unfortunately not," said A.K. Disu, after reflecting a moment or two. "The problem being that we really never announced publicly that we were imposing press censorship. Therefore, we can hardly announce today that we are lifting it."

Word came back from Mr. Disu that Gowon would agree to be interviewed by the Voice of America and Reuters news agency. Both correspondents should present themselves at Dodan Barracks, Nigerian Police headquarters, the following Monday at 10 a.m.

I recall very little of the actual interview, but the impression of Gowon remains quite clear in my mind, fortified by news photographs taken at the time. He was 31 years old, the son of a Methodist minister and the product of missionary schools in Northern Nigeria and various military academies in Britain, including Sandhurst — the British equivalent of West Point.

Gowon was not a tall man, but he had the bearing of an athlete, as well as a soldier. He enjoyed a reputation as an excellent squash player and he wore his uniform easily and well. His communicative skills were less impressive. Under questioning, he seemed shy and inarticulate. He gave the impression of being absolutely sincere in what he wanted to say, but he had trouble getting the words out.

In the months to come, foreign journalists in Lagos would occasionally agree among themselves not to quote him directly on some of the statements he had made to us because there was some confusion as to what he actually meant to say. It would have been easy to quote him verbatim, but we felt — rightly or wrongly — that it would have been misleading to do so. He got better as he grew on the job, and we stopped letting him off so easily.

His opposite number in Eastern Nigeria was a different sort of person altogether.

Lieutenant Colonel Chukwuemeka Odumegwo Ojukwu was born into considerable wealth. His father had become a millionaire in the road transport business and was one of the first Nigerians to be knighted by Queen Elizabeth. After attending private schools in Nigeria and Britain, the younger Ojukwu went to Oxford where his father wanted him to study law, but he got a degree in Modern History, instead. Upon graduating, he joined the Nigerian civil service, but soon gave it up for a career in the military.

The January 1966 coup, mostly carried out by young officers from the East, had put Ojukwu in charge of the Eastern Region and he remained in the job — in spite of the second coup in July. Confident of his position as Military Governor, but reluctant to visit Lagos for any of the conferences scheduled by Gowon, Ojukwu was harder for reporters to reach.

He therefore reached out to bring them to Enugu, his Eastern Region capital. He even set up a charter flight to encourage them to come.

British news organizations accepted the offer, but his invitation posed an ethical dilemma for American correspondents in Lagos. We wanted to cover Ojukwu in Enugu, but we didn't feel we could accept his offer of a free charter flight to get there. When we presented this problem to the managers of the American-run air charter service in Lagos, they quite willingly agreed to charge us directly for the aircraft, instead of sending the bill to Ojukwu's Eastern Region Government.

"We probably wouldn't have gotten our money out of them, anyway," was the way they put it — as we proceeded to quietly hijack their six-seater aircraft and its pilot away from Ojukwu.

When we landed at Enugu, we were told that Ojukwu was about to hold a news conference and it was being held up until we could get there. We were whisked to the official residence of the Eastern Region's governor where we discovered our British colleagues were waiting for us and none too happy about the delay.

"Bloody Yanks holding up the story!" was among the grumblings we heard as we trooped into the room. Ojukwu's entry a few minutes later eased some of the tensions that had evidently been building. He moved very slowly, with considerable solemnity. He wore a full beard, but I noticed, as he passed close to me, the hair on his head was thinning, making his massive forehead even more pronounced. He looked older than Gowon and he seemed, on first impression, to have less military bearing. But then he began to speak.

Ojukwu's voice was strong and commanding. The words rolled out in measured, almost oratorical tones. He began by outlining what he said were his difficulties in obtaining an audience for the views of his government. He accused Lagos of blocking his access to journalists and this was the reason, he said, why he had invited them to Enugu so that he might talk to them directly.

"I am aware of the fact," Ojukwu said, "that the Gowon government in Lagos does feel very touchy about the question of journalists publishing reports abroad about the situation here. For that reason, I have made facilities available to all journalists who may wish to send their dispatches by an alternative means should you need to avail yourself of those facilities."

As Ojukwu went on to attack Gowon's recent statements about the Eastern Region, it occurred to some of us that what he meant by providing an alternative means for filing news stories from Enugu involved using our airplane. He clearly thought it was still his charter. He intended using it to fly correspondents' written dispatches out of the country — probably to neighboring Cameroon — where they could be sent on to London without going through the Nigerian government telegraph system.

Once Ojukwu's news conference was over, we headed to Enugu's main hotel to look for our pilot. We found him in the coffee shop and he promised us we could return to Lagos as soon as he finished his lunch. One of the London reporters overheard him and — fearing our copy would get out ahead of his own — complained to Godwin Onyegbula, Ojukwu's press assistant.

"I am very sorry," Godwin informed us, "but the charter aircraft will be required to fly to Cameroon to provide filing facilities for the other journalists. You can take it back to Lagos afterwards."

Several of us had known Godwin in Washington, when he was the press attache at the Nigerian embassy. Unfortunately, this did not make it any easier for us to explain that we had already taken his charter away from him. He refused to accept our explanation and remained adamant about the plane leaving first for Cameroon, regardless of who had chartered it to Enugu.

Lloyd Garrison of the New York Times had been the principal figure behind the Lagos takeover of the Enugu charter. He turned to Godwin and said, in dramatic tones that resounded throughout the hotel lobby, "Godwin, if that airplane takes off for Cameroon, it will do so over my dead body!"

"Oh goodness, Lloyd," replied Godwin, "there has been so much bloodshed already."

At this point, the pilot strolled out of the coffee shop, and we all casually headed out the front door of the hotel to our waiting car. We drove at considerable speed to the Enugu airport and piled into our charter plane, barely getting the door closed before our pilot fired up the engines and began taxiing to the end of the runway.

But when he radioed the Enugu tower requesting clearance to take off, he was told to return to the airport terminal building immediately. When he advised the tower that he had passengers on board with urgent business in Lagos, the tower operator replied that his instructions were to prevent us from taking off because our aircraft was needed for a flight to Cameroon.

By now, the plane's engines were fully warmed up. As we began moving down the runway, our pilot radioed the tower that he would call ahead to Lagos for another aircraft. We did not hear the tower's reply in the noise of the take-off, but we carefully watched two military helicopters hovering at low altitude near the end of the runway. They didn't bother us, and we sped back to Lagos to send our stories.

I had come to know most of the other foreign correspondents in the Nigerian capital and had met one or two people at the American Embassy, including Helen Bodurtha — the young foreign service officer from Cleveland who had helped Phillip Effiong escape to the Eastern Region.

Helen was kind enough to introduce me to night life in Lagos. We toured the outdoor nightclubs where she patiently led me through the High Life, a complex African dance rhythm that was considerably more subtle than Congolese music. Lagos, in those days, had several good restaurants and Helen, who shared my enthusiasm for a fine meal, seemed to know them all.

I found Helen very attractive and enjoyed being with her, We discovered we had a lot in common — beyond a fondness for dining and dancing. She was three or four years younger than me, but had read widely, loved poetry, and knew considerably more about music — classical, musical comedy, even rock and roll — than I did. When I wasn't out covering politics in Nigeria, I began looking for opportunities to spend more time with Helen.

But the Congo — 1,000 miles further south — remained my home base. As long as there was any chance Ojukwu might come to Lagos, or persuade Gowon to meet him in the Eastern Region, I remained on call for the Nigerian story. When neither possibility appeared to be likely, I flew back to the Congo where I discovered Leopoldville had been renamed Kinshasa in my absence. Most other Congolese cities with Belgian colonial names had also been changed. The renaming process complicated reporting the story from the Congo because many of the Congolese place names had become major news datelines — Stanleyville and Elizabethville, for instance. It took time — and some explanation to the Voice of America listener — for Kisangani and Lubumbashi to establish themselves as replacements.

I wasn't in Kinshasa long before a message from the VOA newsroom summoned me back to Lagos. A mysterious cargo aircraft had crashed in a mountainous area of Cameroon, bordering Nigeria's Eastern Region. It had been carrying a considerable quantity of arms, apparently ordered by Ojukwu. This was being reported in Lagos as further evidence that Ojukwu was now leading the Eastern Region away from any settlement with Gowon and the rest of Nigeria. The question was becoming not so much a matter of whether his Eastern Region would actually secede, but rather when and under what circumstances.

Helen met me at the Ikeja airport in Lagos. She confirmed that the Ojukwu arms plane story had created a major stir in Lagos, but there was still no firm news on the Eastern Region breaking away from the rest of Nigeria. The chances of Ojukwu coming to Lagos seemed very unlikely, however. Helen was driving across the border to Cotonou, Dahomey (now Benin) that week-end and invited me to join her.

I had to pull together a couple of Nigerian stories for week-end broadcasts, but Dahomey, a former French colony, still retained good telephone and telex connections with Paris and I knew I could file from there. Nigeria had recently reimposed military censorship on outgoing dispatches, but I could avoid this by filing from Cotonou. The subterfuge didn't fool anybody for very long, but neither did my BBC colleague, Angus McDermid, a fellow Congo hand who had become a good friend. He would occasionally bypass the Lagos censors with lengthy phone conversations in Welsh with his wife in London. The Nigerians eventually cracked down on both of us.

Cotonou had its own night life and French seaside restaurants that served grilled lobster and a fairly decent sauvignon blanc. Helen and I ventured further afield by driving across the Dahomean border to neighboring Togo. As we approached the capital, Lome, it became apparent that some sort of festivity was underway. Truckloads of palm-waving Togolese were driving at high speed up and down the city's main boulevard.

I spotted an elderly European woman pedaling her bicycle down a side street and I asked her in French what the celebration was all about. "Shhhh," she whispered, putting her finger to her lips, *"c'est une coup d'etat!"*

We pulled into a nearby hotel where I discovered that all international telephone and telex lines were closed. Not wanting to be caught in a situation where I couldn't report whatever the story might turn out to be, I told Helen we needed to get back across the border to Dahomey quickly.

But the truckloads of palm-waving Togolese had become more numerous — and more vocal. They had taken over the only road out of town and were roaring up and down it at break-neck speed. There was an additional problem at the border, itself. The steel barrier was down and no one seemed to be on duty.

Suddenly, a customs official did appear. When he confirmed that the border was closed, I quickly offered to pay him "overtime" to reopen it. He asked to see my passport and, noting my middle name, asked if I was related to John F. Kennedy. This was four years after the president's assassination, but the Kennedy name was still magic throughout Africa. "We are not of the same family," I replied solemnly in French, "but we are certainly of the same tribe."

The Togolese official exploded with laughter and waved up through, without ever stamping our passports or demanding the overtime payment. We drove straight to Cotonou where a colleague at the telex office filled me in on the details in Togo. There had in fact been a coup, but when I got through on the phone to a source at the American Embassy, he told me on background that the change in regimes — "one Colonel in and another out" — would probably not make very much difference to the average Togolese. Since I had been there and could lend presence with an on-the-scene report, I filed a story to VOA, but I don't recall that it made headlines on the evening news.

Helen and I had dinner at an open-air restaurant near the port. Sitting out under the stars with a soft breeze coming in from the sea, I thought to myself that being a foreign correspondent in West Africa occasionally had its good days — along with all the others that didn't turn out so well. There was an expression for the latter. We lumped them together as "WAWA" — short for "West Africa Wins Again".

Looking back, I can see now that Helen and I were headed for a no-win situation, but it didn't seem so at the time — at least not to me. I was moving back and forth between a wife and family in the Congo and a fascinating lady in Nigeria — of whom I was becoming increasingly fond.

It helped that my hotel in Lagos was virtually across the street from Helen's apartment. I began seeing less and less of the hotel. Matters reached the level of a small diplomatic scandal early one morning when several embassy wives came to call on Helen and were told by her Nigerian cook: "Madam is not here. Master is, but he is still asleep."

From that point on, we were usually invited out together — Helen and her fairly constant companion from the Congo. It was, of course, only a matter of time before word reached Anne in Kinshasa. On my return from Lagos, I was confronted with an angry wife and a demand for explanations. "Nothing to worry about," I assured her and, in a move I have long since regretted, I suggested we all spend Christmas together in Nigeria — and she could see for herself.

We did. She saw for herself, and Christmas in Nigeria was a disaster. To complicate matters further, Helen's parents were visiting from Cleveland and her boss at the embassy took it upon himself to lecture them on what he regarded as Helen's wayward behavior. This caused them understandable concern about their daughter's future as a diplomat. The downward spiral continued until we all spent a miserable New Year's Eve at a Lagos restaurant Helen and I had always enjoyed together — under less complex circumstances.

My marriage to Anne was already strained, not just by my deepening relationship with Helen, but also by the fact of my being away from home most of the time. This had left Anne alone with two small boys to raise during difficult times in the Congo. In retrospect, it seems amazing that both the marriage and the relationship with Helen survived — the one in the Congo and the other in Nigeria.

Helen and I were watching a film at a downtown Lagos cinema when a bomb went off a short distance away. The building rocked, but there was no panic. When we got out on the street, we learned that an Ibo had tried to talk his way past the front gate at nearby Dodan Barracks, where Colonel Gowon lived. Failing in the process, he panicked, abandoned the explosives-laden car in a gas station across the street, and fled on foot. It was lucky for us all that the bomb blast did not ignite the gas station or its fuel storage tanks.

But the bombing incident brought the looming conflict in Nigeria sharply into focus for Helen and me. The country which had become so much a part of our own complicated lives seemed poised on the edge of a precipice.

For Ojukwu and his embattled Eastern Region, there seemed no turning back. "I think we are rolling downhill," Ojukwu told Reuters news agency in May, "and it will take a great deal to halt the momentum. We are close, very, very close."

When the actual split came on May 30, 1967, it almost seemed anti-climactic. In a radio broadcast heard clearly in Lagos, Ojukwu solemnly proclaimed the Republic of Biafra. Nigeria had already been placed in a state of emergency by Gowon who simultaneously created twelve new states out of the former Federal regions. In the process, he divided the Eastern Region into three states, only one of which comprised the Ibo heartland: the landlocked East-Central State, which included Enugu — now the capital of Ojukwu's Biafra.

In reporting the emergence of Africa's youngest republic, I noted that Biafra, which now controlled most of Nigeria's extensive oil production, had a fairly respectable economic base to support its newly-independent status. Apart from the oil, which Nigeria would certainly fight to retain for itself, Biafra had coal, palm oil and rubber resources, plus a good transportation network of railways, highways, port facilities, and two international-class airports at Enugu and Port Harcourt.

Perhaps even more important, Biafra could also boast an efficient, well-trained civil service, a considerable portion of which had recently fled Nigeria's top government offices. The same could also be said for its military leadership, from its Chief of Staff, newly-promoted Major General Philip Effiong, on down. Biafra's actual military capability — compared to that of Nigeria — remained very much to be seen, however.

The first shots had yet to be exchanged between the two sides. But there was plenty of fighting taking place elsewhere in the world, and it pushed the Nigeria and Biafra story completely out of the international news. The June 1967 six-day war in the Middle East had broken out and it dominated headlines around the world. Shooting had also started up again closer to home in the Congo.

The main struggle in Nigeria was centering on the nation's oil production which was largely based in the former Eastern Region and was now under firm Biafran control. Both sides stated their claim to the revenues, but Biafran forces commanded the area around the refinery at Port Harcourt and the oil terminal at Bonny. When it became clear that Biafra intended collecting the oil revenues directly from the producing companies, Nigeria promptly mounted a naval blockade against its own coastline — which included Biafra's access to the sea.

As the arguments raged back and forth between the various sides in Nigeria, the troubles in the Congo escalated into a full scale military revolt. I rushed to book a seat on the weekly Pan Am flight to Kinshasa only to be told that the airport there had been closed to all international traffic.

I told Helen this represented the ultimate irony: the conflict in Nigeria I had been sent to cover showed no signs of getting started, while I couldn't fly home to report the war in the Congo where I was supposed to be in the first place.

She smiled and said quietly, "It rather looks as though West Africa Wins Again."

Pan Am was allowed to land in Kinshasa the following week, but its passengers had to be given a military escort into town from the airport. A mercenary-led rebellion had started up the week before in Kisangani (formerly Stanleyville) and had since spread throughout the eastern part of the country. There was considerable anti-white feeling which was heightened by reports that the mostly Belgian and French mercenaries leading the rebellion had committed atrocities against African civilians. An agitated President Mobutu was on the telephone to the American Embassy demanding immediate military assistance.

I wrote Helen from the Congo, telling her how much I missed her, and pointing out that I was stuck in the Congo and probably would not return to Nigeria any time soon. Quite apart from being tied down by the Congo story, I explained that I had to get back to the United States to sort out problems resulting from my mother's death in Nevada the year before. Her estate, which very much involved me as her sole heir, was a mess. I told Helen that it could be months before I got back to Lagos, but that I loved her very much and was trying to work out a solution for all of us.

My two year tour in the Congo (much of the second year having been spent in Nigeria) was coming to an end and I cabled VOA that I had no wish to extend it. I had seen enough pointless chaos in Kisangani's latest mercenary revolt to sour me for all time in the Congo. Nigeria, I said, was another matter. It was a story I would very much like to see through to the end, having been present, as it were, at the beginning.

Washington cabled back that, since I was already overdue for vacation, I should plan to come back to the States, take some time off with my family, and give serious thought to going back to the Nigerian story, later in the year, on a full time basis.

The shooting had finally broken out between

Nigeria and Biafra in early July 1967. If I took the correspondent assignment in Lagos, Anne and the boys would have to remain behind in Washington until the situation in Nigeria became more secure and families were allowed to return. This would give me a chance to decide what I was going to do about my marriage and my wanting to be with Helen.

Or so I thought at the time.

9.

Nigeria: Getting It Back Together Again.

Helen was not at the airport when I landed back in Lagos. Bad sign, I thought. Then it got worse. Helen, as it turned out, had acted on her own — while I was away.

It was true that I had been gone from Nigeria longer than I had originally planned. During this time, Helen had met and fallen in love with Fritz Picard, a new political officer at the American Embassy. Perhaps I should have written more while I was on the road? Maybe I had not made myself clear in stating the hopes that I had for us together — or stated them forcefully enough? Who knows? In many ways, she made the right decision for both of us .

But it took a while for me to come to accept that.

Helen had arrived at the conclusion, on her own,

that she and I had reached the end of wherever it was we were going. Then Fritz had entered the scene. He eventually proposed marriage, which I was not in a position to do — unless I simply broke up my own family. Helen was steadfastly opposed to this. It made a difference, I think, that Fritz was already divorced and his three young children desperately needed the nurturing that Helen could give them.

None of this made it any easier for me to accept, but it didn't seem as though there was much I could do about it, except to try and make Helen unhappy for having gone ahead and made the decision without me. I decided there was little to be gained by my hanging around Lagos and being a spoiler. Better, certainly, to throw myself into my job.

Or try to, at any rate.

Covering the Nigerian civil war was hard work and the heat didn't make it any easier. It seemed to me that I was always sweating and always thirsty. So were the soldiers on both sides. The Nigerian army began moving beer up with their ammunition. This was to discourage their soldiers from being tempted to drink locally-made palm wine which the other side might have poisoned.

I had developed a taste for palm wine, but preferred beer, particularly when it was cold — more often it was not. In those days, Nigerian Star beer was made by Heineken breweries and it was good either way. The food eaten by Nigerian soldiers was laden with pepper and other spices. A strong beer was needed to wash it down. I often found the Nigerian army curries too hot to eat and I would ask the cooks for some fried plantains, which they called *dudu*. These could be spicy-hot, as well, but not as volatile as the curries and the Star beer helped keep them down.

From the standpoint of cuisine, it was not a memorable conflict. You ate and drank to survive.

The war had begun with a series of border probing actions by both sides. The Nigerians and Biafrans had each tried to bring aircraft into play. Biafra had acquired a couple of World War II-vintage bombers on the international arms market, but they were barely serviceable. Of more importance were the DC-3 and Fokker Friendship airliners hijacked earlier from Nigerian Airways. These were deployed, along with the French-built helicopters, on occasional bombing raids over Nigeria.

In one such attack on Lagos in August 1967, the ex-Nigerian Airways Fokker Friendship was pressed into service as a bomber by the Biafrans. According to eyewitnesses, several improvised explosive devices were tossed out its cargo door by hand. The Nigerians opened fire with anti-aircraft guns as the hijacked airliner passed over Dodan barracks where Gowon was living. The guns either scored a direct hit, or — what seems more likely — one of the homemade bombs blew up inside the aircraft.

In any event, the Fokker suddenly exploded in

mid-air, breaking windows throughout one of the capital's more elegant residential areas and showering it with bits of aircraft wreckage and human body parts. One nearly complete corpse crashed through to roof of the Czech ambassador's residence. Eight men had been on board, four Africans and four non-Africans. All wore Biafran military uniforms.

The Nigerians had looked further afield in building up their air force. They acquired British-built Jet Provost fighter-bombers, reportedly from the Sudanese government. Journalists traveling with federal troops first came across the Provosts in October at Makurdi airport, north of the border with Biafra. The aircraft were being serviced by a white mechanic who, when I asked what he was doing in Makurdi, replied in lofty British-accented tones, "Actually, I'm just here on holiday."

I later encountered one of the Provost pilots convalescing in the Makurdi hospital. He had been wounded by Biafran groundfire and was looking forward to leaving Nigeria. Like the mechanic I had seen earlier, he was also British, but a bit more forthcoming in his answers. "This is a silly goddam war," he said, "we're using Shell road maps for navigation and throwing hand grenades out the door for aerial bombardment. Nobody's getting anywhere."

More serious efforts were underway by the Nigerians to acquire Soviet-built Il-28 bombers from the Egyptian air force, jet trainers from

Czechoslovakia and MIG-15 and 17 fighter-bombers from the Soviet Union. When these finally arrived, American Ambassador to Nigeria Elbert Mathews was required by the U.S. Congress to find out from the Nigerians how much they had actually spent on them. He was then obliged to deduct a similar amount from the U.S. aid program in Nigeria. "We managed to find a highway project in eastern Nigeria and pull the funds out of it," he told me with a chuckle years later.

The thrust and parry phase of the war ended in October 1967 when the Biafrans were pushed back from Benin City and across the Niger river, once and for all. It was a major defeat, brought about more through intrigue than outright military force. The Biafrans later said they had been betrayed by their own officers, several of whom were executed shortly before the fall of Enugu.

Radio Biafra, claiming to be broadcasting from Enugu, denied the Biafran capital had fallen to the Nigerians. "We are here," the station proclaimed, inviting journalists to come to the city to see for themselves. In fact, the Biafrans scheduled a news conference to be held in Enugu October 14.

The conference did take place in Enugu a few days later, but it was held by the Nigerians. The Biafrans had fled to the south. Enugu, with a pre-war population of 100,000, was virtually deserted. So was Calabar when I visited it shortly afterwards.

As the Nigerian military began pushing Biafra from both the north and the east, its civilians withdrew into the interior. This pattern continued as the federal forces gradually encircled the former Eastern Region reducing it to an enclave.

Biafra's strongest remaining defensive front was to the west, along the Niger River at Onitsha. The Nigerian army had seized the opposite bank of the Niger, but several attempts by to cross the river at this point had been rebuffed by the Biafrans who had blown up part of the Onitsha bridge.

Back in Lagos, newly-promoted Major General Yakubu Gowon was quietly celebrating his birthday in Dodan barracks. In a reflective mood, he called in the foreign press for an informal chat. Asked how he felt about the way the war was going, he said the prospects for a Federal victory looked very good. He admitted that the army's failure to cross the Niger and capture Onitsha was a setback, but he regarded it as only a temporary one. The damaged bridge would be repaired soon, he said, adding that it was vital to the overall transportation network in Nigeria. Easterners — he pointedly did not call them Biafrans — should return to the cities they had abandoned, he urged, and he gave repeated assurances they would be welcomed back.

General Gowon accused Colonel Ojukwu of using his position to deceive and subjugate his own people. It was fear generated by Ojukwu's propaganda that was keeping Easterners from returning to their own homes, he said. Summing up his hopes for the year ahead, he added wistfully, "We want to keep Nigeria one, and live at peace with one another. If only we could give the nation this gift for this Christmas."

Helen and I had been meeting for lunch in Lagos occasionally, between my trips to and from the war zones. She seemed increasingly pleased over the way her life was working out with Fritz Picard. She noted, however, that he was not too happy about our luncheons together, infrequent as they were. Then she showed me the Alexandrite engagement ring he had brought her from a recent trip to the Middle East.

I think it may have been our last such meeting. I remember going back to my office and thinking how sad it was that our year together in Nigeria should end up this way. I had reached the point where I was looking forward to the briefest of contacts with Helen. Now even those had become an issue between us.

In retrospect, there was little I could offer her except the prospect of a lengthy and conceivably bitter divorce process with Anne. Then, too, whatever happiness we found together would be shadowed by the sure knowledge that it had caused the break-up of a family with two small children. My growing awareness that this should have occurred to me far earlier in the day was not particularly helpful at the time. It was of little comfort to realize that I had only myself — mostly — to blame.

While Anne and I had been back on leave in Washington, we had rented a small town house not far from the Voice of America's head office. I had made it clear that I needed to go back to Lagos alone and see where matters stood with Helen. We would plan from that point onward, but she must understand that I was considering asking her for a divorce so that I could marry Helen.

Anne had gone ahead and put the boys in a Washington school while she waited to hear from me. I now wrote and told her that I would not be marrying Helen, who was in fact marrying someone else. I added that I missed my family and that if she and the boys wanted to come to Lagos to live, I would make a very serious effort towards becoming a better husband and a father. She accepted this, somewhat to my surprise, and said she would try to join me in time for Christmas.

Meanwhile, the civil war ground on. I visited the Nigerian army's newly-created Third Marine Commando Division as it was in the process of occupying Calabar, an historic seaport on the Atlantic. There was still some Biafran resistance and my interview with Lieutenant Colonel Benjamin Adekunle, who lad led the attack on Calabar, was punctuated by the sound of nearby small-arms fire.

While we were speaking, a lone Biafran B-25 bomber of World War II vintage flew low over the city, provoking a nearby Nigerian naval patrol boat to open fire with its anti-aircraft guns. The Biafran bomber kept its bomb-bay doors closed and turned slowly back towards the East, seemingly unpreturbed by the anti-aircraft barrage.

I asked Colonel Adekunle if the Biafrans had put up much of a fight. "No," he said, "it was all over in four hours, but we still have some mopping up to do. And they are keeping some pressure on us while we do it"

Several of the Nigerian army officers I had seen in Enugu had worn, with some degree of pride, the blue berets issued to them just two years before by the United Nations in the Congo. None of Col. Adekunle's officers wore the faded blue berets and I asked him why.

"Very simple," he said, "none of them have been in the army long enough to have served in the bloody Congo! Except me of course — and I don't wear berets"

Colonel Adekunle soon became a highly quotable target for visiting journalists, earning the name "Black Scorpion" in the process. He told me his next move would be to link his Third Marine Commando Division with the First Division forces coming down from the north, thus sealing the border with Cameroon and effectively closing off Biafra on three sides. This would leave open only the Port Harcourt-Onitsha axis along the Niger River.

"We will move on Port Harcourt," he promised,

"early in the new year and we will take it. Just as we did Calabar."

Back in Lagos, Colonel Gowon issued a special Christmas radio and television appeal for "representatives of Eastern Nigeria (he was still not ready to refer to them as Biafrans) to come forward to work for national reconciliation, peace, and reconstruction." But, he added, "we are determined to prosecute this war to the end. We have not even committed one tenth of Nigeria's resources to the struggle."

The prospect of an embattled Biafra, cut off from the outside world, and slowly being pushed in on itself began arousing international sympathy. Pope John Paul appealed for a Christmas cease fire and sent two special envoys to Lagos. Gowon rejected the cease fire proposal and warned the papal delegates that any visit to other side would be at their own risk. They eventually made the trip anyway, traveling to Biafra from Lisbon on a clandestine gun-running flight.

Seizing the moment, Ojukwu declared a unilateral cease fire for the duration of their stay in Biafra. As John Stremlau points out in his study of the Nigerian civil war, the papal delegation's reception in Biafra contrasted markedly with the reserved welcome it had received in Nigeria. Stremlau quotes their report to Pope John Paul where they spoke of a "tumultuous welcome ... roads lined with joyful people waving palm branches ... sometime for an unbroken distance of twenty miles ... "

More to the point, the papal envoys described to the Pope how "the deep conviction of the Ibo people that they are fighting for survival against a campaign of genocide manifested itself in forests of placards held aloft and poured forth in every address of welcome."

Hundreds of expatriate Roman Catholic missionaries had remained behind in Biafra after the war broke out. When the fight intensified, they retreated with their parishioners into the Biafra enclave. Their links with the outside world remained extensive, however, and they were among the first contacts made by overseas journalists visiting Biafra.

The visit by the papal delegation was reported abroad by the newly-organized Biafra Overseas Press Service. It was also passed along by the Catholic missionary network in Biafra to the Catholic News Service in the United States where it was then picked up by American newspapers.

Ojukwu had, in the meantime, contracted Markpress, a Geneva-based public relations firm, to organize foreign (mostly British) press tours of Biafra. The first of these, in April 1968, produced spectacular results in the London press and led to several others, ultimately bringing seventy to eighty journalists to Biafra by mid-1968.

In the midst of all this press attention on the Nigerian civil war, Arnold Smith, a Canadian politician then serving as Secretary General of the

Commonwealth, came to Lagos. He said his mission was to try and set up peace talks between the two sides under Commonwealth auspices. These eventually took place in London in May, followed by a more formal peace conference in Kampala, Uganda.

Neither produced any significant outcome, apart from enhancing Biafra's international posture as a co-equal participant in the bargaining process. Ojukwu had sought to achieve this level of legitimacy from the very beginning of the conflict. Now, his increasing losses on the battlefield were being offset — to some extent, at least — by Biafra's growing international acceptance.

On March 21st, he lost Onitsha, the Niger river crossing point that had held out for nearly six months against the Nigerian army's Second Division. A major market center on Nigeria's main East-West highway, Onitsha was still being contested when I arrived there by taxi and motor boat three days later. It was clear that Federal forces controlled the river crossing and the center of town. But there was heavy machine gun fire to the south of the city and the Biafrans were still firing mortars into Onitsha itself.

When I returned to Lagos later in the day and was sending the story by telephone to the VOA newsroom in Washington, the Africa Desk editor advised me that journalists covering the Biafran side were also claiming to be reporting that day from Onitsha. Did I, by any chance, encounter any of them?, he asked.

For that matter, how could we all be reporting from the same place?

"Onitsha is a fairly good sized town," I told him, "But if the other journalists were at the river crossing, or in the center of Onitsha, they must have been ducking the same Biafran mortar fire I was."

Finding out where you were, precisely, could be a problem in both Nigeria and Biafra. All the road maps had disappeared since the outbreak of the war. It was rumored that the armies of both sides had grabbed them all up once the fighting started. Most foreign journalists brought in their own maps from outside Nigeria. Even these did not solve the problem of knowing exactly where you were at a given moment.

As the Biafrans retreated, they took most of the road signs and mileage markers with them in order to confuse the invading Nigerian army. Vehicle speedometers were only helpful if you knew exactly where you were when you started down a Nigerian road. This might be the case if you began the trip from a fixed, identifiable location like a river or a railway crossing. But most Nigerian speedometers didn't seem to be working, anyway.

It sometimes happened that reporters covering opposite sides of the war ended up reporting from the same town at the same time. Often this was more the result of faulty navigation — and broken speedometers — than poor journalistic ethics.

The Nigerian noose was tightening around Biafra, although Port Harcourt, with its oil refinery and international airport remained in Ojukwu's hands. Nigeria's Third Marine Commando Division, led by Colonel Benjamin Adekunle, had moved west from Calabar. By mid-May, they were poised to take Port Harcourt.

The June 3, 1968 issue of Newsweek magazine carried a fairly long story about VOA. The opening paragraph read: "Covering the bloody Port Harcourt battle in Nigeria's civil war two weeks ago was only half the problem for Voice of America reporter Sean Kelly. To get the news out, he had to rattle overland in a bouncing lorry, skim through the mangrove swamps by motorboat, hitch a ride on an army truck and finally board an airplane for the last leg to the capital city of Lagos. His story, transmitted to Washington, then beamed back to Africa by the VOA, was 24 hours old and only two paragraphs long. But for many Nigerians, it was the first impartial account they heard about the battle."

I was grateful to Newsweek for the coverage, but — along with other reporters covering the war — I disagreed with the magazine's arithmetic. By Newsweek's account, fifty percent of the effort spent covering the war was simply showing up on time at the battlefield. The way we figured it, ninety-five percent of the effort was pure logistics, what was left was devoted to reporting the story.

With the loss of Onitsha, followed by Port Harcourt — which contained Biafra's last remaining international airport — the conflict appeared to have reached a stalement that could only be resolved at the peace table, or by the annihilation of the Biafrans themselves.

The slowed pace of the fighting made it easier for reporters to move about the war zone independently — without having to travel in the large press groups organized by each side. Angus McDermid of the BBC, whom I had come to know in the Congo, was an excellent traveling companion. We made several trips together around the fringes of Biafra, first to Enugu, then to Onitsha and on to Port Harcourt, itself.

We ended up spending much more time in Enugu than we intended, although we were able to get out into the surrounding countryside and see some of the direct effects of the year-long conflict.

At the village of Onuba, on the road east from Enugu towards the Cameroon border, I saw young children, their hair already showing the tell-tale reddish color of kwashiorkor, an advanced state of malnutrition caused by a lack of protein. I had seen it before in the Congo. The normal Biafran diet began by being low on protein and heavy on starch. With fish supplies cut off by the war, protein levels were now virtually non-existent. As usual, the children, always the most vulnerable, were often first to show the effects of the food shortages.

On an earlier visit to Enugu, before the fighting had actually started, I had met with Ojukwu's personal pilot, an American who flew the U.S.-registered Learjet used by the Biafran leader. The pilot told me he was having problems with the Biafran engineers who were building a hangar to house the executive jet. They were using an old British design for a military motor pool building. It called for a grease pit and Ojukwu's engineers were determined to build one.

"I told them," said the Learjet pilot, "that this was a sophisticated aircraft, not a truck. It didn't need a grease pit. But they wouldn't take my word for it. The design called for a grease pit and, by God, they were going to dig one in the hangar floor."

There wasn't much left of the Enugu airport when Angus and I visited it. The terminal had been destroyed by bombing, but we saw a fairly new hangar off to the side towards the end of the runway. We checked it out for a grease pit. There wasn't any. No sign of the Learjet, either.

We were both anxious to get back to Lagos and file our stories. There was no scheduled air service, but we caught sight of a Nigerian Air Force DC-3 coming in for a landing and we headed over to what was left of the terminal building to see if we could hitch a ride on it.

Many Nigerian soldiers were waiting to get on board. We saw that some of them were wounded, but that most seemed to bear few signs of battle damage.

There were more than enough of them, however, to fill the airplane several times over.

When the pilot emerged, we nonetheless tried our luck. He was white, bearded, wearing short trousers, sandals, and a Somali skull cap. Angus recognized him as one the Congo mercenaries. "Bonzo Bill!" he greeted him, "if you are going back to Lagos, could you find room for a couple of journalists?"

"Of course we can," he said, "we can always make room for a couple of journalists. We'll just throw off some of the wounded!."

This drew some rather fierce glares from the soldiers standing in line, but Bonzo made room for us up on the flight deck. We did not see how many Nigerian soldiers managed to board the plane behind us, but the long line was gone when we left.

I sat directly behind Bonzo as he read through the pre-flight check list on the venerable DC-3. When he finished, I watched him fish about in his shirt pocket for a cigaret and a battered Zippo lighter that bore the faded insignia of 5 Commando — Mike Hoare's old mercenary unit in the Congo. Bonzo's hands shook badly when he lit his cigaret, but he was able to steady them as he pushed the throttles forward. The take-off seemed to last forever. I think there were more Nigerian soldiers behind us than anyone — including Bonzo Bill — had counted.

Back in Lagos, I spent some time catching up with my family. Anne had enrolled our sons into the local International school where they had become friends with the Picard children of the same age. Helen and Fritz had since married and occasionally I would see her bringing the children to and from school. I waved from a distance and she would always wave back. Sadly, that was about the extent of our communication.

After more than a year of covering the war from the Nigerian side, I was intrigued with the idea of trying to get into Biafra itself — while it was still Biafra and not occupied territory. The Nigerians had warned all foreign correspondents based in Lagos that we could only cover one side of the war at a time and we would have to choose between the two.

"If you go over to the other side," said Nigerian Information Minister Anthony Enaharo, "you better expect to stay there, because you will not be welcome back here. For security reasons, we do not want reporters crossing back and forth across the front lines, telling Ojukwu's people what you have seen here."

My editors at VOA News made it clear they felt it was more important for me to remain on the Nigerian side — at least for the time being.

I tried neutral ground and flew to Douala, Cameroon where I thought I might cross over to the island of Fernando Po (since renamed Equatorial Guinea) where the International Committee of the Red Cross (ICRC) had begun flying a nightly airlift of food and medical supplies into Biafra.

As is often the case with African travel adventures, just getting to Equatorial Guinea was half the fun. The island of Fernando Po was still under Spanish rule and journalists were supposed to apply to Madrid for entry visas. Iberia, the Spanish airline, operated daily flights from Douala, on the Cameroon coast and I learned from one of their pilots that Americans were able to enter Equatorial Guinea easily without Spanish visas.

"When we land at Fernando Po," he said, "just mention the word 'Mobil' as you pass through customs. It's like open sesame."

I flew over the next morning, showed the customs officials my American passport, and mumbled "Mobil" as though it were some strange new password. It worked — thanks I later learned to the presence of a large number of Mobil oil exploration people in the area.

The airport at Fernando Po was crowded with large cargo aircraft, mostly Douglas DC-6s and 7s, bearing the Red Cross insignia of the ICRC. I told one of the pilots I was an American journalist and I needed to see the man in charge.

He turned out to be Colonel Sven Lampel, a Swedish air force fighter pilot who had earlier commanded the United Nations air force contingent in the Congo. Although we had not met before, we had many friends in common and he gave me a full briefing on the airlift operation. He was sending an average of ten flights a night into Biafra, landing at an airstrip created out of a portion of the new highway that ran between Port Harcourt and Onitsha.

Could this be, I have since wondered, the same highway project U.S. Ambassador Elbert Mathews told me he had canceled because Nigerians had bought aircraft from the Soviet Union? Ironies abounded in the Nigerian civil war.

At one end of the improvised airstrip was the town of Uli, at the other was Ihiala, so the Red Cross pilots were calling it Uli-Ihiala, or Annabelle for short — the name given to it by their French engineers who advised the Biafrans on constructing airstrips out of highways. The other main Biafran airstrip was code-named Caroline by the same French advisers, but it had already been captured by the Nigerians.

I asked Lampel if I could fly into Biafra on one of the Red Cross airlift missions, "Not without a Biafran visa," he said. "What if I stay on board the aircraft?," I asked. "The problem," he said, "is that Biafran security inspects each flight and we have to account for everyone we bring in."

"It is all very sensitive," he added. "because the Biafrans are trying to run arms in at the same time. We refuse to carry military weapons because it would compromise the neutrality of our ICRC mission. But we are not the only airlift flying into Biafra. There is at least one other, operating at the same time we do. It is based on the Portuguese island of Sao Tome. We all end up together in Biafra, maintaining radio silence and no lights, stacked thirty deep every night over Uli-Ihiala. It has become an air traffic nightmare, but we have not flown into each other — so far."

Biafra refused to accept daylight flights because it would mean risking its airstrips to Nigerian attack. By insisting on night flights only, Ojukwu forced the ICRC and other international relief flights to give cover to aircraft flying arms, ammunition, and the occasional journalist into Biafra from Sao Tome.

The war Nigerian civil war was already receiving global news coverage with television crews flying into both sides of the war zone. It was only a question of time before the first journalist would be killed in action. It turned out to be a good friend from the Congo: Priya Ramrahka was shot by a Biafran sniper while filming for the American CBS television network.

Increasingly, the story had less to do with the stalemated war on the ground and more to do with the worsening humanitarian situation in Biafra, which included the international relief effort. I covered both, but found myself spending more time reporting the problems the ICRC was encountering getting into, and out of, Biafra.

In talking to pilots making the nightly relief runs from Fernando Po, I came across fragments of a recurring story which I was never able to pin down. Pilots approaching Biafra's Uli-Ihiala airstrip were required to use an elaborate system of codes and passwords on certain radio frequencies in order to get permission to land. Otherwise, they risked being shot down by Biafran anti-aircraft units. The procedure had to be followed closely before the Biafrans would even turn on the runway lights for incoming aircraft.

Pilots would radio the makeshift Biafran tower, using their identity codes and citing the amount of endurance time they had available before they needed to return home. The Biafrans would then determine which aircraft would get to land first and which ones would have the remain circling over the airstrip. Ojukwu's personal aircraft, I learned, always got top priority. Curiously, it was flown by an American crew using the radio call-sign "Gray Ghost". It was a name I had first heard in the Congo, when it had been used by an American military aircraft. I wondered about this and asked around the ICRC whether any of its pilots had any personal experiences with the "Gray Ghost", or its American crew.

"The 'Gray Ghost' always cuts through the stack," one Swedish pilot told me. "He gets first landing rights at Uli ahead of everybody." Another pilot recounted an experience he had when one of his aircraft's propellors stuck in the reverse position just after landing at Uli.

"It was close to dawn," he said, "and the airstrip was too short to get off on only three engines. While we were unloading, I looked around desperately for help in getting the propellor back to its original position so we could take off. Otherwise, the Nigerians would bomb or strafe the aircraft as soon as it was light enough for them to see it.

He told me he was about to abandon hope altogether when he heard an American voice shout up to him from below the aircraft, asking if he needed help. It turned out to be a crewmember from the "Gray Ghost." The pilot said the American lashed two pieces of lumber around the propellor and manhandled it back into position — just as the sun was breaking out over the field.

"I never got to thank him," the ICRC pilot said. "We pulled of there just as fast as we could and I never saw him again."

The war came to an end when the "Gray Ghost", or an aircraft like it, flew Ojukwu out of Biafra at 2 a.m. January 11, 1970 — just as the Nigerian forces were beginning to close in on Uli-Ihiala.

The final act was played out at Dodan barracks in Lagos. Biafra's acting head of government, Major General Philip Effiong, dressed in civilian clothes, surrendered to his old Sandhurst classmate and chum, Major General Yakubu Gowon. In doing so, he demoted himself to his original pre-war rank, stood at attention and saluted. "Lieutenant Colonel Philip Effiong," he said, "reporting for redeployment, sir."

A more formal surrender ceremony followed.

Later, Effiong passed a message to Helen Bodurtha Picard at the American Embassy in Lagos. "Tell Helen thanks for her help in Kaduna."

I had long since departed for Washington. The Nigerians had been systematically kicking out all the Western journalists who had been covering the war from the beginning. The BBC had already left. My turn came shortly afterwards. I had been unable to get a visa to Biafra before it fell and now the Nigerians wouldn't let me stay. As it turned out, neither side would have me.

Proof, I suppose, that I must have been at least somewhat even-handed in my coverage of their war.

Interviewing Colonel Ochoa on Salvadoran warfront (Chapter 1).

Interviewing guerrilla soldier guarding a rebel roadblock in El Salvador (Chapter 1).

With Nixon on 1967 visit to Nigeria (Chapter 2).

From Armed Forces Radio to NBC
Television, Air Force-style (Chapter 3).

With Kenneth Kaunda, Zambia's founding father
(Chapter 6).

REBELLES?
DEPOSEZ VOS ARMES!

JE VIENS DE
DONNER TOUTE MA
PUISSANCE AU
GOUVERNEMENT
CENTRAL

LA REBELLION
EST MORTE!

Les rebelles qui ne déposent pas leurs
armes sont des hommes finis

MAMA ONEMA

Congolese
propaganda
poster with
rebel sorceress
Mama Onema
(Chapter 7).

George Clay's gravestone at Stanleyville (now Kisangani), DRC (Chapter 7).

With international observers at Biafran ambush site in Eastern Nigeria (Chapter 8).

Borrowing a Nigerian armored car for a VOA
publicity photo (Chapter 8).

Nigerian Colonel "Black Scorpion" Adekunle and staff
(Chapter 9).

Nigerian soldiers wearing plastic flowers looted from local cemetery for helmet decorations (Chapter 9).

A Biafran homemade tank that died defending Port Harcourt, Nigeria (Chapter 9).

A C-130 of the type that once flew over Laos and answered to the name of "Cricket" (Chapter 10).

Reporting, with others, Henry Kissinger in Laos (Chapter 10).

With Captain Charlie Pepper, FAC pilot in
Vietnam (Chapter 11).

1972 Vietnam battlefront north of Hue (Chapter 11).

Bringing home the Space Shuttle (Chapter 15).

Burying Diane Fossey. Author at upper left (Chapter 16).

Campaigning to be South Africa's first democratically-
elected president (Chapter 16).

10.

Laos: Somebody Must Have Called "Cricket".

In southern Laos, near the border with Cambodia and Vietnam, the Bolovens Plateau rises straight up from the steamy Mekong River valley, reaching an altitude of nearly four thousand feet. The land changes at that elevation, becoming cool, moist and fertile. Lao farmers have raised food and livestock on the Bolovens Plateau for years. But in 1971, the Plateau and the people who lived on top of it found themselves abruptly pushed into the war in neighboring Vietnam.

So did three reporters, named Arbuckle, Daniel and Kelly, who went up to the plateau to cover the Battle for the Bolovens — and almost didn't make it back.

In those days, the eastern edge of the Plateau looked down upon the main north-south military supply route for the North Vietnamese army and its Pathet Lao and Viet Cong allies. This loose network of bicycle trails, truck routes and hidden storage depots had become known at the Ho Chi Minh Trail. It sustained the North Vietnamese war effort in South Vietnam and Hanoi was determined to protect it all costs.

The United States was equally bent on shutting it down. Washington had been trying to disrupt the flow of traffic down the Ho Chi Minh Trail for years — without much success. No expense had been spared in the effort. Highly secret projects with code names like *Igloo White* spent millions of dollars trying to track movement down the Trail electronically. Ground sensors would be dropped along the Trail. These would feed data into computers which would then launch strike aircraft from neighboring Thailand. At one point *Igloo White* claimed a response time of less than five minutes between sensor activity and air strike. Still, thousands of North Vietnamese soldiers managed to make their way down the Trail, bringing with them many tons of equipment.

In 1971, U.S. President Richard Nixon decided to attack the Trail directly, using South Vietnamese troops airlifted into Laos by U.S. Army helicopters. As part of the operation, which was code-named LAM SON 719, American jet fighter-bombers were used to soften up North Vietnamese defensive positions.

One major effect of the attack was to push the Ho Chi Minh trail further west, up into the Bolovens

Plateau. LAM SON 719 ended in April 1971 with South Vietnamese fighting their way back across the border into Vietnam. Shortly afterwards, fifteen hundred North Vietnamese soldiers stormed up the eastern side of the Bolovens and captured it. They seized the town of Paksong, the Plateau's main administrative center, and dug in around it, eventually building a network of fortified bunkers. Then they brought in Soviet-built tanks and artillery to secure their occupation of the Plateau, creating a new Western flank for the Ho Chi Minh Trial.

After considerable prodding from the American Embassy in Vientiane, the Royal Lao Army decided to take the Plateau back. Additional military forces were moved south to the Mekong river port of Pakse, along with helicopters and T-28 fighter-bombers to support them.

Thus the stage was set for the Battle of the Bolovens.

I had just arrived in Bangkok with wife Anne and our two small sons. We had spent the past year in Washington and had begun settling into a Thai-style house on the edge of one of Bangkok's old canals — the Thais called them *klongs*. We were busy negotiating the purchase of a small boat for the kids to paddle about the *klong* when Leon Daniel of United Press International called. Leon had been in and out of Southeast Asia for years, and, as a new-comer, I welcomed his wisdom and experience.

He had been tipped by a colleague in Laos that the Americans were getting ready to move Lao troops by helicopter onto the top of the Bolovens, as part of an assault on the North Vietnamese forces occupying the town of Paksong. If we could get to the Pakse airport, on the Mekong, we could probably catch a ride up to the Plateau with the troops.

Would I be interested in the trip?

Emphatically.

Leon figured the best way to get there would be by railway from Bangkok east to Ubon Ratchatan. This meant traveling virtually all the way across Thailand, but it could be accomplished in an over-night train ride. In Ubon, there were taxis that would take us to the Mekong where we could cross the river by boat to Pakse.

The trip across Thailand by train was easy, but the taxi in Ubon turned out to be a problem. None of the taxi drivers wanted to go beyond the Laotian border which was necessary in order to reach the Mekong. "Lao road number ten", one of them put it succinctly, using a worsening ten-point scale to rate the condition of the road surface. We finally found a willing driver who got us all the way to the Mekong river bank just as the sun was setting.

There was no shortage of canoe operators willing to motor us across the wide and fast-flowing Mekong. On the other bank, a couple of young men on motor-bikes gave us each a ride into Pakse. We passed by the airport on the way into town, but it seemed to have closed down for the day, so we headed for the hotel. It was a fairly minimal establishment, six rooms over a noodle shop. A good Chinese meal, washed down with several cold Thai beers, and the austerity of our living accommodations didn't matter too much.

In the morning, after a steaming bowl of Vietnamese soup for breakfast, we set out to find the Americans.

"What we usually look for, " said Leon, "are the antennas and the air conditioners. The American military can't seem to operate in Southeast Asia without a lot of them."

A short time later, we came across a large house with a diesel generator operating outside, several air conditioners punched into the walls, and a roof that bristled with antennas. Behind it was a Huey helicopter and several jeeps, all well shielded from the road,

We found two U.S. army Captains and a Major inside. They seemed to be expecting us. "We heard there were several reporters in town," one of them said. "What can we do for you?"

"What about a ride up to the Plateau?", asked Leon.

"Let me first of all lay down a few ground rules," said the Major. "We're willing to help you out, but we can't be quoted because, officially, we're not even here. So don't use our names and keep us out of your photographs. Is that agreeable?"

We said it was, but we still needed to go up to the Plateau.

"There was some action up there last night," reported one of the Captains. "The North Vietnamese sent a patrol down Route 23 from Paksong. It was led by a tank, a Russian PT-76. The Royal Lao forces took it out with a rocket and the patrol retreated back up the road to Paksong. The tank is still there by the side of the road and we want to check it out to see what kind of rocket they used.

"We've been training them on the LAW — our light anti-tank weapon — but we didn't know they had started using them yet," said the Major. "You're welcome to ride along in the jeep as long as you stick with the ground rules and stay out of trouble."

We assured them we would.

The North Vietnamese tank had been heading down the center of Route 23 when it was hit by the rocket, a Soviet-made one, as it turned out. The tank had since been pushed over to the side of the road and was now straddling a drainage ditch. The PT-76 was an amphibious tank, similar to those in use by the U.S. Marine Corps. It didn't appear very sea-worthy, but it had two small propellors at its rear. Against such a light-weight target, the armor-piercing rocket had done its work well, leaving a large hole just below the gun turret and blasting into oblivion the two Vietnamese crew members inside.

Leon, who had been a Marine in Korea, insisted

on climbing up the side of the tank and peering down into its turret. He did this with some difficulty because his right leg was encased in a plaster cast from his knee down to his ankle. He told me he had broken several bones in his ankle when he was in the Marines and was now having them reset. Bulky as it was, the cast did not seem to slow him down very much.

Leon wanted to file a story to UPI on the North Vietnamese tank and I wanted to look around Pakse a bit, so we caught a ride back down the highway into town. The American Major told us he planned to take a quick trip around the edge of the Plateau in the helicopter after lunch and we could ride along, if we wanted.

We said we did.

"Be at my place no later than 1500 hours," he said.

We assured him we would.

Back in Pakse, we ran into Tammy Arbuckle of the Washington Star, he had flown down from Vientiane that morning with the news that the Royal Lao Army did indeed intend to launch their Plateau offensive with the next 48 hours. It was going to be led by Colonel Suchai Vongsavanh, who recently had returned to Laos from training in the United States.

"Colonel Suchai likes to have the press around him," said Arbuckle. He's something of a hot-shot, not your usual Lao army Colonel."

I noticed that Arbuckle seemed to be rather pale and shaky. It turned out he had a roaring case of malaria, but had come down from Vientiane because he couldn't afford to miss the Bolovens Plateau story. His main competition, the Washington Post correspondent, was off in Vietnam and Arbuckle, despite his malaria, was happy to have the Bolovens all to himself.

We told him about our deal with the American Major and the helicopter trip, thinking there would probably be room for him if he wanted to show up with us. He begged off. "Colonel Suchai said he would take us all up in his command chopper," he said. "I'll wait for that. In my present state, I'm only good for about one trip up that mountain, anyway."

Later, I understood what Arbuckle had meant when we rode with the Major up to the Plateau in his Huey. We had door gunners on each side of the helicopter and everything was open. It was very breezy, particularly when we got up above five thousand feet. The Plateau itself was around 3,600 feet, but it was surrounded by higher mountains and the Major was being deliberately circuitous in his approach. We ducked in and out of several valleys on the way to Paksong and then only saw the town from a distance. It was very chilly until we got back down to the Mekong.

"The weather might be a problem for tomorrow's operation," said the Major. "It is basically going to be a helicopter insertion on top of the Plateau. Colonel Suchai will give you more details, but we are looking at the movement of several hundred Lao troops, mostly brought in by the Royal Lao Air Force. Of course this will be preceded by tactical air strikes in which there will be some U.S. involvement, although Laotian T-28s will carry the burden of the operation. There shouldn't be any problem if the weather stays decent."

Arbuckle was waiting for us when we got back to the hotel in Pakse. The state of his health had not improved, but he had some good news from Colonel Suchai. We were to be at the Pakse airport operations center at 7 a.m. Suchai would brief us and take us up to the Plateau where the operation should be well underway.

In the meantime, Colonel Suchai had a Pathet Lao defector we could interview, if we were interested.

Between Arbuckle, who spoke some Lao, and the Royal Lao Army interpreter, who would no doubt put official spin on whatever the defector said, we figured there might be a story in why he came over to the government side.

He told us he was Lieutenant Kamporn and he had been with the Pathet Lao for sixteen years. He identified his unit as Company Two of the Twelfth Pathet Lao Battalion, based, apparently, on or near the Trail. His unit's main job was to transport food and ammunition down a ten kilometer portion of the

Trail. The work was done by hand, he said. There were no trucks or push carts available and the men carried the loads on their backs, making the 20 kilometer round trip in a day's time. Another Pathet Lao unit would pick up the food and ammunition for the next portion of the Trail.

Lieutenant Kamporn said he had been trained as a soldier in North Vietnam, but had rarely seen combat. He said the North Vietnamese forces in Laos did not trust the Pathet Lao units under their command. For that reason, the Pathet Lao were mostly used for supply and other non-combat tasks. When I asked him why he came over to the government side, he replied that increased North Vietnamese taxation and forced labor were causing many Pathet Lao to consider making the move. He had brought twenty members of his company out with him, he said, and was now going back to try and bring out more.

I taped the interview to send to the VOA Lao Service in Washington and telexed a story to the Newsroom entitled "Conversation with a Pathet Lao" which drew a small note of praise from the Chief of the News Division. He then went on to caution me about conducting news interviews in a language I didn't understand. He didn't seem to share my confidence in Arbuckle's knowledge of spoken Lao.

We asked Arbuckle how he was feeling and he said he had taken another dose of quinine to help him deal with the malaria. He was in no mood for food or drink that night and wanted to turn in early. He asked us to please check his room if we didn't see him at breakfast time. "I need this story," he said. "I just wish it had come along at a better time."

Leon and I wandered around Pakse that evening, ultimately finding a modest riverside cafe overlooking the Mekong. Fish was on the menu, along with fried rice. Thai beer was everywhere, on both sides of the Laotian border in those days, and, miraculously, it was almost always cold. How local shop owners managed to serve it that way, given the prevailing tropical weather and the general lack of electricity, remained one of the best kept secrets of the Indochinese war.

Day One of the Battle for the Bolovens dawned early, but not very brightly — nor very quietly, for that matter. The tactical air strikes got underway up on the Plateau at first light. We could hear the distant explosions in town and it was clear from the noise of the jet aircraft that it was not the Royal Lao Air Force that was carrying, as the Major had put it, most of the burden of the operation. The Laotians flew relatively slow moving, propellor-driven T-28s. What we were hearing from the Bolovens was not the sound of T-28s, but American jet fighter-bombers seriously softening up the North Vietnamese defensive positions around Paksong. The difference in sound and volume was unmistakable.

The sky was overcast when we arrived by taxi at

the Pakse airport. Colonel Suchai was not in sight, but we were met by a young Laotian Lieutenant who said he had been assigned to look after us. His English was not very strong and his French even less so. Arbuckle spoke to him in Lao and this seemed to be our most likely means of communication. To make matters worse, he gave the impression of being extremely nervous and excitable for a Laotian military officer. Arbuckle learned that he had been slightly wounded earlier in the year during LAM SON 719. We noted he spoke frequently into a hand-held field radio and was obviously in touch with some higher authority. Under the circumstances, this made us all feel a bit easier.

Whatever his shortcomings, he loaded us into a Royal Lao Air Force Sikorsky troop-carrying helicopter and told us we were headed up to the Plateau. We took off almost immediately. Unlike the Huey, the Sikorsky's engine was in front, just below the pilots. We were further back in the aircraft with no view forward. The open side door gave us our only perspective on the landscape we were flying over. It was rugged countryside and we had the impression we were climbing up through a series of valleys. We were in loose formation with another Sikorsky which we assumed was Colonel Suchai's command chopper.

The landscape below abruptly turned into lush farmland, flanked by occasional rows of trees. We crossed over an unpaved road and headed towards a hilltop where there appeared to be a military outpost of some kind. Soldiers waved at us as we approached and someone set off a red smoke grenade, indicating there were wounded needing immediate evacuation.

We descended through red smoke and suddenly Laotian troops were everywhere. They grabbed the landing gear struts and clambered on board the Sikorsky even before it touched the ground, causing it to veer awkwardly to the right.

"We got to get out of here!" shouted Leon. "These guys are panicking. They are going to swamp us!"

In quick reaction, the Laotian pilot applied power and the Sikorsky seemed to strain against the weight of the oncoming soldiers. We bumped once and I pushed away from the aircraft, hitting the ground hard. I ran head down, stumbling into a sandbagged foxhole. Leon was already there. Arbuckle and the Laotian Lieutenant were close behind. As the helicopter was pulling away from us, Laotian soldiers were still hanging onto its landing gear struts.

At about that time we became aware that the sky had clouded over and it had started to rain. We could still hear the sounds of the fast-moving jet fighters, but we could no longer see them. They were not attempting to break through the cloud cover. They had stopped their close air support of the Royal Lao troops trying to retake the Bolovens Plateau.

We were close enough to Paksong to see the

North Vietnamese soldiers defending the town. Now that the American fighter-bombers had been forced by the weather to stop their air strikes, the North Vietnamese started moving out of their fortified bunkers and were setting up mortar positions. Leon, whose plaster cast was beginning to disintegrate in the rain, had brought binoculars and was watching the North Vietnamese soldiers with fascination.

"We are going to have to get off this hill," he said. "Those mortars are being aimed at us."

I had never been in a sustained mortar attack before, but I argued that if we left the hill, the Royal Lao Air Force might have trouble locating us again. "Right now," I told Leon, "they know where we are. Once we leave, it may not be so easy for them to find us."

The first mortar round fell well short of our position, but it was close enough to be taken seriously. "They're still working out our range," said Leon. "The next rounds will be a lot closer and we don't have any real cover up here at all. We've got to move out."

I noticed that our nervous Laotian army Lieutenant was still with us and was talking excitedly into his radio. We had no idea what he was saying, or who he was talking to. Arbuckle, who was curled up, shivering in a poncho, mumbled something about calling "Cricket".

Who is "Cricket?", I asked.

Leon replied that "Cricket" was the radio call-sign for a U.S. Air Force C-130 outfitted as an airborne command post. It flew daily orbits over southern Laos, keeping track of what was happening on the ground and serving as a radio relay point for downed pilots, friendly troops in trouble and possibly even the occasional journalist under fire. At night time, "Cricket" was replaced by another C-130 with essentially the same mission, but named "Moonbeam". The system worked around the clock, seven days a week.

Arbuckle crept over to the Laotian Lieutenant and spoke to him quietly. I could see that the Lieutenant was very agitated, but he seemed to understand whatever it was that Arbuckle was explaining. He nodded repeatedly, and began screaming into the radio. Occasionally, I could make out the word "Cricket" in the torrent of Lao delivered by the Lieutenant. Arbuckle seemed satisfied and curled back up into his poncho.

As the North Vietnamese mortar rounds began exploding on all sides of our exposed hill top, closing in on our position, I began thinking this first visit to Laos could very well end up being my last. There did not seem to be any way out of our present situation and it was becoming increasingly clear we were not going to be able to remain alive on the hill top much longer.

I thought of Anne and the boys in Bangkok,

setting up our new house, paddling about the *klong* in the just acquired boat. "Is this the way it ends?," I asked myself. "Here I am, in a country I barely know and care even less about, covering a minor military operation that was badly planned and now has gone off track and I'll probably never know why."

I even thought of Helen, gone now from Nigeria to God knows where — a place I did not know and could not even picture in my mind. How was she? What was she doing? Would she ever learn what happened here?

The mortar rounds seemed to diminish in number, but new explosions shook the hilltop. Added to them was the wonderful war-movie roar of the propellor-driven T-28s. The Royal Lao Air Force had begun working over the North Vietnamese mortar positions in Paksong. Their T-28s, slow-moving training aircraft modified to carry bombs and machine-guns, were getting in below the weather and had forced the North Vietnamese back into their bunkers. The threat of mortar fire had eased, but then the weather got worse and the T-28s went away.

The Laotian Lieutenant had gathered up the few soldiers that had remained behind when the Sikorsky had left and he motioned for us to join them. We moved along with them, single-file, off the hilltop. By this time, the rain and mist had become so heavy we could no longer make out Paksong and we assumed the North Vietnamese probably couldn't see us either. At any rate, they made no effort to stop us.

The going was slow. Leon Daniel had found some plastic material to keep the rain off what was left of his leg cast, but the downhill slope was difficult for him. Tammy Arbuckle's raging malaria made any movement at all a personal challenge. The Lieutenant and his Laotian soldiers were eager to get off the Plateau and away from the North Vietnamese, but they stayed with us until we reached a level clearing.

There, to our very great surprise, was a Royal Lao Air Force Sikorsky, its rotors turning slowly. We clambered on board and took off down a ravine and into the mist toward Pakse and the Mekong.

"How did we manage to get out of that mess on the Plateau?," I asked Leon.

"I think the Lao Lieutenant must have finally got through to somebody on the radio," he replied.

"And then," mumbled Arbuckle, "somebody must have called 'Cricket'."

Back in Bangkok, a week or so later, we heard that Colonel Suchai had hit the Bolovens Plateau a second time — with the weather in his favor. He eventually cleared it of North Vietnamese soldiers.

Peace talks followed and an agreement was reached requiring all foreign military forces to withdraw from Laos, including Laotian airspace, by twelve noon of a certain date. At 11:05 that day, several reporters were sitting in Vientiane, listening to an air operations radio. An American voice broke through the static.

"This is Cricket. We are now departing this area. We have enjoyed being of service over the years, but the time has now come for us to go. Good-bye. See you next war."

11.

Vietnam: Hanoi's Easter Surprise.

When the attack finally came on Good Friday, March 30, 1972, it still caught nearly everyone by surprise. The American military had plenty of evidence that North Vietnam was planning a new offensive against the south, but had no clear idea when it would take place. Or how it would begin. Or, perhaps most importantly, where Hanoi would strike first.

The signs were all too evident by early February. More North Vietnamese men and supplies were observed moving down the Ho Chi Minh Trail. Tanks and heavy trucks were rolling south at a greater rate than ever before. More ominously, Hanoi was, for the first time, positioning Soviet SA-2 surface-to-air missile (SAM) batteries along South Vietnam's northern border areas.

In Saigon, it was being widely predicted the

attack would coincide with *Tet*, the Vietnamese lunar New Year, as had been the case four years earlier. Once again, the South Vietnamese capital would be the major target. This timing would coincide with U.S. President Richard Nixon's historic first visit to China in February, possibly even stealing some of its thunder.

It didn't happen. Saigon was full of foreign correspondents, myself among them, waiting for the offensive to begin in early February. But Hanoi did not oblige and Nixon's visit to Beijing captured all the headlines it deserved. The only story to report from Saigon at the time was the massive exodus of American troops. Nearly sixty thousand American soldiers returned home from Vietnam between February and April 1972. Historians have since called it the largest single troop reduction of the war.

Ironically, it was taking place just as the North Vietnamese were building up their own troop levels in preparation for the coming offensive. The Americans were withdrawing from South Vietnam at an unprecedented pace, mainly because the war was becoming increasingly unpopular in the United States. 1972 was an election year. Richard Nixon, running for re-election in November, had committed his government to a program of "Vietnamization" in the war. A key element of this policy was a phased withdrawal of American troops in South Vietnam.

After many years of direct American participation, the war was finally being turned over to the South Vietnamese to fight.

American advisers were to remain on the scene and U.S. combat air support would continue to be available, but most of it would be coming from Thailand or from aircraft carriers in the South China sea — and not from U.S. bases in South Vietnam itself. These were being closed down. Their facilities, often including their aircraft, were being turned over to the South Vietnamese. The Americans, at long last, were going home.

But when the opening North Vietnamese shots were fired at noon on Good Friday, Nixon's "Vietnamization" plan had already gone seriously askew. American forces were headed home faster than the South Vietnamese troops were prepared, or willing, to replace them. Aware of this growing imbalance, the North Vietnamese army, after a massive artillery bombardment, stormed across the border into South Vietnam. Three North Vietnamese Army divisions, nearly forty thousand troops, poured across the Demilitarized Zone into Quang Tri province while three more NVA divisions prepared to attack further south from sanctuaries in neighboring Laos and Cambodia. A total of 130,000 North Vietnamese soldiers moved into South Vietnam, supported by as many as 1,200 tanks and other armored vehicles from the north. It would become America's last major battle in Vietnam, and, in many respects, the most important of the war.

Two days into the invasion, an incident occurred that demonstrated how little the Americans and their South Vietnamese allies were prepared for what was taking place. A U.S. Air Force EB-66 radar surveillance aircraft was shot down by one of the first North Vietnamese SA-2 missile batteries recently introduced into the border area. The EB-66 crew had not been briefed that a massive new North Vietnamese offensive was underway, nor were they warned about the threat posed by the repositioned missile sites.

The EB-66 navigator, Lieutenant Colonel Ical Hambleton, managed to bail out successfully, but he landed directly in the middle of the North Vietnamese invasion force. For the next twelve days, his radio call-sign "BAT-21", became the focal point for a major air and ground rescue effort. Two U.S. rescue helicopters, their crews unaware of the North Vietnamese invasion or the existence of the SAM sites, were also shot down, as were several observation aircraft.

Painful as these losses were, the most damaging result of the BAT-21 incident was that it led to the creation of an immense no-fire zone around the downed Lieutenant Colonel, until he could be rescued. This meant that no American or South Vietnamese military operations could be carried out while the rescue effort was underway. For twelve days, the South

Vietnamese Army was denied artillery and air support in an area and at a time where it was needed the most —- just as the North Vietnamese soldiers were swarming across the border. As one American adviser put it, the exclusion zone gave the North Vietnamese "an unprecedented opportunity to advance at will."

The first South Vietnamese city to fall was the provincial capital of Quang Tri, just south of the border area. I was in Saigon, having flown over from Bangkok once the extent of the North Vietnamese invasion had become clear. It seemed to me that Hue, the old imperial capital located sixty kilometers south of Quang Tri City, would be the next likely NVA objective. I set about to see how I could get there before the North Vietnamese did.

There was a daily Air Vietnam flight north to Danang from Saigon's Tan Son Nhut airport. If I could get on it, I would be a lot closer to Hue. Buying a ticket proved no problem, finding a seat on the airplane was another matter altogether. I was told at the Air Vietnam counter that the flight was completely full. So was the flight the following day. Luckily, I managed to intercept the pilot on his way to the aircraft. He was an American and, after I explained my problem, he invited me to sit behind him on the flight deck.

The aircraft was a vintage Douglas DC-4. I had a chance to browse through its log book while I was waiting for the engines to start up. I noted that it had originally been in the service of Air France before joining Air Algerie in North Africa and ultimately ending up in Southeast Asia wearing the green and white colors of Air Vietnam. It had seen a lot of miles along the way.

Once the engines were started, the flight deck filled with smoke, but the pilots opened their side windows as we taxied out to the runway and the air inside the cabin soon cleared. We had to wait a while before we could take off. Tan Son Nhut air base was also serving as Saigon's international airport. It had become increasingly active since the outbreak of the Easter invasion. Taxiing along the flight line, we saw incoming fighter-bombers, heavy troop transports, rescue helicopters and light observation aircraft, as well as civilian jetliners loaded with American soldiers headed back to the United States.

We took off for Pleiku in the Central Highlands, our only stop on the long flight to Danang. Weather was good and my seat behind the pilot gave me a clear view of the passing landscape. It was the first time I had flown north out of Saigon and I followed the changing scenery closely. Vietnam seemed to me a remarkably beautiful country, in spite of the war. From the air, the soft green contours of its valleys and hillsides gave little hint of the ongoing havoc taking place below us.

The airport at Pleiku brought me back to reality. A mortar attack got underway while we were unloading passengers near the terminal building and the pilot decided to cut short our stay. I could see the explosions from my seat on the flight deck as we started up engines and the crew got the last of the Pleiku passengers off the aircraft. The mortar rounds were hitting closer to the aircraft, and I noticed the pilot and copilot cut short the usual preflight check list procedures. After a very abrupt takeoff, we circled back over the field and could see several airport buildings burning, including the terminal where we had parked.

Danang had recently been a major headquarters for the U.S. Marines in Vietnam, but most of them had left, taking their legendary press operations center with them. Searching for the Americans who might still be around, I followed Leon Daniel's wisdom and looked for a building with air conditioners and a lot of antennas. It turned out to be the office of John Hogan, a senior provincial adviser who has been my boss at VOA while I was in Nigeria. He gave me a warm welcome, found me a ride on a military helicopter to Hue, and promised me a cold beer and a hot shower when I got back to Danang.

Hue, the old imperial city, had been heavily fought over four years earlier during the 1968 *Tet* offensive. There had not been much in the way of reconstruction, but one of the old riverside hotels remained in business. It was filled with journalists, many of whom I knew from Bangkok, or Nigeria, even the Congo. Staying there was a little like attending an old boys' school reunion.

We were all waiting for the North Vietnamese to come down the highway from Quang Tri City. They were barely forty miles to the north, practically within artillery range. Retreating South Vietnamese troops had swept through Hue several days before. Very few of them stayed behind to defend the city. We figured it would only be a matter of time before the North Vietnamese army showed up, in one form or another.

There didn't seem to be much to slow them down, let alone stop them along the way. Or so we thought at the time. From Hue, it was not yet possible to gauge the extent of President Nixon's reaction to the North Vietnamese offensive. The first indications came from the flood of refugees moving south, fleeing down the highway from Quang Tri City.

Along with several other reporters, I fell victim to the false notion that these refugees were, as I phrased it in one broadcast report I have since come to regret, "voting with their feet." They didn't want to become North Vietnamese, so they fled south — as thousands had done less than twenty years before, on Bernard Fall's historic "street without joy." But the explanation in 1972 was not that simple.

Shortly after the last American was extracted by helicopter from the battered citadel in Quang Tri City on May 1, B-52 heavy bombers were brought in to level what was left of the provincial capital. The

North Vietnamese victory celebrations, if any, must have seemed rather hollow to the victors. They had captured, and were now holding, a lunar landscape, composed for the most part of broken masonry and twisted metal. Now the B-52s were coming back, as Winston Churchill once phrased it, "to make the rubble bounce."

Any citizen of Quang Tri City still unfortunate enough to be in the area would have headed south, not necessarily to choose freedom but to avoid the destruction from the B-52s which flew so high their approach could often neither be seen nor heard. This served to make their attacks all the more fearsome to those on the ground. The B-52s could drop thirty tons of high explosive in an area not much bigger than a city block. To me, even their code name — Arc Light — seemed ominous.

What the B-52s missed, American fighter-bombers soon destroyed on the road south of Quang Tri City. President Nixon had dramatically raised the number of tactical aircraft in South Vietnam, as well as in neighboring Thailand, and on aircraft carriers in the Tonkin Gulf. He also brought in naval artillery, using warships off the coast. All of this was directed on the North Vietnamese forces stretched out along the road between Quang Tri City and Hue. The added American firepower quickly became evident to any journalist venturing up the highway from Hue to seek out the war.

I drove up the highway every day for a week or so in early May 1972, until it seemed as though the North Vietnamese offensive had bogged down at a point roughly halfway between Quang Tri City and Hue. A breakthrough was still possible, but Hanoi would pay an very heavy price to achieve it.

In the meantime, the beer and the good Chinese food was holding out well on the rooftop restaurant at the riverside hotel in Hue. I have forgotten the hotel's Vietnamese name, except that it sounded close to the Thai words — *hung nam* — for toilet, and we may have called it that, deliberately.

Every morning, at first light, charter aircraft flying out of Danang, or our "fallback" airport at Phu Bai, south of Hue, would buzz the hotel roof-top, looking for infantry signal panels set out during the night by the American television networks. These would indicate, by color code and arrangement, whether the network television crews had film to be picked up at Phu Bai, or simply wanted to be picked up themselves, or whatever other administrative requirements needed to be met. The networks were highly competitive with each other and didn't want their messages to be seen by their competition. Hue's telephone system was out of comission, so the networks communicated their needs by coded signal panels whose colors had sometimes faded, requiring the charter pilots to make repeated low altitude passes at the hotel roof.

It made for an interesting start to each day. After a dawn breakfast at the hotel, we would make our way across the river, past the old Imperial citadel and then north up Route One — until the first sound of gunfire was heard. Then we would stop, put on our hot, sweaty flak vests, and discuss the next move.

You learned to watch for on-coming traffic. Any sustained lack of it could mean danger ahead, as could battle-damaged vehicles headed south. Basically, you felt your way north, talking to as many people as you could, trying to get a sense of what was taking place. It was a frustrating process, particularly as it became clear that the real war was being fought closer to Saigon.

Filing stories to VOA in Washington from Hue or Danang was necessarily done on military circuits. Over the years, VOA had worked out an exchange arrangement with the military in Saigon giving us access to Defense Department satellite circuits. This meant we could call Washington from practically anywhere in Southeast Asia, providing we could get past the Vietnamese telephone operators with the right-sounding code numbers, most of which, as it happened, we made up as we went along.

"Hello Phu Bai, this is VOA Correspondent Sean Kelly with an immediate call for Washington. Can you put me through?"

"OK, VOA. What's you code number?"

"Delta Alpha Foxtrot Four Three Zero."

"OK, you going through to 'Washington Switch'."

I never found out where 'Washington Switch' really was, except that it was presumably somewhere near the nation's capital and the operator there could then dial into the 24-hour VOA Operations Studio number: 737-0015.

On one memorable occasion, neither the Phu Bai nor Nha Trang operators could raise 'Washington Switch.' I tried later to no avail and the Phu Bai operator suggested, in a perfectly straightforward way, that maybe 'White House Switch' could take my call. It was late in the day. I needed to drive back to Danang to catch a Saigon flight the next morning. I figured what the hell, it was worth a try.

"This is the White House."

"Operator, this is VOA Correspondent Sean Kelly in Hue. South Vietnam. I am trying to reach the Voice of America studios in Washington at 737-0015. Can you please put me through?"

"The White House is not a switching agency!"

"I know ma'am, but I can't get through any other way from here and it is an urgent call. It's five in the afternoon here. It must be five in the morning in Washington. There is shooting going on here. Can't you possibly take the call?"

"I'll put you through this one time, but don't ever use the White House switchboard again!"

I didn't, but the call did succeed in getting me out

of Hue at the last possible minute. The sun was close to setting and Route One over the Hai Van pass to Danang was closed during hours of darkness. I drove the borrowed jeep hard, heading south to Danang in a race with the sunset. As I approached the top of the pass, I suddenly heard the sound of machine gun fire on both sides of the road. The bursts were too short to make any sense, until I realized the gunners were just clearing their weapons and I was not their target.

I crossed the long bridge into Danang just as the South Vietnamese sentries were beginning to pull the reinforced barbed-wire barrier across the highway. "Bao Chi!" I yelled out the window. It supposedly meant "journalist" in Vietnamese, but I doubt that it mattered that much to the South Vietnamese sentries who waved me through.

The jeep belonged to John Hogan, who had invited me to stay at his house near the Danang air base. The promised hot shower was a treat after several bathless days in Hue and John's company was always a pleasure. Several whiskies, a good dinner and a bottle of wine later, sleep came easily. In fact, I slept right through a Viet Cong rocket attack on the nearby air base. It destroyed the empty Air America terminal without causing any casualties. Happily, it did not even delay the departure of my flight to Saigon the next morning.

The Easter offensive had become stalled in the north, in large part due to President Nixon's Operation

LINEBACKER which was aimed directly at North Vietnamese attempts to move down Route One towards Hue. A front line had developed at My Chanh, a river village about halfway between Quang Tri and Hue. By mid-May, neither side had advanced much beyond that point, although South Vietnamese marines were reportedly planning to push north, across the My Chanh river.

The heaviest fighting of the war was actually taking place not far from Saigon, along Route 13 — the old colonial highway connecting Saigon with the Cambodian capital of Phnom Penh. Several North Vietnamese army divisions — as many as thirty thousand men — had pushed across the border from Cambodia and were attacking the village of Loc Ninh with tanks and heavy artillery.

According to U.S. Army Captain Mark A. Smith, who took part in the defense of Loc Ninh, South Vietnamese Colonel Nguyen Cong Vinh — the ranking South Vietnamese officer — tried to give the village over to the North Vietnamese on April 7th by pulling down the South Vietnamese flag and running up a white t-shirt to indicate surrender. Captain Smith promptly pulled the t-shirt back down again, raising the yellow and red South Vietnamese flag in its place. Smith, the most experienced of several American military advisers in Loc Ninh, was later forced to call in repeated U.S. air strikes on his own position, as North Vietnamese soldiers overran the village.

Badly wounded in the battle for Loc Ninh, Smith was captured by the North Vietnamese and held prisoner in Cambodia until the war's end. He was awarded the Distinguished Service Cross, the nation's second highest medal for valor. Captain Smith was eventually recommended — unsuccessfully, as it turned out — for the top award: the Medal of Honor.

Meanwhile, Hanoi's Easter offensive raged on. The North Vietnamese troops, once they had finally taken Loc Ninh, pushed further south toward Saigon. Having arrived back in Saigon from Hue and Danang, I drove up Route 13 with several colleagues to see how close we could get to the action. We were stopped well south of the battle line. The South Vietnamese had put a barrier across the highway and were not allowing journalists further north.

I tried another approach and asked the press office at U.S. military headquarters in Saigon if I could cover a Forward Air Control mission along Route 13. Forward Air Controllers — FACs for short — flew light observer aircraft over the combat zone, serving as a link between ground commanders and fighter bombers circling overhead. The FAC pilots knew the local area well and were in close radio contact with the troops on the ground. Many of them had completed previous tours in Vietnam as fighter pilots, so they were in a good position to deal with the strike aircraft on the scene and could call in additional resources if needed. Slow moving, and lacking any defensive armament, the FACs were highly vulnerable to ground fire. They were a risky way for journalists to report the war.

My request got a quick response from the military press office. I was told to be on the flight line for a preflight briefing at Tan Son Nhut air base early the following morning. The mission would take me up along Route 13 towards Loc Ninh and would last approximately five hours. "Eat a good breakfast," the press office advised, "there won't be any food and beverage service along the way."

The FAC aircraft was a Cessna 02, known affectionately in the Air Force as a "Zero Deuce." It was basically the standard "Push-Pull" twin-engined Cessna I had used several times in Africa on charter flights. One engine pulled from the front and the other "pushed" from the rear. In between there was space for a pilot and maybe five passengers — depending on size. The Air Force 02 version of the Cessna had room for a FAC pilot and one observer who sat in the right seat. All the other seats had been removed to make room for the additional radio equipment needed to communicate with ground units, as well as strike aircraft. Air-to-ground rocket pods had been attached to the wings and an improvised aiming sight had been added to the control panel.

Journalists flying FAC missions in the Cessna 02 normally sat in the right seat and wore flying helmets containing earphones connected to a radio console in front of them. The console, with its row of push button pre-set frequencies, made it possible to eavesdrop on air-to-ground conversations, as well as radio contacts between units on the ground and between aircraft in the area. FAC missions were a front row seat on the war and, apart from the risks of being shot down, I wondered why more journalists didn't take advantage of them.

My first such mission was on May 10, 1972. My pilot was Captain Charlie Pepper, a red-haired ex-fighter pilot who had come back to Vietnam to fly FAC aircraft. He briefed me on the special equipment I was to wear, including the flame-retarding Nomex flying suit which carried, to my concern, a Major's oak leaf insignia on each shoulder.

"Isn't there some way we can take the oak leaves off?" I asked. "I'm a civilian journalist — an ex-Air Force Sergeant, actually — and I am reluctant to impersonate a military officer, particularly over a combat zone."

"Sorry, but regulations require you to wear a Nomex flying suit on a FAC mission and this is the only one in your size," was the reply. "We can't cut the oak leaves off this particular type of suit, so if you want to fly the mission, you have to wear it. There is no other choice."

So I flew as a Major, not that I really minded impersonating an officer, apart from the obvious complications if we should happen to come down behind North Vietnamese lines. In that case, it might be a bit difficult to establish my noncombatant status as a journalist. For this reason, I also declined the .38 caliber service pistol that came with my survival vest. No one insisted I carry it on the mission — for which I was grateful.

The survival vest itself did have a number of potentially useful items tucked away in its many webbed pockets. There were rocket flares and a signal mirror for attracting the attention of any rescue crews that might come my way — were I to find myself on the ground unexpectedly. There was also a small, hand-held radio for communicating with my rescuers. Ingeniously, a further radio was embedded in my parachute harness, triggered to beep a signal automatically once the canopy opened. The parachute itself was the last item to be donned before climbing into the Cessna 02 "Zero Deuce."

Charlie explained the workings of the radio console in front of me. This would permit me to overhear his communications, as well as any others I cared to tune in on. He didn't expect me to transmit on the console, but if I had to, my radio call sign would be "Chico Zero Niner Alpha." Charlie was "Chico Zero Niner." I was the "Alpha", indicating I was the passenger.

The only other survival item needing explanation was the procedure for exiting the Cessna in an emergency, Charlie pointed out that the only door was on my side and I would be controlling it. It had a large handle which, when I gave it a hard pull, would cause the door to fall clear of the aircraft.

"We will be working over An Loc today and it is a very active sector. Lots of ground fire. If we get hit and start to burn," said Charlie, "I'll tell you to pull the door handle and bail out. I'll be right behind you. Try to avoid hitting the rear propellor or the tail boom before you pull the chord to open your chute."

"What happens," I asked, "if we get hit, but are not on fire?"

"In that case, I'll try to put her down on a road somewhere, but we will still jettison the door so we can get out easier once we are on the ground."

I thought all this over as Charlie started up the engines and we taxied out to the Tan Son Nhut runway. What I did not know, but have since learned, was that May 10, 1972 was one of the heaviest days of fighting in the Easter offensive and that most of the action was centered in, and over, An Loc. The North Vietnamese had pushed down Route 13 from Loc Ninh and had succeeded in blocking the highway between An Loc and Saigon. The South Vietnamese forces still in An Loc — as well as their American advisers — could now only be resupplied, or reinforced, by air.

The situation was not unlike Dien Bien Phu in 1954 when the French army allowed itself to be cornered by the Viet Minh and could only be reached by air. In the end, air power was not enough against determined Vietnamese nationalists and the French were forced to give up both the battle and ultimately the war.

Captain Charlie Pepper, having completed his climb out of the Saigon area, now began to busy himself with the specifics of his mission. I could hear him on the radio, contacting American troop positions in and around An Loc. He would note their map coordinates and radio call signs. He would then mark the data on the Cessna's windscreen with a yellow grease pencil. By the end of the day's mission, his portion of the plastic windscreen would be virtually covered with his yellow scribblings.

He then called on another radio frequency to find out which American strike aircraft were available, what type of ordnance they carried, and how long their fuel supply would allow them to remain in the area. These included Air Force, Navy, Marine Corps and South Vietnamese fighter bombers circling nearby. Some of them had flown out of South Vietnamese and Thai air bases, others had taken off from aircraft carriers patrolling in the South China Sea. Each strike aircraft offered different possibilities for Charlie, depending on their load, endurance, and his own personal estimate as to their accuracy.

"Sometimes the ground action is so close," he

told me, "it's like door-to-door, sometimes hand-to-hand. It can almost look like World War One trench warfare."

In such cases, fast-moving jet fighter bombers, like the F-4 Phantom, flown by all three American services, could prove worse than useless. Much more suitable were the slower propeller-type aircraft used by the South Vietnamese air force, or the A-37 "Dragonfly", a converted Air Force trainer operating out of Bien Hoa air base, north of Saigon. The A-37, which could bomb and strafe with far greater accuracy than the F-4, was particularly popular with Charlie Pepper when the troops on the ground were in close contact. Unfortunately, there were not many of them, while the F-4s seemed always available.

We overflew the Route 13 roadblock well south of An Loc where several of my colleagues — Leon Daniel of UPI among them — were trying to talk their way further up the highway. I could see them out of the Cessna side window, arguing in the hot sun, trying to convince the South Vietnamese soldiers to let them through the roadblock. Later in the day, I would compliment Leon in Saigon on his newly-acquired sun tan. For the moment, I was much happier to be above it all.

Our first target of the day was a cluster of North Vietnamese tanks and other heavy vehicles taking cover in the big Michelin rubber plantation that ran parallel to Route 13, south of An Loc. Charlie pulled the Cessna up and over on its left wing and I could feel pressure tighten me against my shoulder harness as we began a steep, roller-coaster dive towards the green ocean of rubber trees below us. Suddenly there were two sharp blasts as Charlie fired off smoke rockets to mark the ground target.

"OK, you guys," he radioed the two F4 PHantoms rolling in behind us, "hit my smoke!"

It seemed to me that we pulled out down among the rubber trees themselves, much harder I thought than the Cessna was ever designed to take. I felt myself forcefully pushed down into my seat, my socks literally dropping around my ankles.

Charlie was back on the radio, getting a report from a nearby American ground adviser on the accuracy of the air strike. It turned out that one Phantom had been on target, but the other had been way off. We were asked to try again.

Charlie lined up another set of fighter bombers and directed them in on the target. This time I had a clearer expectation of what was about to happen and I was better prepared for the roller-coaster dive and the sudden force of the pull out.

Our next target was easier to find. It was close to the "Peanut Pond," a small hour-glass shaped lake to the south of An Loc, often used as a rendezvous point by American fighter pilots. A nearby French rubber processing plant had been taken over as a field headquarters by the North Vietnamese army. Their troops had managed to burrow under the plant's heavy concrete flooring, creating an improvised underground command and control bunker.

The building showed up clearly from the air, but friendly troops were nearby and Charlie, evidently unimpressed by the accuracy of the previous air strikes, wanted slower moving fighter aircraft. He turned down several offers by F4 Phantoms circling overhead and sent out an urgent radio call for A-37s from Bien Hoa. In the meantime, he dove repeatedly on the old French building, firing off smoke rockets on the way down.

"The explosion of the rocket doesn't do much damage," he explained, "but the noise makes them keep their heads down inside the bunker. Besides, they don't know when the next smoke rocket isn't going to come with a bomb behind it."

Two A-37s showed up from Bien Hoa and Charlie, the ex-fighter pilot, suggested what seemed to be the best approach to the target. He would head in across Route 13, planting his smoke as close as possible to the rubber processing plant. The A-37s would come in low from the north, crossing over An Loc and aiming for Charlie's smoke. The first A-37 would use his Gatling-type machine gun to strafe on the way to the target, the second aircraft would follow close behind and drop napalm on the building itself.

Charlie warned the pilots to expect plenty of ground fire on the way in to the target.

"Most of the anti-aircraft seems to be on the out-skirts of An Loc," he said. "The town itself looks to be pretty quiet for the moment."

"Roger that, Chico Zero Niner," said the lead A-37 pilot. "We'll strafe on the way in to keep their heads down."

"...and I'll be right along behind you," piped in the second A-37 pilot. "I'm going to lay this shit right down the main street of town."

Charlie hit the target perfectly with the smoke rockets. By that time, he had taken plenty of practice runs on the building. He brought the Cessna up into a climbing turn in time to see the A-37s stream in from the north at low altitude. The napalm went off direct-ly on target and the rubber processing plant was soon engulfed in black smoke. There were some second-ary explosions indicating the North Vietnamese had stockpiled fuel or ammunition nearby.

Our time on station over An Loc was coming to an end and Charlie had expended all his smoke rockets, so we headed back down Route 13 towards Saigon. We met the relief FAC on the way up and Charlie briefed him on the situation he could expect to face over An Loc.

The battle for the town continued to rage for sev-eral days, worsening with the introduction of a serious new weapon by the North Vietnamese. We had heard rumors of a new ground-to-air missile sighted in var-ious parts of the country, and on May 11 — the day after Charlie and I were over An Loc — these were confirmed. The North Vietnamese had introduced the Soviet SA-7 Strela, a shoulder-fired, heat-seeking missile with devastating effect. Two Cobra helicopter gun ships were shot down over An Loc, so were both FAC aircraft, and an A-37 fighter bomber. There were no survivors.

The A-37 crash produced a curious historical aftermath — one that made me think once again about ever wearing a Major's oak leaf insignia into a combat zone. Because of the intensity of the fighting around An Loc, it was six months before investigators could reach the A-37 crash site. By that time, it was not immediately clear who had been the pilot. Eventually, the human remains found near the A-37 were declared unidentifiable and were buried, with considerable ceremony, in the Tomb of the Unknowns at Arlington National Cemetery, near Washington, D.C. on Memorial Day in May 1984.

Fourteen years later, and twenty-six years after the event, the pilot of the A-37 was determined by DNA evidence to have been Lieutenant Michael J. Blassie and therefore no longer an unknown warrior of the Vietnam war. His remains were disinterred from Arlington and reburied in the Jefferson Barracks National Cemetery in St. Louis, Missouri.

When I read the news at the time, I had to wonder what might have happened if Captain Charlie Pepper and I had flown over An Loc on May 11, instead of

May 10 and I was wearing my borrowed Nomex flying suit with the rank of Major.

By June 1972, the battle line south of An Loc appeared to be holding against the North Vietnamese Easter offensive. On the northern front, there had even been some progress pushing the invasion back towards the DMZ. I flew north to Hue to report on the progress of the war along the My Chanh line, halfway between Hue and Quang Tri City along Route One.

President Nixon's Operation LINEBACKER was working. The North Vietnamese invasion, now entering its third month, had weakened — thanks to a massive resupply effort by the Americans to their South Vietnamese allies. I saw heavy artillery being flown into Danang air base directly from the United States in giant C-5 cargo aircraft. B-52 bombers had been increased in number at air bases in Guam and Thailand, as had the jet refueling tankers used to support them. More U.S. naval vessels arrived off shore to provide additional artillery and fighter aircraft of their own. It looked as though LINEBACKER had saved the day.

But then, on June 22, 1972 — while I was still in Vietnam — an event took place thousands of miles away which helped bring the war — and President Nixon's political career — to an end. It was an attempted robbery at a Washington, DC office building, called the Watergate.

The next time the North Vietnamese came down Highway One — in April 1975 — there was no LINEBACKER to stop them, and Watergate had driven President Nixon from office.

12.

Washington:
Kissinger and Watergate.

Watergate, by the time I arrived back in Washington in July 1973, had become a full fledged national scandal. Its bizarre narrative was being rehashed daily in a Senate investigation broadcast live across the country on radio and television. The opening event, a bungled burglary at the Democratic Party's national headquarters, had quickly been traced to the White House. President Nixon predictably denied any involvement, although several of the men captured at the Watergate crime scene had clearly been employed by his re-election campaign. Others had links to the Central Intelligence Agency. When the televised Senate hearings revealed that the President had secretly been tape recording all his office conversations, the Senate immediately moved to subpeona the tapes as evidence. Nixon, claiming executive privilege, refused to turn them over — thus provoking a constitutional crisis of major proportions.

In a totally separate investigation, Nixon's Vice President, former Maryland governor Spiro T. Agnew, was facing serious charges of bribery. He was accused of accepting thousands of dollars delivered to his White House office in unmarked vanilla envelopes. While this had nothing to do with Watergate, it did little to advance the public's perception of the moral climate prevailing during the Nixon administration.

All of this was taking place, not in some backwater banana republic, but in Washington, DC. After years of witnessing corruption and crises of one sort or another in Africa and Southeast Asia, it never occurred to me that I might some day encounter the same in my own nation's capital.

Naturally, I hoped to cover the story.

I was in Washington at my own request. My return to the States from Southeast Asia had been prompted by the fact that I had spent the previous two years in more or less perpetual orbit from Vietnam to Cambodia, to Laos and back again. I had, as a result, seen very little of Anne and the boys at the house by the *klong* in Bangkok. My sons were growing into teenagers without my being around to exercise much influence over their behavior and the results were beginning to show. Matters reached a head when they were both kicked off their school bus for being rowdy. As further punishment they were obliged to take Thai public transportation to and from the Bangkok International School which was located a considerable distance across the city from our house. The daily trip involved several bus changes in route and therefore had to be launched much earlier than normal, if they were to get to school on time. At one point, it seemed to me they were on the road well before dawn.

I decided it was time to head back to Washington, put the boys into decent schools, and try to be more of a father to them both. It meant walking out on the very active Saigon-Vientiane-Phnom Penh story, but Washington — thanks to Watergate — was developing into a fascinating political beat of its own which, by its very nature, would tend to keep me more at home than on the road.

As it happened, the Watergate story was already being sufficiently staffed, in VOA's view, but the correspondent position covering the State Department was opening up and I was told I should apply for it. This would mean reporting from the State Department on a full time basis. The assignment would tend to keep me away from the VOA News Room, which I would readily welcome, and the small amount of travel with Secretary of State William P. Rogers would be manageable, since he did not leave Washington all that often. Nixon's National Security Adviser, Henry Kissinger, had been undercutting Rogers for years, conducting foreign policy directly out of the White

House through back channel communications and highly secret, but often well-publicized, missions abroad.

I told VOA to put my name in for Diplomatic Correspondent, got the job, and arrived in Washington just as Nixon named Kissinger to be his new Secretary of State. I had barely unpacked before I was asked to go to New York to cover the new Secretary's meetings at the annual meeting of the United Nations General Assembly.

So much for spending more time at home with my family!

And it got worse.

My first actual encounter with Kissinger was in the lobby of the Waldorf Astoria Towers. He was coming out of the hotel elevator, accompanied by his bodyguards. Several other journalists and I moved foreward to ask him a question and were brusquely pushed aside by his bodyguards. I noticed that they were not the beefy, slow-moving State Department security detail that had accompanied Secretary Rogers prior to his resignation.

"Best not to argue with them," warned a colleague. "They are part of a Secret Service detail out of the White House."

"Since when", I asked , "does the Secretary of State rate a White House bodyguard ?"

"When he is also the President's National Security Adviser," I was told.

It then struck me that Kissinger was doing both jobs at once. In a move that was historically unprecedented, he had taken over the two most powerful foreign policy positions in the government. It was a measure of how deeply Watergate had eroded the Nixon administration. The President had been obliged to fire Bob Haldeman, his Chief of Staff, and John Erlichman, his Domestic Policy Adviser. The Attorney General had since resigned. The Vice President was facing bribery charges. Henry Kissinger remained the most senior member of the original White House staff not to have been touched by the worsening scandal and Nixon had put him at the top.

In the meantime, the Nixon White House was being hit repeatedly by demands that the secret Watergate tapes be released. The recordings had become evidence needed to complete the Senate Watergate investigation, as well as the several court cases that were emerging. Nixon's failure to release them was being seen as an obstruction of justice, possibly an impeachable offense.

This level of constitutional chaos placed a special burden on the new Secretary of State to maintain some degree of diplomatic continuity with foreign allies and adversaries alike. The annual opening session of the United Nations General Assembly in New York presented Kissinger with an exceptional opportunity to bring his legendary persuasive skills to bear on foreign ministers from all over the world. It took place at a time when these talents were especially needed. He quickly proceeded to make use of them.

There was also the strong likliehood that his meetings in New York would serve to draw the focus of press attention away from Watergate, thus easing pressue on the White House and its beleaguered occupant.

Kissinger instructed his staff to set up a series of one-on-one sessions between himself and visiting foreign ministers in New York. On October 4, I wrote about his less formal approach to the delegates in a correspondent report I entitled "Dinner at Henry's":

"The United Nations General Assembly suspended debate on South Africa Thursday night and went to have dinner with Henry Kissinger. General Assembly President Leopoldo Benites of Ecuador told delegates: "We have a difficult situation here, but we also have a dinner ahead of us, so I propose that we adjourn until ten-thirty Friday morning."

There were no objections.

The dinner in question took place at New York's elaborate Metropolitan Museum of Art: an immense neo-classical structure built at the turn of the century. Some four hundred and sixty foreign ministers, diplomats, businessmen, and members of the press were invited. They were served roast veal and California wine amidst Greco-Roman antiquities and the "Strolling Violinists" of the United States Army.

Museum staff members confessed privately that the dinner arrangements posed some unusual problems. First of all, there were the security considerations. Some of those attending were not on speaking terms. Then there was the question of the menu itself: many of the guests had rather firm dietary restrictions.

The party went on, nonetheless. And the roast veal was followed up with a lemon mousse and some California champagne. The guests enjoyed themselves, and the museum's fluted columns and thirty-meter high ceilings positively pulsated to the music and the vibrant conversation.

In his remarks to his guests, Secretary Kissinger issued a word of warning. He said: 'To those of you who are diplomats, be mindful of what you say, for you are surrounded by members of the press.' And he added: 'To those of you who are members of the press, be careful not to take too seriously everything you hear, for you are surrounded by diplomats.'

He then asked them to join him in a toast to the United Nations, which he called the treasury of man's noblest aspirations.

It was over all too soon. The guests left, the museum darkened, and preparations got underway for resumption of debate here at the United Nations."

Reporting the United Nations was not all fun and champagne. There were dull stretches that seemed to last interminably. For the Voice of America, the surroundings were quite spectacular, even though the story itself often did not measure up to them. Our bureau in the UN headquarters building had huge windows overlooking the East River which, in those days at least, offered a unending parade of maritime traffic. To a visiting correspondent, the view alone could make up for the slower pace in activity. When there was a story to file, the bureau had leased its own broadcast and teletype circuits direct to the VOA Newsroom in Washington which vastly simplified the process.

The tempo could change rather suddenly, however.

At 6:15 a.m. on October 6, Secretary Kissinger was awakened in his apartment at the Waldorf with the news that Israel, Egypt and Syria were about to go to war. He picked up the telephone and began a series of calls aimed at halting the hostilities before they could be launched. Significantly, one of his first was to his long time friend the Soviet Ambassador in Washington Anatoly Dobrynin, waking him up in the process. What follows is Kissinger's transcript of their conversation:

K: "The Israelis are telling us that Egypt and Syria are planning an attack very shortly and that your people are evacuating from Damascus and Cairo."

D: "Yes."

K: "If the reason for your evacuation…"

D: "For our…"

K: "Yes. The Soviet evacuation, is the fear of an Israeli attack, then the Israelis are asking us to tell you, as well as asking us to tell the Arabs…"

D: "The Israelis?

K: "Yes. They have no plans to attack."

D: "Yes."

K: "But if the Egyptians and Syrians do attack, the Israeli response will be extremely strong."

D: "Yes."

K: "All right. From us to you. The President believes that you and we have a special responsibility to restrain our respective friends."

D: "Yes."

K: "We are urgently communicating to the Israelis."

D: "You?"

K: "Yes."

D. "Communicate to the Israelis?

K: "If this keeps up — there is going to be a war before you understand my message."

The Secretary finally succeeded in getting his point across to the Soviet Ambassador who agreed to pass Nixon's message (about "the special responsibility to restrain our respective friends") to Moscow. By day's end, Kissinger had spoken at least eleven times with the Soviets, twelve with the Israelis, four with the Egyptians, and three with UN Secretary General Kurt Waldheim. In between, he had also found time to brief President Nixon and Alexander Haig, his former NSC Deputy, who had since replaced Bob Haldeman as White House Chief of Staff. But by then, the war had broken out anyway.

The Egyptians had begun it with an artillery and rocket attack across the Suez Canal into Israeli-occupied Sinai at 2 p.m. local time (8 p.m. New York time) as the Israelis were celebrating Yom Kippur, their holy Day of Atonement. The Syrians followed up quickly from their side with an artillery barrage along the Golan Heights, Israel's eastern border. Israel was thus being hit simultaneously from both directions. The Egyptians then began using high-pressure water hoses to blast holes in the sand embankments on the Israeli side of the Canal. This opened the way for thousands of their infantrymen to cross the Canal and push their way into the Sinai. The Syrians, in a coordinated attack, began moving hundreds of Soviet battle tanks up the Golan Heights which, like the Sinai, had been captured and occupied by Israel in the June 1967 war.

"Why?", I asked a more senior colleague, "would the Egyptians launch a war against Isarael at two in the afternoon? Why not at dawn when most wars start?"

The answer, as it it turned out, was that the Egyptians wanted to wait until the Yom Kippur celebrations were well underway and, perhaps more importantly, until the Israeli defending troops in the Sinai would have the fierce African sun directly in their faces. The Syrians, of course, did not have that advantage, but they went along with the Egyptian plan, anyway.

Kissinger, acting in his capacity as President Nixon's National Security Adviser, called General Brent Scowcroft, his deputy in Washington, to set up an emergency meeting of the Washington Special Actions Group (WSAG), an NSC crisis committee, in order to obtain the views of the rest of the government. Then, putting on his Secretary of State hat, he followed up with a request for a separate assessment that day from State's own Bureau of Intelligence and Research (INR). Returning to his role as the President's National Security Adviser, he ordered up a similar same-day assessment from the CIA.

"Clearly, " he later wrote, "there was an intelligence failure, but misjudgment was not confined to the agencies. Every policymaker knew all the facts. The Israelis were monitoring the movement of every Egyptian and Syrian unit. The general plan of attack, especially of the Syrians, was fairly well understood. What no one believed — the consumers no more that the producers of intelligence — was that the Arabs would act on it. Our definition of rationality did not take seriously the notion of starting an unwinnable war to restore self-respect."

Kissinger's remarkable ability to sense the Arab motive for launching the war was key to his later success in negotiating an end to it. The restoration of

Arab self-respect, he said, drove the Egyptians and Syrians to the attack on Israel. This motive was given further clarification by Egyptian journalist Mohamed Heikal, an intimate confidant of President Anwar Sadat, when he wrote: "By 1973 Egypt had become the laughing stock of the Arab world. We claimed to be the leader and protector of the Arabs, but we gave no lead to our own people and showed ourselves unable to protect our own territory. We asked others to use their oil weapon but showed no sign of using our own weapons. Each day that passed was a day of humiliation for Egypt."

"From the onset," wrote Kissinger in his own account of the period, "I was determined to use the war to start a peace process. Nixon in the following days enthusiastically agreed. A big piece of the puzzle was Soviet intentions. What had the Soviets known about the imminence of war? Would they encourage its continuation with equipment and diplomatic support? Or would they cooperate in ending it?"

As he moved forward to sound out the Soviets on the possibility of a cease fire, Kissinger came face to face with the realities imposed by the Watergate scandal. Nixon was facing a losing court battle in holding on to the White House tapes, and the first indictments against his former aides were being handed down by the courts. Vice President Agnew was resigning after being charged with accepting bribes while he was governor of Maryland. This had nothing to do with

Watergate, but it forced Nixon to appoint Agnew's successor at a time when his attention was increasingly dominated by the Watergate scandal. Agnew's departure from the Nixon administration left the Vice Presidency open, thus raising the issue of Nixon's successor. The possibility of Nixon himself being driven from office was now beginning to seem very real.

Nixon evidently never seriously considered Agnew up to succeeding him politically. He once said, only partly facetiously, wrote Kissinger, "that Agnew was his insurance policy against assassination." The President had obviously not considered his impeachment as a possibility at that time. At least he did not mention it to Kissinger.

Two days into the conflict, as the Israelis counterattacked, Kissinger received a reply from the Soviets confirming they had contacted the leaders of the Arab states and hoped to get a reply shortly. The Secretary found some encouragement in the Soviet assurance that Moscow intended to act in cooperation with the United States — "...in the broad interests of maintaining peace and developing Soviet-American relations."

"By the next day," Kissinger later recalled, "we were convinced the Israeli offensive would prevail, the Security Council would then call for a cease fire in place. Our ally would have repulsed an attack by Soviet weapons. We could begin a peace process with the Arabs on the proposition that we had stopped the Israeli advance and with the Israelis on the basis that we had been steadfastly at their side in the crisis. It was becoming apparent even at this early stage that we were the only government in contact with both sides. If we could preserve this position, we were likely to emerge in a central role in the peace process."

Then the Israelis began adding up their losses on both fronts. The total was staggering. In an urgent appeal for additional American weapons, the Israelis told Kissinger they had already lost forty-nine aircraft, including fourteen U.S.-supplied F4 Phantom fighter-bombers, as well as 500 tanks, 400 of them on the Egyptian front alone. Apparently, the Soviet surface to air missiles and anti-tank rockets had made the difference.

"I never doubted," said Kissinger, "that a defeat of Israel by Soviet arms would be a geopolitical disaster for the United States. I urged a quick victory on one front before the UN diplomacy ratified Arab territorial gains everywhere." The Israelis replied that they were concentrating now on a fast Syrian victory. The Egyptian front, they admitted, would take them a bit longer.

Kissinger took the arms supply problem to Nixon who agreed that all of Israel's aircraft and tank losses were be replaced, if necessary by means of an airlift. Still concerned with the need to preserve Arab self-respect, the Secretary hoped the process of re-supplying the Israelis might be kept to as low a profile as possible. No U.S. military aircraft were to be used in the airlift, at least for the time being. The Israelis would provide their own transports, or rely on U.S.-chartered civilian aircraft.

By October 10, however, it had become clear that the Soviets were launching an airlift of their own, but on a much larger and more public scale. It was obvious to Kissinger that planning for the Soviet effort must have been underway for several days and this was troubling. He complained about it in telephone discussions with his friend the Soviet Ambassador:

"K...Just a minute Anatoly, before you go into one of your wild charges.

D. You understand that...

K. You're engaged in a massive airlift in the Middle East and that is not helpful because we have been very restrained.

D. I don't know.

K. I'll be glad to send you the figures."

The fact that the Soviet arms airlift was continuing at a time when the U.S. was having trouble getting its own started became a matter of concern both to Kissinger and the Israelis. Reporters covering the State Department were told on background that the Soviet airlift was being watched and attempts were being made to ascertain both its size and its significance. I had returned to Washington from New York and filed a story to VOA quoting State Department officials as cautioning that "if the airlift turned out to be massive, it might tend to put a new face on the situation" — although they would not take the point any further. Kissinger, who had also returned to Washington, announced he would be postponing a long-standing speaking engagement in London because of the Middle East crisis. He scheduled his first full scale news conference the following day.

Kissinger's dealings with the press were especially important to his way of conducting his simultaneous roles as Nixon's national security adviser, as well as Secretary of State. In the White House, his leaks to the press during Nixon's first term were widely known, as was his continual concern that other members of the Nixon administration were leaking information he considered detrimental to his own position. As he was reported to have explained: "Well, you know, even paranoids have enemies."

At the State Department, however, press relationships were more structured. The main flow of information was conveyed through the official spokesman, at the traditional noon briefing. When Kissinger's appointment as Secretary of State was announced, the existing spokesman — Charles Bray — abruptly resigned out of loyalty to former Secretary William Rogers whom Kissinger had been alternately undercutting and upstaging for years. This left the position of official spokesman vacant at a critical time and Kissinger simply drafted Robert McCloskey, who had been very effective in the job before before Bray, but who was currently U.S. Ambassador to Cyprus. McCloskey handled the situation well both in New York and in Washington, but it was clear he wanted to get back to Cyprus and the search went out for a new spokesman.

When Kissinger finally got around to naming the new man, he announced that it was going to be someone named George West. No one in the diplomatic press corps had heard of George West and this sent all of us scrambling to find out who he might be. It turned out that his name was really George Vest and that Kissinger, overcompensating for his heavily Germanic accent, had misconverted Vest to West. George Vest turned out to be an excellent spokesman, particularly during the difficult days of the 1973 Middle East crisis.

Kissinger's October 12, 1973 news conference at the State Department, his first since the outbreak of hostilities in the Middle East, gave him the opportunity to describe the Soviet behavior as less provocative — less incendiary — than it had been during the 1967 Arab-Israeli war. Nonetheless, he said, "we don't regard their appeal for more Arab nations to join the conflict to be particularly helpful, nor is their current military airlift to the Middle East." However, he added, "we do not consider that they have acted irresponsibly — so far."

An hour later, he learned from General Haig at the White House that the Soviet Union had alerted three airborne divisions. "Well," he replied, "I am seeing Dobrynin for lunch. If they did that, that's it."

"They are going to force us to counter," warned Haig. "We can't ignore that."

"Absolutely," said Kissinger. If they do that, we are going in. I will tell that to Dobrynin at lunch, but we better alert some of ours ."

The next day, which Kissinger later described as "the turning point of the war," the wraps were lifted on the American military airlift to Israel. Ten C-130 transports were ordered to fly in ammunition directly into Tel Aviv, followed by 15 larger C-141s, and three C-5s, the largest of the American cargo aircraft. Much of the impetus for the increase came from President Nixon himself. As he told Kissinger, " It's got to be the works…we are going to get blamed just as much for three planes as for three hundred."

The Secretary conferred with his colleages on the NSC and reported back to Nixon: "Oh, it is a massive airlift, Mr, President. The planes are going to land every fifteen minutes."

"Get them in there," ordered the President, "if we are going to do it, don't spare the horses."

"One of the lessons I have learned from you," said Kissinger admiringly, "is that if you do something, you might as well do it completely."

Transcripts of the recorded telephone

conversations between the two men —some released by Kissinger himself, others made public years later — reflect Kissinger's willingness to flatter Nixon to a degree that now seems frankly hypocritical. Robert Dallek, who years later explored in considerable depth the relationship between Kissinger and Nixon, commented on this tendency in some detail: "Henry also despised Nixon's incessant demands for ostentatious displays of deference, which Kissinger readily provided as the best way to ensure his influence with the President. Kissinger's constant stroking of Nixon, again so abundantly clear in their recorded conversations, left Henry feeling compromised and sullied."

Ironically, it was at this high point in their effort to raise the tempo of the Middle East War, that Kissinger learned he had won the Nobel Peace Prize for his efforts to bring an end to the war in Vietnam. Nixon immediately offered his congratulations, Kissinger replied that it was the President who really deserved the award. Later, he added: "Perhaps the most important goal any administration can set for itself is to work for a world in which the award will become irrelevant, because peace will have become so normal and so much taken for granted that no awards for it will have to be given."

For the President himself, the crisis of his Vice President's resignation had been lifted by the appointment of Gerald Ford, a popular Republican

Congressional leader, as Agnew's replacement. But the confrontation with the Senate over the release of the Watergate tapes continued and there was already an effort underway in the House of Representatives to launch impeachment proceedings against the President.

On the Middle East warfront, the Egyptians, anxious to relieve pressure on their Syrian allies, ventured deeper into the Sinai for the first time, taking their army well beyond the range of its air defense system along the Suez Canal. It turned out to be a rash move. The Israeli Air Force, resupplied with newly-arrived Phantoms and A4 Skyhawks from the United States, destroyed over three hundred Soviet-supplied tanks, forcing the Egyptians back towards the Canal. Meanwhile, to the south of the Canal near the Great Bitter Lake, the Israelis had managed to send twenty-five tanks across the Canal, outflanking the Egyptians, in an attack on their surface-to-air defensive missile installations. On the Syrian front, they were threatening to shell Damascus with their American-supplied 175 mm heavy artillery.

Israeli journalist Matti Golan described the arrival of the first American cargo aircraft in the new airlift: "Citizens in the Tel Aviv area could hear the drone of the giant jets above their heads. No one complained about the noise. Cars stopped on the roads, windows opened in apartments. People went out into the blacked-out streets, their eyes turned to the skies — to the approaching flickering lights. Some people were crying. Many others .. were murmuring, "God bless America."

Kissinger decided it was now time for press for a standstill cease-fire at the UN while simultaneously accelerating the American military airlift to Israel and seeking to calm Arab reactions to it. Taking stock of the military situation on the ground, the Soviets pressed for immediate cease-fire negotiations and asked Kissinger to come to Moscow quickly to discuss the details.

Initially, Kissinger saw the Soviet invitation as an advantage. It would, he said, keep the issue out of the United Nations "until we had shaped an acceptable outcome. It would discourage Soviet bluster while I was in transit and negotiating. It would gain at least another seventy-two hours for military pressures to build."

Then Nixon let the other shoe drop. He intended coupling the announcement of Kissinger's Moscow trip with the news that he had just negotiated a major agreement over the release of the Watergate tapes. Kissinger called the juxtaposition of the two announcements a disaster. "My honest opinion," he told Nixon's Chief of Staff, "is that it is a cheap stunt. It looks as if he is using foreign policy to cover a domestic thing. I would not link foreign policy with Watergate. You will regret it for the rest of your life. It will forever after be said he did this to cover Watergate."

Kissinger's views prevailed. Nixon agreed to keep the two annoumcements separate. Kissinger left for Moscow secretly in the middle of the night, October 20, almost two weeks after the outbreak of the war. While he was in route to Moscow, he learned that the President had fired the Special Watergate Prosececutor, resulting in the resignations of the Attorney General, his Deputy, and the Acting FBI Director — an event that came to be known in Washington as the Saturday Night Massacre. He also learned that Moscow had alerted seven of its eleven airborne divisions. He and his traveling UN expert, Joe Sisco, sat up all night hammering out details of a proposal couched in language sufficiently vague, in Kissinger's words, "to have occupied diplomats for years without arriving at an agreement."

I was not on the flight. The press pool had been kept to a minimum. When details of the agreement reached in Moscow hit the wires in Washington, I got a quick call from a colleague in VOA's Arabic Service asking me to get official clarification on one of its specific terms. It was of course crucial that the Arabic translation of the English text be precise, otherwise there could be misunderstandings throughout the Middle East — wherever VOA's Arabic broadcasts were heard. I took the query up with the State Department's press office and was blithely informed that some degree of "constructive ambiguity" was bound to be a factor in any treaty. I can't recall whether this explanation was of any real help to the Arabic Service. I suspect it may not have been.

Despite its complexities, the treaty brought a temporary halt to the fighting in the Middle East. But the notion of a "stand-still cease fire" quickly evaporated. The Israelis had succeeded in cutting off a major portion of the Egyptian army in the Sinai and were now involved in restricting access roads from the Egyptian side. Many thousand Egyptian soldiers were trapped in the desert without food and water. Their attempts to break out of their predicament were quickly labelled as cease fire violations by the Israelis who proceeded to move against them.

This produced a reaction from the Soviets accusing the United States of allowing the Israelis to get away with violating the spirit of the agreement reached in Moscow. The Soviet Ambassador followed up by telling Kissinger that Moscow would be supporting a resolution at the UN calling for the introduction of Soviet and American peacekeeping forces to the region to police the cease fire. Kissinger exploded. He called the White House: "I want to bring you up-to-date on what is happening," he told General Haig, Nixon's Chief of Staff. "The Soviets are taking a nasty turn. They realize they were taken. They now are telling us they are approving a resolution introduced by the noncommitted members which (1) condemns Israel for violation of the cease-fire and (2) asks for introduction of military peacekeeping contingents, including Soviet and U.S. troops — I told Dobrynin this is mischievous and outrageous. We are totally opposed to the introduction of any military forces."

"Is it going that far?" asked Haig.

"We may have to take them on," replied Kissinger.

"We knew this wouldn't be easy," said Haig.

"I think we have to be tough as nails now," said Kissinger.

Convinced that Moscow intended the proposed resolution as a means of introducing its own forces, Kissinger accused the Soviets of using the Watergate crisis to their own advantage. "I don't think they would have taken on a functioning President," he told Haig. "They find a cripple facing impeachment and why shouldn't they go in there?"

Accompanied by other members of the Washington Special Action Group, the two men met at the White House Situation Room a short while later. Their meeting lasted until 2:00 a.m. early Thursday, October 25. A few hours later, around dawn, I got a call at home from the VOA overnight shift editor. "You better get down to the State Department," he said. "Something crazy is going on. Nixon has put the military on world-wide alert and activated the 82nd Airborne Division for possible deployment."

"What next?" I asked, not totally in jest. "Martial law? Suspension of the Constitution?"

It struck me that the embattled President, as

Commander-in-Chief, might well have decided it was time to circle his wagons around the White House. Was the Watergate drama, which had started out as a failed B-movie burglary, now advancing itself to the level of a genuine Hollywood horse opera? More realistically, was Nixon now attempting to use the military to draw public attention away from the scandal itself.

It turned out that I was not alone in my cynicism. When Kissinger held a news conference later in the day, he was asked point blank whether the military alert had been generated for domestic rather than foreign policy reasons. He replied heatedly: "We are attempting to conduct the foreign policy of the United States with regard for what we owe not just to the electorate, but to future generations. And it is a symptom of what is happening to our country that it could even be suggested that the United States would alert its forces for domestic reasons."

He went on to lecture us in our responsibilities as journalists. "We are attempting to preserve the peace in very difficult circumstances. It is up to you ladies and gentlemen to determine whether this is the moment to try to create a crisis of confidence in the field of foreign policy as well…"

Secretary Kissinger's emotional news conference had barely ended when word was received from New York that the proposed Security Council resolution involving Soviet and U.S. forces had been dropped.

In its place was one calling for a UN observer force that would specifically exclude permanent members of the Security Council. In a more detailed piece the following day, I reported that the United States was phasing down its worldwide military alert and was now prepared to join an expanded United Nations *observer* force — as opposed to a *peacekeeping* mission.

The alert crisis was over, but Nixon's motives in declaring it would continue to be questioned while he remained in office — and afterwards. Ultimately, Kissinger would admit that the nuclear alert had been an error. "Let us concede," he said, "that we had an American President who found himself in a difficult position and who decided to take maximum precautions in order to reassure himself and to reassure others."

The remaining problem was the Egyptian Third Army which was still stuck in the Sinai desert, surrounded by the Israeli soldiers who had cut off their supplies of food and water. Sadat complained to the Soviets who put pressure on Kissinger to get the Israelis to open a relief corridor to the beleaguered Egyptian Third Army. It took Kissinger several days and nights of phone calls, including more than one with Israeli Prime Minister Golda Meir herself, to get agreement on the relief corridor sorted out. Finally, at 1:30 Sunday morning, October 28, Israeli and Egyptian military representatives met for direct talks, under UN auspices, for the first time in 25 years. Shortly afterwards, the first UN relief convoy delivered food, water and medicine to the Egyptian Third Army.

The shooting had stopped and the way was now open to negotiate more permanent peace arrangements. Kissinger had prevailed, in spite of Watergate. I continued covering him, traveling to the Middle East in January, on the famous Kissinger diplomatic shuttle between Egypt, Israel, Syria, and Jordan. Then on to Moscow in February, and a mad one-day dash to Panama and back in March.

He was not an easy man to report. I found that his spoken sentences often tripped themselves up and their meaning became difficult to fathom. I was not alone in this. One of his senior ambassadors cabled Washington for a clarification on the key Kissinger quote: "I am not saying that there is no circumstance where we would not use force." "What does this really mean?", asked the perplexed diplomat.

I enjoyed Kissinger's sense of humor, except on those not infrequent occasions when it was directed at his immediate staff. He often made his aides the butt of some of his joking in front of the press. I eventually came to feel a sense of unease being around him, particularly when we were thrown into close contact on his plane. He was virtually running the entire American foreign policy establishment of which the Voice of America was a small, but not insignificant (to me, at least) part. I thought he was in a position to do me, and my employers, irreparable harm — if he thought it would advance his own position in some way. Kissinger, his spokesman George Vest told me in confidence, once mentioned to Jordan's King Hussein that he was prepared to shut down the Voice of America altogether if the monarch was seriously offended about how he was being reported on VOA. Fortunately, Hussein, after thinking it over, said that he was not. I never heard anything more about it, but when, years later, the Washington Post revealed that King Hussein had been on the CIA payroll for decades, I wondered at Kissinger's offer.

It all seemed a bit incestuous to me and I welcomed a way out. The U.S. House of Representatives actively began deliberating Nixon's impeachment in April, and I happily gave up the diplomatic beat to join VOA's newly-formed Watergate Coverage Unit. Apart from my interest in the story itself, there was the very real possiblity of spending more time with my family in Washington.

13.

Exit Nixon, Painfully

Nobody ever thought Watergate was going to be an easy story for the Voice of America to cover — least of all, those of us working there. I was convinced the biggest obstacle might well prove to be within the organization itself. Many of VOA's top managers owed their first loyalty to the United States Information Agency, the government's overseas public relations organization. I wondered how far they would go along with our reporting all the facts about Watergate.

VOA was very much a part of USIA in 1973. The White House had appointed James Keogh as USIA Director and had approved his annual budget — which included VOA's operating expenses. The proverbial wisdom, then and now, has generally been that he who pays the piper calls the tune. Would the

White House call the tune for VOA, or would we be left alone to report Watergate without USIA's official spin? I felt the odds were against us from the start.

There was also the problem of the peculiarly home-grown nature of the story itself — not easily explained to an overseas audience. When I was asked in Saigon for local reaction to the June 17, 1972 break in at the Democratic party's headquarters in the Watergate building, I had to report back to Washington that Vietnamese were having trouble understanding what all the fuss was about. Political dirty tricks were routine happenings in Southeast Asia, as they were in many other parts of the world. What made the difference in Washington? The White House spokesman had already dismissed Watergate as "a third-rate burglary." So what made it news?

The internal pressures were already being felt. Philomena Jurey, a VOA correspondent who had become a close friend of mine over the years, was running the Newsroom during the early days of Watergate. She describes how she was called upstairs to the Director's office and asked: "Do we have to call Watergate a scandal?" Somewhat astonished, she argued that VOA was most certainly obliged to do so. It was clear that Watergate had, in fact, become a scandal and was generally accepted as such, but, under front office pressure, she reluctantly agreed to drop the word — for the time being.

The pressure mounted. In June 1973, while the

televised Senate Watergate hearings were underway, USIA Director Keogh issued a directive forbidding VOA News from carrying Watergate stories based on unidentified sources. As a result, Jurey says one VOA story was actually killed. It had quoted the New York Times and the Washington Post , both citing "reliable sources" that ex-White House Counsel John Dean was prepared to testify that Nixon knew of the Watergate coverup — which, as it turned out, he did. Both the Times and the Post also carried a White House denial. VOA argued successfully that it could not very well broadcast the denial without including what was actually being denied. Jurey says the Newsroom then wrote a new version of the story, leading with the denial and then getting into the reports by the Times and the Post. She adds that Keogh later clarified his position by saying "My guidance has been to cover Watergate factually, but to not use rumor, speculation, hearsay or anonymous accusation." On the other hand, he added, "If an accusation is important enough to warrant a denial, it's a different thing."

For years, the Newsroom had followed a fairly strict two source rule on stories that did not come from its own correspondents. However, if Newsroom editors felt that a story deserved VOA coverage, even though it was based on a single source — such as, for instance, the Washington Post — the story would be reported on the VOA newswire, credited to the Washington Post. Keogh's ruling would have forced VOA to ignore most of the early reporting on Watergate, particularly the work of the Washington Post's enterprising team of Bob Woodward and Carl Bernstein. Both of them were relying on a source as anonymous as the man they called "Deep Throat" — who later turned out to be an extremely reliable senior official of the FBI.

Bernard Kamenske, who had become chief of VOA News, told me he got around the Keogh ruling, and other Nixon administration restraints, by dispatching a Newsroom copyclerk in a taxi to the Washington Post to pick up the earliest obtainable edition of the newspaper which he would proceed to scour for Watergate news leads. On discovering one, he would then seek a denial from the White House spokesman and the VOA story would lead with the denial, but report all the details, as well.

To facilitate this process, Kamenske assigned Philomena Jurey to cover the White House on a full-time basis. Looking back on the period, she feels VOA managed to convey to an overseas audience the sense, feel, and dynamics of the Watergate story. She says that an essential ingredient of the coverage was the additonal background and explanatory material VOA provided to its listeners abroad. She cites as an example the report she wrote on May 9, 1974 as the House of Representatives Judiciary Committee began its hearings on whether there were sufficient grounds to impeach President Nixon:

"This is an impeachment proceeding, as provided for in the Constitution. Under the Constitution, a president shall be removed from office on impeachment for — and conviction of — treason, bribery, or other high crimes and misdemeanors. When the Judiciary Committee completes its work — which will be weeks from now — it will report to the full House of Representatives, which then will decide whether to vote impeachment. If it does, President Nixon would be tried by the Senate … " .

By that time, the Watergate story had reached a point where its very complexity demanded a new approach to VOA's coverage. Happily, it also coincided with my leaving the Kissinger diplomatic beat. Bernard Kamenske had launched a special Watergate Coverage Unit which would operate directly out of the Newsroom. I felt honored when he asked me to join it.

The Coverage Unit consisted of two correspondents, two news writers (one of whom, Nancy Smart, would also edit all copy and direct assignments) and a senior news analyst who would handle what Kamenske light-heartedly called the Department of Further Amplification — thoughtful examinations of the day's Watergate events with all of the detailed backgrounding the story required for an overseas audience. As a team, we covered the Nixon impeachment process from beginning to end, including the Watergate-related trials, investigations,

Congressional hearings, and so forth. Our stories were transmitted in English on teletype circuits that went out to the fifty or so language services that made up the Voice of America. They constituted VOA's main source for Watergate coverage.

The impeachment inquiry underway in the House of Representatives became a daily focal point for news coverage. This increased Congressional pressure led Nixon to make what he called a full disclosure regarding the Watergate tapes. Up until this point, he had held off their release, fighting subpoenas from both the Special Prosecutor and the Senate Watergate investigation where the existence of the tapes had first been revealed a year earlier. On April 29, 1974 he came up with a compromise he hoped might work.

He addressed the American people on nationwide television in a broadcast that was carried live to the rest of the world, as well as in simultaneous translation by many of VOA's language services. He began by noting that it had been almost was two years since the Watergate break-in by men who turned out to have been working for his reelection campaign. Since then, he said, there had been allegations and insinuations that he knew about the planning of the Watergate burglary and that he was involved in an extensive plot to cover it up. He noted that the House Judiciary Committee was now investigating those charges.

He then turned to a large stack of folders that appeared on a table to his left. "These folders," he said, "are more than 1,200 pages of transcripts of private conversations I participated in between September 15, 1972 and April 27, 1973 with my principal aides and associates with regard to Watergate. They include all the relevent portions of all the subpoenaed conversations that were recorded, that is, all portions that relate to the question of what I knew about Watergate or the coverup and what I did about it."

The President then announced he was turning the transcripts over to the House Judiciary Committee and inviting the Committee's Chairman, Peter Rodino, and its ranking Republican member "to come to the White House and listen to the actual, full tapes of these conversations so that they can determine for themselves beyond question that the transcripts are accurate and that everything on the tapes relevant to my knowledge and my actions on Watergate is included. If there should be any disagreement over whether omitted material is relevant, I shall meet with them personally in an effort to settle the matter."

In retrospect, I have to admit that Richard Nixon sounded to me as though he was making a good faith effort to level with the American people. He seemed caught between honestly trying to answer the demands of the Judiciary Committee while at the same time retaining some vestige of control over his rapidly declining authority as President of the United

States. He gave the impression he was doing his level best to meet the country halfway between the two challenges, even if it meant revealing more of his personal way of conducting the nation's business than he might have wished at the time.

Fortunately, not everybody saw it my way. Judge John J. Sirica, who had prosecuted the original Watergate defendants, knew better. He had already listened to some of the earliest tapes and had formed his own opinions. For a start, he said he was shocked at the level and degree of Nixon's profanity. "I had come up the hard way," he said, "and the language was far from unfamiliar to me. But the shock, for me at least, was the contrast between the coarse, private Nixon speech and the utterly correct public Nixon speech I had heard so often. As I first realized the barnyard quality of his conversations, I couldn't help remembering the rather self-righteous attack Nixon had made, during the 1960 television debates with John F. Kennedy, on Harry Truman's salty language."

Much of the bad language was edited out of the transcripts Nixon handed over to the Judiciary Committee. The sanitized verson soon entered the public record. "Expletive Deleted" was the term used by the White House to substitute for the original text and it soon became a national joke. Judge Sirica was not laughing.

"I'll never forget," he said, "hearing the president

tell his aides on the March 22 tape, 'And, uh, for that reason, I am perfectly willing to — I don't give a shit what happens. I want you all to stonewall it, let them plead the Fifth Amendment, cover up or anything else, if it'll save it — save the plan."

"From that moment on", said Judge Sirica, "there was no longer any doubt in my mind that there had been a conspiracy to obstruct justice operating inside the White House."

When Judge Sirica compared the White House transcripts with the original tapes, he was immediately struck with some startling differences. Among them "the editing out of long and critical sections of the conversations. I checked the printed transcripts against my own memory of the March 22 tapes and found the stunning 'I don't give a shit...' quote missing." The transcripts of other tapes bore, he said, "little resemblance to the original, with the most incriminating statements by the president either fuzzed over or missing altogether...If he could get away with releasing just the transcripts, he must have reasoned, the issue of his guilt would be blurred enough to avoid impeachment, It was Nixon's last big lie in the years of lying about Watergate".

On my first day covering the House Judiciary Committee impeachment inquiry — which took place in the ornate Rayburn House Office Building on Capitol Hill — I learned several rules about reporting from a Congressional television camera stake out: find a good place to sit down and bring along something interesting to read. But stay alert to what was taking place around you. Story opportunities could occasionally — but not often — come up fast.

The Judiciary Committee was meeting behind closed doors in their hearing room down the hall. Every once in awhile, some of the members would emerge and make their way down the corridor to cast a vote or answer a quorum call. Sometimes they might stop at the camera stake-out and answer a question or two. Often they did not and reporters would tag along as far as the elevators and hope to gain some insight into what was actually taking place behind the closed doors. At the end of the daily session, there would frequently be some sort of formal briefing on the day's developments.

Not much news was at hand during the early phase of the impeachment inquiry. Bob Lodge, VOA's Congressional Correspondent, and I would split up the day's gleanings, pooling any new facts we had heard along the way, and then phone in our daily correspondent reports to the Newsroom. We would often meet with Nancy Smart and other Newsroom colleagues during the day at what became a favorite lunchtime venue at the foot of Capitol Hill — halfway between the Rayburn Office Building and VOA headquarters. A new federal building was then under construction across Independence Avenue from the

National Botanical Gardens and a mobile diner had been opened nearby. Known as the Hard Hat Café, it produced excellent steak sandwiches and cold soft drinks. It was mid-summer in Washington and the cool gardens offered a welcome escape from omnipresent air conditioning. The Hard Hat Café al fresco luncheons gave the VOA Watergate Coverage Unit an opportunity to caucus on a fairly regular basis. More important for Bob Lodge and myself, we could get briefed on Watergate developments taking place away from the Rayburn Office Building where, for the moment at least, not much semed to be happening at all.

I was thus more than ready when Nancy Smart suggested I start covering the Watergate story from across the Washington Mall at the Federal Courthouse where the trial of the White House "Plumbers" was about to get underway. It was close enough for me to still manage the occasional Hard Hat Café luncheon meeting.

The "Plumbers" had been created by the White House to stop leaks — unauthorized disclosures — to the press. Their story, which involved Henry Kissinger, went back several years, well before Watergate. In fact, the publication by the New York Times of what became known as the Pentagon Papers led directly to the creation of the White House "Plumbers" unit. It was one of the reasons Watergate happened. The 7,000 page study given by Daniel

Ellsberg to the New York Times was a highly classified analysis of the Kennedy and Johnson programs
and policies in Indochina. It did not include the
Nixon years and therefore did not directly involve
the Nixon administration, but its publication drove
Kissinger into a fury.

"The fact that some idiot can publish all of the
diplomatic secrets of this country on his own is damaging to your image," Kissinger told Nixon, "And it
could destroy our ability to conduct foreign policy.
If the other powers feel that we can't control internal
leaks, they will never agree to secret negotiations."

"Nixon took the view," Kissinger later wrote in
his memoirs, "that failure to resist such massive, and
illegal, disclosures of classified information would
open the floodgates, undermining the processes of
government and the confidence of other nations."

For Nixon and Kissinger, this was not a purely
theoretical concern. They were at that very moment
preparing for Kissinger's secret trip to Peking. They
were also engaged in secret talks with Hanoi which
they thought — incorrectly, as Kissinger now admits — were close to a breakthrough on a settlement
in Vietnam. Discussions were underway over a possible summit with Moscow, together with a whole
range of sensitive negotiations from a Berlin settlement to SALT.

"I shared Nixon's views", says Kissinger, "I almost certainly reinforced them."

Kissinger's actual reaction, according to the testimony of several White House eyewitnesses, was more volatile than his memoirs suggest. Walter Isaacson, one of Kissinger's principal biographers, cites several senior staffers describing how Kissinger provoked President Nixon to "near hysteria" and "then they started cranking each other up until they both were in a frenzy." He quotes John Ehrlichman, Nixon's chief domestic affairs adviser: "Henry managed to raise the heat so high that Nixon was giving orders left and right that could only lead to trouble."

Another White House adviser quoted by Isaacson was Charles Colson who later testified to special prosecutors investigating the Watergate scandal: "Without any question, Kissinger's great alarm over the Pentagon Papers was the primary motivating influence in the formation of the "Plumbers". I was in private meetings with Henry," said Colson, "when he told the President that this must be stopped no matter what we had to do to stop it. It was over the next few weeks that the "Plumbers" were formed as a direct response."

The trial revealed that the White House, in recruiting for the "Plumbers" team, had turned to E. Howard Hunt, recently retired after a long career with the CIA. Hunt had specialized in Latin America and had been involved in the failed Bay of Pigs invasion as well as subsequent, less well publicized CIA operations run out of Miami. He had recruited Cuban exiles, many of them also with CIA experience, to take part in the "Plumbers". Their first assignment was the burglary of Daniel Ellsberg's Los Angeles psychiatrist, Lewis J. Fielding.

Hunt testified at the "Plumbers" trial that the planned operation was plagued from the beginning by a series of mishaps. In a July 1, 1974 correspondent report called "The Bungled Break In", I wrote that, "Although Hunt and what he described as his entry team had thoroughly gone over their procedures in advance and had visited Doctor Fielding's office earlier in the day, when they got there for the actual entry they found, to their apparent surprise, that the doors were locked and they had to smash their way in."

Hunt, meanwhile, had positioned himself at Fielding's home. When he discovered that nobody was there, he immediately attempted to alert the entry team by radio that Doctor Fielding might show up at his office while the break-in was in progress. But it turned out that the walkie-talkie radio specially purchased for the operation didn't have sufficient range to reach the entry team.

So Hunt rushed to the office by car, instead, only to find that the entry team had given up looking for the specific file they had been sent to find. In order to cover up for their activities, however, they tried to make it appear as through the doctor's office had been broken into by narcotics addicts. They smashed open cabinet doors and scattered bottles of medicine about.

Hunt told the court that they later got together in his hotel room. Their operation had not been a success, but they sent out for a bottle of champagne, anyway. It was, as he put it, for morale purposes — an explanation which provoked widespread laughter in the courtroom.

Members of Hunt's entry team — most of whom were later involved in the Watergate break-in — attempted to establish that they understood the burglary to have been legitimate government business conducted in the interests of national security. They were, after all, recruited by Hunt who worked at the White House, and he had given them each an advance payment of a hundred dollars.

The "Plumbers" trial took on a whole new turn a few weeks later when two men being held prisoner in the Federal Court House basement overcame their guards, broke into the armory, and proceeded to take over the Court House. This had nothing to do with the trial itself, which was then in progress, and Judge Gerhard Gesell had the good sense to order the jury out of the room before he told the rest of us what had taken place.

"The prisoners are heavily armed," he said, "and they have taken hostages. We have been asked by local police to clear the building. Those of you who want to leave should do so by the front door as quickly as possible. Anyone who chooses to remain behind may be here for a considerable period of time."

I had no intention of leaving and I quickly gathered up my notes and headed for the Press Room down the hall. VOA engineers had earlier installed a telephone there and a microphone line so that I could broadcast news from the trial directly from the Federal Court House building. I called the Newsroom and dictated a quick bulletin which reported the takeover by the prisoners and the fact that the "Plumber's" trial now appeared to be in suspension.

Several editors got on the line, wanting more details about the prisoners. I said I would find out what I could and get back in touch within the hour. When I ducked outside the Court House Press Room and saw the empty corridors, it seemed to me as though the building had been completely emptied although I could hear some sounds of movement that seemed to be coming up from the basement. I headed down a nearby staircase, hoping to get a sense of where the prisoners might be holding their hostages.

The atmosphere in the building had now changed completely. Gone was the stately decorum of the high court. Devoid of people, the long corridors took on a sinister aspect. I moved cautiously down the hall, uncertain what lay beyond the next corner.

"Stay right where you are!" I was face to face with a heavily-armed Federal Marshal. "We are bringing in riot police," he said, "Special Weapons and Tactics, a SWAT team. They want us to keep the corridors clear. We are asking all reporters to wait in the Press Room. We will be briefing there in just a few minutes."

When I got back and called VOA, I learned that the prisoners had been on the phone from the basement to the AP and other news agencies. The demands were now being carried on the wires, along with the prisoners' names, background details, and the names of their hostages. I was asked to stay on hand and keep filing updates. The prisoners intended to hold a news conference shortly. Meanwhile, the story of a Washington court house under siege was getting a big play overseas. The imagery was near perfect. We were, after all, within a few city blocks of the House of Representatives where President Nixon was facing his own siege at the hands of the Judiciary Committee's impeachment proceeding.

It was eighteen hours before I left the Court House. Under a special arrangement, journalists were allowed to be relieved by their news organizations on a one by one basis and I was replaced by a colleague from the Newsroom. As I made my way through darkness across the Mall to the VOA building on Independence Avenue, it occurred to me that the Watergate story was now reaching a point of becoming virtually beyond belief.

I was soon pulled back to reality by the trial's verdict which had to be delivered in yet another Federal

Court House — Judge Gesell's building was still under siege. John Ehrlichman and the "Plumbers" were all found guilty of conspiring to violate the civil rights of Ellsberg's psychiatrist by breaking into his office to conduct an illegal search. Three members of the team had later participated in the break-in at the Watergate and had already been found guilty of that burglary.

In reporting Judge Gesell's instructions to the jury, I had noted his emphasis on those protections contained in the Fourth Amendment to the U.S. Constitution which offers guarantees against unreasonable government searches and siezures. He had told the jury: "An individual cannot escape criminal liability simply because he sincerely but incorrectly believes that his acts are justified in the name of patriotism, of national security…or that his superiors had the authority to suspend without warrant the protections of the Fourth Amendment."

National security was of course the argument being presented by President Nixon to justify his witholding the evidence contained in the White House tapes. It seemed to me that the multiple challenges to this argument were about to get the better of the President. It was hard to imagine, as I wrote a colleague at the time, "anything other than impeachment, conviction, removal from office, and a series of criminal indictments. At some point in all of this", I said, "Nixon might resign, or become very ill…"

In the end, he quit. Faced with the liklihood of impeachment by the House of Representatives, conviction by the Senate, and criminal indictments afterwards, Nixon resigned from office — becoming the first president in American history to do so.

Years later, it became clear that he may have struck a pretty good bargain along the way.

On August 1, 1974 Alexander Haig, Nixon's chief of staff, had visited Vice President Ford to tell him of Nixon's intention to resign. He then presented Ford with a list, prepared by Nixon's lawyers, of "permutations for the option of resignation." which would allow Nixon to step down without running the risk of criminal indictment. These included one option that would have Nixon leave office with the understanding that Ford, the new President, would eventually pardon him. According to his own Chief of Staff, Robert Hartmann, Ford, after examining Nixon's proposal, apparently called Haig back and told him "to do whatever they decided to do; it was all right with me." Ford later issued a statement designed to cover up any suggestion that a deal had been struck, but it was clear — to Hartmann, among many others, that one had — much as Ford might later deny it.

The reaction to Ford's pardon of Nixon was both immediate and widespread. His press secretary, Jerry TerHorst, having assured reporters less than a month before that there would be no pardon, resigned in protest shortly after Ford's announcement. Calling the pardon untimely, the New York Times, in a next day editorial , said it held "horrendous implications" for the future and that "it does not end Watergate." The Times editorial noted that Ford failed to explain how a presidential pardon would resolve "allegations and accusations" hanging over Nixon's head like a sword. And veteran Times correspondent Tom Wicker, calling the pardon a "horrendous blunder," predicted it would have an impact on the 1976 U. S. presidential election. As usual, he was right.

Looking back on it, Judge Sirica wrote "The truth is that Richard Nixon left office because he was on the verge of impeachment. He was on the verge of impeachment because there was overwhelmingly convincing evidence…that he had committed criminal acts. It wasn't politics that drove him from office. It was the evidence against him, the proof of his own acts…"

Judge Sirica was convinced that Nixon should have been indicted after he left office, and then, no matter how long it took, he should have stood trial. "I take this view not because I would wish any more suffering on Nixon or his family, but because I felt it would have been better for the country if the legal process had been allowed to run its course — either to acquit the former president or find him guilty."

The House Judiciary Committee recommended impeachment and the full House of Representatives voted in favor of it. But by that time, Nixon was no longer in office. Gerald Ford was in the White House. The VOA Watergate Coverage Unit had completed its mission — and I found myself out of a job.

VOA had, in the meantime, managed to cover Watergate and Nixon's exit without getting itself too heavily manipulated in the process. Its reputation for straight news reporting was intact. There were congratulations all around. The heat was off — for the time being.

14.

The Fall of Saigon and the Making of a VOA Dissident.

I started looking around for another assignment as a correspondent.

We had bought a comfortable house on Reno Road in Northwest Washington. My sons were in good schools and, over the past year, had successfully re-entered American life. We had no wish to go back overseas right away. It seemed more important that we stay in Washington for the time being, maybe get the boys through high school before going abroad again. VOA News Chief Bernard Kamenske proposed that I attend a political economy seminar organized by the Brookings Institution and then take on the faltering U.S. economy as a full time assignment. I agreed — with Watergate gone — it seemed the best story in town.

Looking back on it over the years, I have to

admit I was a terrible Economics Correspondent. Brookings Institution notwithstanding, the figures and the statistics made little sense to me, and I had no talent for tracking economic assumptions, let alone for finding any political significance in them. As winter approached, a paralyzing national coal strike came to my rescue. It was a story I could embrace more readily than abstract assumptions and I busied myself interviewing miners and union officials. This got me through the end of the year. The background briefing sessions for President Ford's first national budget and his state of the union message took me well into January.

Then I had a lucky break, before I got into serious trouble. Help was on the way from a totally unexpected source.

Vietnam — more than a year and a half after I had left it — re-entered my life. Henry Kissinger's painstakingly constructed ceasefire, for which he had won the Nobel Peace Prize in 1973, was already starting to unravel by December 1974. The North Vietnamese army had begun a series of probing actions from Cambodia, quietly occupying several district towns across the border in South Vietnam's Phuoc Long Province. Resistance from the South Vietnamese side was weak. On January 6, 1975, the North Vietnamese attacked and quickly overran Phuoc Long's provincial capital of Phuoc Binh. It marked the first time since the fall of Quang Tri City — early in the 1972

Easter Offensive — that a provincial capital had been lost to the North Vietnamese.

These actions did not pass unnoticed in Washington. Anxious to build public support for its continuing military aid program in Southeast Asia, the Pentagon began drawing attention to the increase in North Vietnamese activity. One night in February, after a slow day on the economic front, I got a call from Bernard Kamenske asking me to drive over to the Pentagon and cover a special press briefing.

"We're short-handed," Bernie said, "and you know your way around the military. Try and find out what's really happening in Vietnam."

The immense building was a total mystery to me. I had seen it from a distance over the years, but had never set foot in it. I was instructed to leave my car in the press parking lot outside the Mall Entrance. My White House press pass got me past the front door and I eventually found my way to the briefing room. To my great pleasure, I ran into several old friends from Saigon — journalists, mostly, but some of the military press people, as well. It almost seemed like coming home again.

After the briefing, I wrote a long, fairly thoughtful piece about how the war appeared to be starting up again. The following day, I got a call from Kamenske telling me to forget about the U.S. economy. I should move over to the Pentagon, he said, and start covering the daily press briefings on a regular basis. I had served in the military and I had seen the war in Southeast Asia first hand as a reporter. He felt I was more valuable to VOA as a Pentagon correspondent than an economics reporter. I was very much inclined to agree.

The military situation in Vietnam got steadily worse, particularly after the March 11 surrender of Ban Me Thuot in South Vietnam's Central Highlands. It soon became quite evident that a major North Vietnamese offensive was under way, not unlike the 1972 Easter invasion. Several divisions of Hanoi's army were pushing their way south, crossing over the Cambodian and Laotian borders at several points. The South Vietnamese army, with some notable exceptions, was fleeing before them.

Hue fell March 25. Danang followed at the end of the month. Having secured much of the northern part of the country, as well as the Central Highlands, the North Vietnamese Army now proceeded to march on Saigon.

I began sharing desk space in a small office just down from the Pentagon's E-Ring briefing room that had been set aside for radio and television correspondents. VOA engineers brought in a broadcast line and what was known as those days as a "loud mouth" microphone. It had an off/on switch which also served as a volume control. When I needed to broadcast, I would telephone VOA Master Control and request them to open the line for me. This got around the union restrictions prohibiting non-engineering staff from directly handling broadcast lines. When the situation demanded it, we could broadcast live from the Pentagon directly into an on-the-air VOA broadcast, but this was an exception reserved for breaking stories of unusual significance — like the fall of Saigon.

The Pentagon's main press office was across the corridor. Each of the military services maintained information desks there staffed by officers who were available to answer questions in their respective areas of expertise. Correspondents got to know them all fairly well and they were usually most helpful. On request, they would also set up appointments for interviews with other military professionals who could add even further background to a story. This sort of activity would take place after the daily Pentagon news briefing which usually got underway around noon — once the White House had completed its own morning meeting with the press. This highly-choreographed timing — White House, Pentagon and State Department press offices were frequently on the phone to each other — would often allow a reporter to cover both the White House and the Pentagon or State Department news briefings, but rarely all three in the same day.

I found my working arrangements more congenial than those at the White House, where the VOA broadcast booth was in a basement that had formerly served as the presidential swimming pool. There seemed to be fewer opportunities at either the White House or the State Department to "enterprise" a story beyond the daily briefings and the handouts. Also, the tree-shaded view out across the Potomac River from my Pentagon window was much more pleasing to the eye than what could be seen from the White House basement, or the VOA broadcast booth at the State Department. Lunch at the Pentagon was also better, particularly at the Flag Officer's Dining Room where accredited correspondents were welcome.

Henry Kissinger, who had managed to retain his official positions in both the White House and the State Department during the transition from Nixon to Ford, was leading the effort to sustain the level of U.S. military aid to South Vietnam. But he faced a new Congress, elected since Watergate. Many of its members seemed to me to be determined to prevent even symbolic U.S. assistance to the failing regimes in Vietnam and Cambodia. Kissinger later wrote:

"President Ford and I had no illusions about the outcome of the tragedy. But we thought it important not to compound the evolving calamity by a deliberate and public abandonment of peoples who had linked their fate to American promises. We thought cutting off aid to an ally *in extremis* was shameful and could have a disastrous impact on nations relying on America for their security."

Kissinger had a further motive in asking Congress

for the *in extremis* funding. He was concerned that the government in Saigon, fearing it was being abandoned by Washington, might panic and turn against the six thousand Americans who remained in South Vietnam — possibly even using them as hostages. He saw the need to buy time; above all, to avoid taking any action that might trigger a hostile reaction from the South Vietnamese.

Food and ammunition were running short in Saigon and an airlift of emergency supplies had been underway for several weeks from American bases in the Philippines. On April 3, 1975, President Ford announced that he was directing the Pentagon to make these military aircraft available to fly refugees out of Saigon on their return flights. Specifically, he intended them to be used to pick up several thousand South Vietnamese orphans who were in the process of being adopted by American families. But he said he was also ordering all available U.S. naval ships to stand off the coast of Vietnam and do whatever was necessary to assist in the movement of refugees. There had been a steady stream south since the North Vietnamese offensive had increased its intensity in February.

A few days later, he deployed armed U.S. Marines to several of the ships to help handle the security of the refugees whose numbers had swollen to over a hundred thousand since the fall of Danang in late March. Among the refugees were remnants of the South Vietnamese army, many of whom had retained their weapons. One such group commandeered a U.S. civilian contract vessel and forced its captain to take them to a port near Saigon, rather than the island of Phu Quoc where a refugee camp had been established. The same situation arose on two other ships, but Pentagon officials reported that American crewmembers managed to persuade the Vietnamese troops to disembark with the rest of the refugees. The assignment of the U.S. Marine guards ended any further attempts at refugee mutinies.

Meanwhile, the chaos and the panic had begun to settle in. The airlift of orphans out of Saigon ran into a serious delay when one of the giant C-5 military transports suffered what the pilot later reported was a massive explosive decompression in flight, possibly due to enemy groundfire. The Pentagon told us the pilot had lost most of his hydraulic controls, but was nonetheless able to turn the aircraft back towards Saigon and begin his descent. As he approached the airfield, he saw that he was losing altitude too rapidly and couldn't reach the runway — so he attempted an emergency landing in a rice paddy. The giant aircraft hit the ground at a high rate of speed, bounced several times, and began disintegrating before catching fire. There were two hundred and forty-three children on board — very few survived.

In early April, with North Vietnamese troops approaching Saigon in division strength and Khmer

Rouge forces closing in on Phnom Penh, President Ford formally asked Congress for $722 million in further military assistance for the South Vietnamese. I drove over to Capitol Hill and covered the congressional hearing. Fresh from a hurried visit to Saigon, the Army Chief of Staff, General Frederick Weyand, was testifying in support of the President's request. He did not receive a particularly friendly response.

I reported that he told the Congress that South Vietnam was at a crisis point in its survival as a nation. The South Vietnamese people, he said, needed to feel a sense of support from the United States. Asked whether he thought this would encourage the South Vietnamese army to stand and fight, in view of its lack of resistance so far, he said there was no question in his mind but what they would do so. They had been through what he described as a very traumatic experience, but he thought they would be able to survive, providing they continued to receive American assistance.

As balance, and by way of indicating what I considered the prevailing congressional reaction, I quoted Congressman Robert Legget as noting that equipment provided to South Vietnam by the United States within the past two weeks was being abandoned to the other side — apparently without a battle. Much of it, he said, was simply left in place unused and fully operable for the North Vietnamese to acquire in their march south. Wouldn't it just be easier, another Congressman asked, to give the weapons to the North Vietnamese in the first place?

I received a phone call from the Newsroom immediately afterwards. I was asked to edit out the negative congressional comment and revoice the piece. When I refused to do so, I was told the story would be killed. It had already run on the VOA in-house teletype, so the Newsroom had to issue a "Note to Editors" an hour and a half later. "Make no further use," it said, of the following correspondent report: Kelly/Congress — "Weyand and Congress."

I was outraged, not just at being over-ruled on a story, but also because I knew that Ford's request had litle chance of getting through Congress, in its present mood. I felt strongly that my reporting should reflect this and that the Voice of America owed its listeners as much. I re-wrote basically the same report, giving it another title. This time around I used a quote from Senator Hubert Humphrey, noting that he was both a former U.S. Vice President and a presidential candidate who, in calling South Vietnam "a disaster", said he was sickened "at the sight of South Vietnamese troops fleeing from battle and mistreating civilians." Humphrey added that he was "not prepared to give any more money to people who won't stand up and fight for their existence." This time the story ran and nobody complained. But I kept copies of both reports, fully intending to raise the whole issue of censorship at a later point — once the dust had settled.

There was no real hope that the arms would reach Saigon in time. U.S. Marine helicopters were sent into Cambodia a few days later to rescue the 82 Americans remaining at the U.S. Embassy in Phnom Penh. Across the border in Vietnam, large numbers of North Vietnamese troops were moving south towards Xuan Loc, the last South Vietnmese defense line before Saigon. President Ford was taking the precaution of ordering all non-essential American government employees flown out of the city.

On April 14, the new VOA censorship policy was finally put in writing, after weeks having been passed along to correspondents by word of mouth. It appeared in a Newsroom directive known as a "slot note" to be read by all personnel as they came on duty at the beginning of each Newsroom shift. Most of us who read it felt ashamed that VOA management had caved in to what was obviously a USIA instruction. It read: "In relation to the question of evacuation or phasedown of Americans and Vietnamese associated with them from Vietnam, we are to use only official statements of the White House, and Departments of State or Defense, and Congressional actions (e.g., a vote) until further notice. This instruction stems from a very volatile situation in Saigon which raises concern for the lives and safety of these individuals and recognition of a responsibility to protect them."

My copy of the new directive was handed to me just as I was sitting down to have lunch on Capitol

Hill with several colleagues from other news organizations, including the Washington Post and the New York Times. I was so irked at VOA management for having knuckled under to pressure from higher levels — something we had managed to avoid doing during Watergate — I decided to share my discontent. I passed the directive around the press table, noting as I did so, that news this bad deserved a wider audience. The VOA directive thus entered the public domain.

My experience with the new censorship regime was by no means unique. Philomena Jurey, VOA's White House correspondent, recalls being informed by the Newsroom that "there were strictures on the subject of evacuation and we weren't supposed to mention it." She says she refused to rewrite her story, arguing that she would rather not do the piece at all if an important part of it would be left out. Instead of killing the story outright, as had been done with my report from the Congress, the Newsroom went ahead and manipulated her story to match the directive. She says she was incensed when she learned what had been done behind her back. The episode soon found its way into the Washington Post, along with an attempt by a USIA spokesman to clarify the matter.

"We have got a fluid situation," said the USIA representative, "a situation where we have to be very conscious at all times about adding to the complications already existing — even to the extent of placing American lives in jeopardy." Then he added: "Normally the news coverage of VOA is not limited to congressional actions or official expressions. But the situation in Saigon is not normal."

USIA's direct censorship immediately brought up the controversial issue of the VOA Charter. This statement of mission was written during the Eisenhower administration while VOA was undergoing its major programming expansion under Henry Loomis. The Charter had become the guiding news policy for VOA ever since. Although there had been occasional challenges by USIA, the original language had remained in force: "The long-range interests of the United States are served by communicating directly with the peoples of the world by radio. To be effective, the Voice of America must win the attention and respect of listeners. These principles will govern VOA broadcasts:

1. VOA will establish itself as a consistently reliable and authoritative source of news. VOA news will be accurate, objective, and comprehensive.

2. VOA will represent America, not any single segment of American society. It will therefore present a balanced and comprehensive projection of significant American thought and institutions.

3. As an official radio, VOA will present the policies of the United States clearly and

> effectively. VOA will also present re-
> sponsible discussion and opinion on these
> policies."

The Charter, unfortunately, had no force of law. It had never been approved by Congress nor had it been given any formal presidential sanction. Over the years, it had occasionally become a source of friction between USIA and VOA, particularly when USIA management felt that VOA was not being sufficiently responsive to the Agency's policy guidelines. USIA had created for itself an elaborate "policy" apparatus which sought to establish what U.S. official policy *was* on a given issue. This effort had kept many people employed at the higher echelons of USIA, but it was in basic conflict with the principles proclaimed in the VOA Charter — much as USIA policy officers might argue to the contrary.

In the long run, most of us felt that U.S. government policy was determined by many points of view, including those of the Congress, and that these were best reflected by having a professional team of news correspondents regularly covering the White House, State Department, Pentagon, Capitol Hill, and other Washington centers where policy statements emerged. Creating an office known as Policy in USIA to provide "guidance" to VOA News also seemed to us to suggest dictatorship and propaganda. Its irony was perhaps best summed up in a joke that was popular around the corridors of VOA at the time:

"Query: What, after all, *is* U.S. policy anyway? The reply: U.S. policy is what Policy says it is."

When the VOA Newsroom moved down to the basement in the 1960s in order to acquire more working space, there was still a USIA Policy Office functioning up on the first floor, with windows that overlooked the Mall. We used to phone Policy from the Newsroom for a weather report to find out whether we needed rain coats and umbrellas when heading out to lunch. That was pretty much the extent of "policy guidance" in those days. Not long afterwards, the Policy Office closed altogether.

If we had thought the days of USIA policy guidance were history, we were soon mistaken. They re-emerged suddenly on April 23, 1975 when President Ford, in a speech at Tulane University, declared that the war in Vietnam was over. His remarks, which Kissinger later claimed had not been cleared by his office, effectively changed the policy of not saying anything that might panic the South Vietnamese.

Ironically, the Tulane speech almost turned out quite differently. Robert Hartmann, Ford's favorite speech writer, had urged Ford to use the line declaring the Vietnam war "over". The President, according to Hartmann, was hesitant. "I am not sure," he said, "Henry would approve."

Hartmann pointed out that Kissinger and others had been saying pretty much the same thing. However, he told Ford, "You have to say it to make it official. Nobody declared this war, but you can declare the end of it."

When they reached the Tulane fieldhouse, acccording to Hartmann, the floor and grandstands were packed with students who had come to see and hear Ford. When the President exclaimed: "Today, America can regain the sense of pride that existed before Vietnam. But it cannot be achieved by refighting a war that is finished as far as America is concerned," the audience went wild with applause.

"His final words," Hartmann says, "were drowned out as soon as the students heard the word 'finished'. They almost literally raised the roof with whoops and hollers. Pandemonium lasted for several minutes and continued to erupt through the remainder of Ford's speech."

Hartmann found the President feeling quite pleased with himself on the trip home, particularly after he had read the UPI bulletin that began "To the standing ovation and cheers of six thousand Tulane University students in New Orleans, President Ford called the Indochina conflict 'a war that is finished as far as America is concerned."

When reporters on board Air Force One asked to see the President, Hartmann told Ford, "I wouldn't go. You can't make tonight's story any better." But, says Hartmann, "He was in no mood not to miss any more praise, especially from the press."

I was in Washington, covering a related story. I had

planned to include the President's Tulane University remarks. When I called into the VOA Newsroom, I was told that we were not to report the President's Vietnam war comments under any circumstances. I couldn't believe what I was hearing.

"Since when did we start censoring the President of the United States?," I asked. "If you try to include Ford in your story," I was told, "we will cut it out of your copy. So don't do it!"

Cooler heads eventually prevailed and Philomena Jurey, who had not travelled with the President to Tulane, attempted to put the story into context afterwards by reporting from the White House that "Even though President Ford says the Vietnam war is finished as far as America is concerned, he has not abandoned his belief that additional military aid would help stabilize the situation and would help being about a ceasefire or negotiated settlement."

Coming on the heels of my being censored over the earlier story, I was furious at this latest effort at news management. Censoring both the President and the Congress seemed to me to be the worst possible violation of VOA's Charter. Worse yet, it involved VOA in what amounted to a cover up. We were put in the position of trying to delude the Vietnamese into thinking we were not pulling out of Saigon. The fact that this might cause the needless loss of Vietnamese lives did not seem to occur to those who were imposing the censorship.

Somehow I sensed Henry Kissinger's hand at the National Security Council in all of this. We had been told that the orders to VOA to show America's resolve by not reporting Congressional or presidential comments had come down from the White House. Whether they originated in the White House or at USIA, their objective was plainly to delude the Vietnamese. I felt sickened at having been made part of the subterfuge and I wanted to stop it from ever happening again.

Senator Charles Percy, an Illinois Republican, had long been a friend of VOA at budget time. His district included a large number of Americans with close family links to Czechoslovakia, Hungary and Poland — which may well have contributed to his interest in international broadcasting. I telephoned Scott Cohen, his legislative assistant, and asked if we could meet privately on a matter involving VOA censorship.

Cohen told me that Senator Percy was acting temporarily as chairman of the Senate Foreign Relations Committee and, as such, would soon be presiding over USIA's annual budget hearings. He said the Senator felt that VOA should be pulled out of USIA and made an independent entity — free, as he put it, from the control of what was essentially a public relations agency. I couldn't agree more. Cohen then suggested I bring him specific examples of recent Charter violations, particularly those that involved censorship of Congressional or presidential statements.

When Senator Percy had USIA Director James Keogh on the witness stand, the issue of charter violations became the main topic of the day. "I have been given information," said the Senator, "which indicates that VOA news is not always accurate, objective and comprehensive. For example, during the last two months of April, as the evacuation of Americans from Vietnam became a preoccupation of the world press, the Administration and the Congress, VOA news was not similarly preoccupied."

Senator Percy then noted that instructions were passed by word of mouth at VOA to the effect that the evacuation of Americans from Saigon was not suitable material for VOA news. "VOA staffers were told by the editors that — under no circumstances — would the possibility of an evacuation of Americans from South Vietnam be reflected in VOA broadcasts." Later, said the Senator, these instructions were put in writing.

The USIA Director admitted that special restraints had been placed on VOA news reporting during the evacuation, but he disputed the charge that President Ford's remarks had been censored. He said he would look into the matter and report back to the Committee.

Senator Percy then charged that White House and State Department intervention had led to management of VOA news in violation of both the charter and common sense. He added that such violations demonstrated the need to increase the Voice of America's autonomy. "If VOA is to be believed," said the Senator, "it must be left free to tell the truth."

Greater autonomy for the Voice of America was already being discussed by several blue-ribbon investigative panels, notably two separate commissions led by CBS broadcast executive Frank Stanton and former Undersecretary of State Robert Murphy. The topic was thus getting a fairly thorough airing in Washington. Senator Percy proposed taking it considerably further, but he wasn't sure he had the votes to do so. He suggested, as an interim measure, that the VOA Charter be given the force of law by including it in an amendment to USIA's annual budget. For this to happen, he said we would need to get additional support within the House of Representatives, preferably from a Democrat — to give the measure full bipartisanship.

I had been covering the VOA discussions on Capitol Hill, while working somewhat clandestinely with Senator Percy's office, and was surprised to hear that Congresswoman Bella Abzug, a Democrat from New York, had been in touch with Bernie Kamenske, my Newsroom boss, on VOA censorship matters. Bernie was not aware of my contacts with Senator Percy's office. There was no way I could tell him without revealing that I had been the source for most of the information Senator Percy had used in attacking USIA Director James Keogh over the VOA Charter violations. And I didn't want to put him in the position of not being able to deny that he knew which member of his staff had become the VOA Dissident. It turned out that Bernie was doing fine on his own in getting Bella Abzug to generate bipartisan support for VOA in the House of Representatives.

Eventually, Percy's aide Scott Cohen tacked the VOA Charter onto the Foreign Relations Authorization Act for the next fiscal year — 1977. As Alan Heil noted in his detailed history of VOA, "The amendment went forward virtually unnoticed, a nearly verbatim text of the Eisenhower directive... Who, after all, could object to chartering America's Voice. Its provisions for objective news and broadcasting about American policies appeared innocuous to congressional authorizers, somewhat akin to a Mother's Day resolution — as American as apple pie."

It took several months for the Percy amendment to work its way through the legislative process before it reached President Ford's desk for his signature. He signed the VOA Charter into law on July 12, 1976. A great shout of approval went up from the VOA Newsroom, even from those of us who felt that, while it was a great first step forward, it wasn't enough. We went on to press for even more autonomy from USIA. Giving the VOA Charter the force of law might protect the Newsroom from ever having to censor the President or Congress again. Whether it would help VOA chart its own course past the troublesome intersection of journalism and diplomacy was another challenge altogether. The basic problem being, as VOA Director John Chancellor was fond of pointing out: "the practice of one of these disciplines negates the practice of the other."

In a Chicago speech November 30, 1976, Senator Percy said: "I want to do something to help the Voice of America to become truly a voice of America, speaking the truth clearly and without bureaucratic impediment. I don't want American diplomats and bureaucrats distorting VOA newscasts anymore." He then pledged to introduce legislation "to…make the Voice of America independent of USIA, operating under an oversight authority similar to that which now oversees Radio Liberty and Radio Free Europe."

In February 1977, I wrote an article in the Foreign Service Journal, a monthly magazine published by the American Foreign Service Association in Washington. It was entitled "Shall Truth Be Our Guide? A Proposal for Reforming the Voice of America." I called for "entrusting control of VOA to an independent board — or to the Corporation for Public Broadcasting — with the responsibility for overseeing a Voice of America that speaks for all Americans, and by its broadcasts exemplifies their belief in freedom of expression."

I delivered copies of the article, along with several supporting documents, to members of President-elect Jimmy Carter's transition team involved in drafting policy positions for the new administration. Then I took a year's leave of absence from VOA and became a research fellow at the Georgetown University Center for Strategic and International Studies. While there, I wrote a book entitled "Access Denied: the Politics of Press Censorship" which was published by Georgetown the following year. It took up, once again, the issue of greater VOA autonomy.

By that time, President Carter had created a whole new entity out of USIA, calling it the U.S. International Communication Agency and giving it additional responsibilities, notably in the field of international exchanges. In his message to Congress outlining the principles that had guided him in shaping the reorganization plan for the new agency, he said that among the most important was "keeping the Voice of America's news gathering and reporting functions independent and objective." He further pledged that under his new administration "VOA will be solely responsible for the content of its news broadcasts — for there is no more valued coin than candor in the international marketplace of ideas."

Almost immediately, VOA locked horns with the State Department over the question of news access to international organizations the United States did not officially "recognize," such as the Palestine

Liberation Organization. VOA maintained its reporters needed access to any bonafide news source and that such access should not necessarily be seen as conveying any sort of diplomatic recognition by the U.S. Government.

The incident led to the creation of yet another panel of outside experts to look into the status of VOA correspondents abroad and whether they should function as journalists or "governmental officials". The issue, said Peter Straus, Carter's appointed VOA Director, "lies at the crux of the problems that can arise when a news organization is also a government agency: can a reporter be independent if he receives a security clearance, carries an official passport, is paid from government funds, and has 'high visibility' in many areas of the world just because he is a VOA correspondent?"

Unlike previous panels of outside experts, this one was mostly made up of working journalists. It was led by a former Washington Post diplomatic correspondent, Chalmers Roberts, who had just published a scholarly history of his newspaper which described how the Washington Post had dealt successfully with the pressures brought upon it by the Pentagon Papers and the Watergate scandal. Mr. Roberts was no stranger to the problems of journalistic access and I looked forward to working with him and his distinguished panel.

My own book "Access Denied" was coming

out and had already been favorably reviewed on the Op-Ed page of the Washington Post by Charles B. Seib, the newspaper's ombudsman. I was still at Georgetown's Center for Strategic and International Studies and wrote, as one of their occasional "CSIS Notes", a paper entitled "The Voice of America Correspondent: Journalist or Diplomat?" which was delivered to members of the Chalmers Roberts panel and subsequently reprinted in the Foreign Service Journal.

The Roberts panel came to the conclusion that VOA needed its correspondents abroad, that they should be free of diplomatic restrictions, and that their status should be as close as possible to that of correspondents of commercial American news organizations. The panel also recommended that "VOA correspondents should use regular passports, apply for journalists' visas and relinquish such diplomatic perquisites as PX and commissary privileges." Furthermore, they should not have access to classified material.

In return, recommended the panel: "Ambassadors and other American government personnel abroad would accord VOA correspondents the same courtesy, consideration and assistance extended to any other American correspondent — no more, no less."

For once, the outside experts were taken seriously and their recommendations put into effect. I resigned my commission as a career foreign service

officer and accepted assignment as VOA Nairobi
Bueau Chief, agreeing to put the new correspondent
status to the test. Shortly after arriving in East Africa,
I joined correspondents from the New York Times
and Newsweek Magazine and travelled to Ethiopia's
disputed Ogaden region with guerrilla soldiers from
the Somali Liberation Front. Our reports from the region were carried by VOA, as well as the New York
Times and Newsweek. The trip was the subject of a
protest to VOA by the U.S. Embassy in Ethiopia ,
but the new VOA guidelines held — at least for the
time being.

   The incoming Reagan administration would prove
less faithful to them, particularly in El Salvador.

15.

Of Space Shuttles and Other Bold Beginnings

There was not a lot of chaos to chase when I got back to Africa in 1979, after an absence of ten years. A war was still simmering in Ethiopia's Ogaden, but Idi Amin had been forced to flee Uganda and Rhodesia was well on its way to becoming Zimbabwe. The big change in South Africa was certainly overdue, but no one could predict how soon it would come. I welcomed the opportunity of a return to the peaceful pursuits of the American space program, especially when it seemed I might report them from the Seychelles — instead of Cape Canaveral, or the Johnson Space Center in Houston, where I had last pursued them.

The Seychelles form a loose collection of palm-fringed islands located, as the guidebooks say, "a thousand miles from anywhere" — out well beyond

Madagascar towards the middle of the Indian Ocean. I had been trying to get to them for years. Suddenly, they were within reach.

Five years earlier, I had covered the final Apollo space flight, an unspectacular rendezvous in orbit between American and Soviet spacecraft that turned out to be more a demonstration of political *détente* than an accomplishment of technology. Apollo-Soyuz, as it was called, marked the end of an era when U.S. astronauts were carried into space in rocket-launched capsules and returned to earth in a parachute landing, usually to be picked up at sea. I wrote a story from Houston called "The Last Splash Down Party" which described the traditional victory celebration at the end of a successful Apollo mission, but noted, with some regret, that the next U.S. manned space flight was at least five years away and there would be no splash down. The new spacecraft would be flown back to earth like a space glider and it would be called the Space Shuttle.

The Seychelles had first came to my attention during a visit to East Africa in 1960. At that time, they were only accessible by ship which took a week to reach the islands. In later years, the United States built a space satellite tracking station on Mahe, the main island. It was reached by a flying boat service operating out of Kenya. When I asked in Nairobi, I was told it was impossible for me to get a seat on it.

No airport existed in the Seychelles until 1971

when one was finally created out of landfill near Mahe's harbor. Scheduled airline service started up shortly afterwards and the islands were opened for tourism. I learned that the U.S. satellite station had become, in the meantime, an important link in the world-wide tracking network developed to support the expanding space program, including the new Space Shuttle project. The first flight of the Shuttle was scheduled to take place in a few months and I drew VOA's attention to the fact that the Seychelles would be involved in the success of the inaugural flight.

Once it reached space orbit, the Shuttle spacecraft would have to separate from its empty external fuel tank. The command for this maneuver would be relayed by the Indian Ocean Tracking Station on the Seychelles which would then track the descent of the large empty tank back into the earth's atmosphere. The expectation was that most of the tank would burn up on re-entry. The remaining pieces would fall — it was hoped — into an uninhabited part of the Indian Ocean. But scientists were not certain. This was, after all, the Shuttle's first flight.

I persuaded VOA that it made sense for us to try to broadcast live from the Indian Ocean Tracking Station during the first mission. We would first of all have to get permission to do so from NASA — the national space agency. We would then have work out the technical details in time for the first Shuttle launch.

NASA and VOA were old friends — neighbors, even — in Washington. We had covered the manned missions to the moon from the very first test flights into space. VOA loved the space program. It was easy and relatively inexpensive to cover. In return, it helped draw a huge international audience. We had based a broadcast trailer at Cape Canaveral for years, and had maintained permanent studios, as well, at the Johnson Space Center in Houston. We had already begun coverage plans the first flight of the Space Shuttle — from lift off at Cape Canaveral to its planned desert landing at Edwards Air Force Base in California. Adding the Indian Ocean Tracking Center would give the broadcast an overseas presence that was bound to appeal to listeners around the world. Washington sent me to the Seychelles to check out the technical details.

The beauty of the remote islands lived up to my expectations — as spectacular as the guidebooks described them — "silvery sands, secluded coves bounded by granite boulders, misty mountain peaks cloaked in verdant forest and coral reefs extending into the warm ocean." I felt obliged to dash off a few feature stories to help ease my sense of guilt at being there on expenses. I interviewed several local officials on the new impact of tourism on the economy. I asked about the politics of the Seychelles and the extent of their relations with their neighbors — a thousand miles away on the African mainland. I also met with U.S. officials at the Indian Ocean Tracking Station.

They seemed very enthusiastic about my publicising the role of the station in the Space Shuttle program. It was several years before I found out why.

The Seychelles station turned out to be part of a tracking network that supported the Vela system of space satellites designed to detect nuclear explosions. Some months earlier, on September 29, 1979, a Vela satellite had detected the characteristic double flash signal of a nuclear detonation in the Indian Ocean or South Atlantic area. South Africa was known to be working on the development of a nuclear weapon. So was Israel. In fact, both countries had carried out nuclear research together. Had either one, or both, conducted secret tests that were picked up by the Vela satellite?

A controversy raged behind the scenes in Washington over what Vela had, or had not, seen. 1980 was an election year and not an ideal time for President Jimmy Carter to be in a position of having to take action against Israel — a close ally — should Vela's detection of a nuclear explosion prove to be accurate. Carter, after all, had established nuclear non-proliferation as a top priority of his administration. Nor, for that matter, did he look forward to defending himself against charges that he had failed to impose sanctions. Either way, it was a losing proposition for him and he moved quickly to diffuse the controversy. He appointed a panel of eminent scientists to investigate all available data. Ten months later, they came to the conclusion that there was no clear evidence of a nuclear explosion. Vela had probably witnessed natural phenomena, they said. There were, however, many scientists who did not agree with the panel's findings.

In any event, the Indian Ocean Tracking Station on the Seychelles was happy to have the Vela controversy go away. Its staff welcomed the opportunity of demonstrating the station's role in the Space Shuttle program. NASA, which ran the Shuttle project, was involved in the peaceful exploration of space. The space agency put astronauts on the moon. It didn't concern itself with detecting nuclear explosions.

I quickly arranged with the local Cable and Wireless office to run broadcast lines up to the Tracking Station so that we could connect with VOA Washington by commercial satellite. This would make it possible for me to converse back and forth with the Washington broadcast studio. The VOA coverage plan for the first Space Satellite flight was programmed around an anchor man in the Washington studio who would be joined by various NASA experts to explain the more technical aspects of the mission as they occured. Correspondents at Cape Canaveral and the Johnson Space Center would also be brought in live during the launch and throughout the mission — so would I, since the Shuttle would be passing repeatedly over the Indian Ocean Tracking Station. As the flight drew to a close, another correspondent would pick up coverage of the landing at Edwards Air Force Base in the California desert.

We did several dry runs, chatting back and forth to test the lines out. All went well and we began the wait for the first Space Shuttle mission to begin. It turned out to be longer than anyone had expected. The Shuttle's three on-board computers could not agree with each other on whether it was safe to go ahead with the launch, so NASA interrupted the count down just seconds before the scheduled blast off. It took a week to reschedule the mission. I didn't mind at all. The Seychelles remained as beautiful as ever and I set about to explore as many of them as I could.

There are three main islands: Mahe, Praslin and La Digue — all within a few miles of each other. Others, such as Aldabra and Cosmoledo, take days to reach by boat and I saved them for another trip. Each island has its own distinct landscape and, in some cases, its own distinct birdlife — such as the rare Black Parrot on Praslin, and the Seychelles Black Paradise Flycatcher on La Digue. Altogether, the tiny Seychelles islands have seventeen land bird species not be found anywhere else in the world. I was never much of a birdwatcher, but I was sent to the Seychelles to track a spacecraft that was having trouble getting off the ground. Somehow, it seemed not too inappropriate to look for birds capable of managing the task without a problem.

When the Shuttle "Columbia" finally did blast off from Cape Canaveral, it was a matter of minutes before it would pass over the Seychelles. I heard the Washington anchorman toss me an advance cue: "VOA Correspondent Sean Kelly is standing by at the Indian Ocean Tracking Station in the Seychelles islands and we will be going to him in a few minutes for a report on the separation of "Columbia's" main fuel tank."

I was ready but the technology was not. I could hear the Washington anchorman, but he couldn't hear me — nor could anyone else. He tried again after a few minutes: "If Sean Kelly is ready in the Seychelles, we'll switch live to him now." In the background, I could hear someone muttering at the Washington end of the line: "He ought to be ready in the Seychelles, he's been out there for two weeks on expenses!" It was probably some envious soul from the VOA's senior management.

We finally got the broadcast going the way it was planned. I don't know how much light my contribution from the Indian Ocean Tracking Station shed on VOA's overall coverage of the mission, but I had fun making it. The rest of the mission went as planned and the "Columbia" spacecraft landed successfully in the California desert. I spent several days dismantling the broadcast lines from the Station to the Cable and Wireless office and then headed back to Nairobi to deal with an outbreak of electoral violence in Uganda. The Seychelles, however, would soon be heard from again.

On November 25, 1981, Mike Hoare, the legendary mercenary commander whom I had last covered fifteen years earlier in the Congo, arrived at the Seychelles capital on Mahe, intending to carry out a coup d'etat. He was leading a group of fifty South African and ex-Rhodesian mercenaries posing as members of a beer-drinking fraternity known as the Ancient Order of Frothblowers. Each man carried an over-night bag stuffed with toys and candies to be handed out to school children. The bottom of each bag had a cleverly designed styrofoam compartment containing an AK-47 assault rife with a folding stock.

When Hoare's advance team met the Frothblowers at the Mahe airport, they succeeded in loading most of the men on a rented bus, but as the last mercenary was passing through Seychelles customs, his AK-47 was discovered — as well as the coup.

At that point, most of Hoare's men had off-loaded their Frothblower over-night bags on top of the bus. They were quickly thrown down by one of the advance men and a fire-fight erupted in the Mahe airport terminal. Unfortunately for Hoare, the Tanzanian army, fresh from having thrown Idi Amin's troops out of Uganda, was guarding the airport area at the request of the Seychelles government that Hoare was trying to overthrow. Joined by nearby reinforcements, the

Tanzanians were beginning to close in when Hoare's men managed to hijack an Air India Boeing that had landed in the midst of all the shooting. It still had enough fuel on board to fly them all to South Africa where Hoare and his men were promptly arrested and jailed for the skyjacking, but not for trying to launch a military coup in the Seychelles. Two men had been killed during the shooting at the airport and several others wounded.

The South African hand was quite obvious in the whole affair. The AK-47s had been drawn from the South African army — Hoare produced a hand receipt at his trial to prove it. South Africa negotiated the release of six of the mercenaries left behind on the Seychelles, including one man known to be a South African security agent. Hoare was sentenced to ten years in prison, but got off with much less. As did all the others.

Why South Africa had allowed itself to become involved in an attemped coup d'etat in the Seychelles was not clear. But during the period following Robert Mugabe's 1980 election victory in Zimbabwe, South Africa had begun to see itself facing what its president, P.W. Botha, declared to be "total onslaught" from the outside world. To counter this, Botha had developed a policy of not only destabilizing unfriendly regimes among his immediate neighbors, but also carrying out military interventions further afield.

In 1981, the year of Hoare's attempted coup,

South Africa managed to carry out attacks on all its neighbors: Angola, Botswana, Lesotho, Mozambique, Swaziland, Zambia and Zimbabwe. The following year, it bombed the London offices of its principal opposition movement, the African National Congress. No target seemed too distant for Botha's forces — even one located "a thousand miles from anywhere".

Like most African independent governments, the non-aligned Seychelles regime was not particularly friendly to South Africa. Maybe Botha saw an opportunity to install a government he thought South Africa might be able to deal with. The Seychelles offered certain strategic advantages in its airfield and harbor facilities. And then there was that pesky Indian Ocean Tracking Station spying on any nuclear activity that might — or might not — be taking place in the area.

Several years later in Los Angeles, on what was to become my last VOA assignment, an old school chum and I put together a film scenario involving the Seychelles, South Africa, and the Indian Ocean Tracking Station. My friend, with whom I had graduated from high school, but who prefers to remain nameless, had become a highly successful screenwriter and film producer in Hollywood. Along the way, he had developed a reputation for being able to salvage good films out of bad scripts. Paramount Studios had asked him to take over a story about a fading TV journalist who had become a network anchorman, but now missed chasing chaos and who sought — just one more time — to get back in the action. For added color, the story was to be set in an exotic location, ideally one that had not been used before in a film — or at least not too recently.

He called me and I immediately thought of the Seychelles. Suppose, I suggested, our proposed hero gets tipped off to an upcoming coup well enough in advance so he can assemble his television crew and get on the scene as the action takes place. We could then restage Mike Hoare's short-lived invasion of the Seychelles. The real purpose behind Hoare's raid would be to knock out the Indian Ocean Tracking Station so that the South Africans could test the nuclear weapon they have been working at for years. Our hero stumbles on this bigger story by accident and eventually gets a front row seat at the big blast.

It seemed close enough to real life to be plausible and so we took the story to Paramount. There were several meetings, but no serious commitment. Then both of us got the word that Paramount was no longer interested. We had a drink together that night and the next day we heard that the studio had suffered a mysterious and devastating fire. "That will teach them," I said, "not to mess about with African folklore."

I was in Los Angeles helping VOA get ready for the 1984 Olympic Games. East Africa, the Seychelles notwithstanding, had turned out to be less interesting than I had hoped. After a year or so, when I was asked whether I might consider volunteering for the Mexico City bureau, I accepted the offer gladly. The job meant covering the turbulent politics of Central America, including a messy civil war in El Salvador. But having spent the past couple of years in Africa, I hadn't realized the level of the Reagan administration's active interest in the Salvadoran conflict until I got caught up in it.

When I began reporting the situation as I saw it, I quickly found myself running into problems with Washington. I was accused of spending too much time covering just one side of the conflict. I was striving for what I thought was balance in our reporting, but this was interpreted by VOA management as my seeming to take a position contrary to the Reagan administration. When I cited the provisions of the VOA Charter we had worked so hard to get passed into law, I got nowhere.

In the midst of the Salvadoran crisis, I received word from the Cuban Embassy in Mexico City that my long-awaited visa to cover the Caribbean Games in Havana had come through. VOA had not been able to send a correspondent to Cuba for years. Neither Havana nor Washington had been encouraging travel between the two countries. The Reagan administration had, in fact, imposed strict restrictions on U.S. citizens trying to visit Cuba. But exceptions were being made by both sides for journalists and the

Caribbean Games provided an excellent occasion, particularly since Fidel Castro wanted very much to make a success out of them.

From my own point of view, my Caribbean Games visa would make it possible for me to report a story I had longed to cover for years: everyday life in Fidel Castro's Cuba. Accordingly, I didn't spend much time at the games. I walked around Havana visiting stores, reporting what I found on their shelves. I interviewed African students from Angola and Namibia and had them describe their courses of study. I visited Ernest Hemingway's house and reported on its restoration as a national museum. And I met Fidel Castro.

The encounter was by no means casual. Journalists covering the games were invited to a farewell reception hosted by the Cuban government. We were taken to an official visitor's center in downtown Havana, but not allowed to bring cameras or tape recorders. I was standing, talking to a Cuban radio correspondent who had recently returned from Africa, when a familar grizzled figure dressed in military fatigues suddenly appeared before me, extending his hand in greeting. I shook his hand, and introduced myself in Spanish, but it was clear that our conversation was going to be through an official interpreter and fairly one-sided at that.

Castro started jovially, remarking that, given our respective heights, we should play perhaps basketball together. I agreed, but then he headed off into a tirade about Reagan's policies towards Latin America. When I could get in a brief word without appearing to interrupt him, I asked him what he thought about the recently inaugurated Radio Marti broadcasts aimed at Cuban listeners. They are not important, he said, but if Washington wants to send its broadcasts here, certainly there should be no objection to our playing Cuban music loudly across the United States.

He then moved on, as abruptly as he had appeared. As an interview with a head of state, it was not going to lead the news in Washington, but I thought it might make a nice light item on the breakfast shows. I filed it over the phone from my hotel room. The next morning I got a call from my office in Mexico City. There was a telex message from my boss — no longer Bernard Kamenske. who had moved on to CNN. "I want you," the message read, "on the next available flight to Washington."

An hour or so later, there was another telex message relayed by the Mexico City office: "I want you on the next available COMMERCIAL, repeat COMMERCIAL, flight to Washington." Apparently, VOA management was afraid I might charter a plane all the way from Havana.

It turned out I was being called on the carpet, not for anything I had written, but because there were critics of the Reagan administration who felt VOA had no business being in Cuba, let alone broadcasting a conversation with Fidel Castro. Furthermore, there was the reporting I had done on rebels in El Salvador. When I was shown clippings from several right-wing publications attacking me directly, I said that I was amazed that anyone took them seriously. "This administration takes them all seriously," I was told. "What we need right now in our Central American coverage is some benign neglect. We are currently over-exposed."

I flew back to Mexico City and stayed away from the political scene for a few weeks. But on my next trip to El Salvador, I was condemned to death — along with several other journalists — by a group of right-wing extremists. From Washington's point of view, it might have been better if they had been Marxists. I was already in enough trouble with the Reagan administration's hard-core conservatives.

Once the death list was published in the New York Times, any hope of benign neglect went out the window. I was offered the choice of opening a bureau for the 1984 Olympic Games in Los Angeles, or coming back to Washington to write feature stories. I had seen the corridor where the VOA feature writers had their cubby-hole offices. It was known as "Liberal's Lane" during the Reagan years.

Which is how I happened to be in Los Angeles when Helen Bodurtha Picard came back into my life, after an absence of eighteen years. I had heard somewhere that she and Fritz had moved to Iran and that he had died there. What I didn't know was that she had since rejoined USIA and had come back to Washington. Her assignment to Kigali, Rwanda had just been announced.

I decided to give her a call.

When she answered, the sound of her voice brought back memories that had lain dormant for decades.

"It's Sean," I said. "Do you remember me?"

"Of course," she replied, catching me by surprise. I had expected the need for explanations. We spoke for a long time, catching up on the years we had been out of touch. She said she was leaving shortly for Central America on a pleasure trip. I mentioned some of my favorite haunts in Costa Rica and Guatemala and suggested we might talk about Kigali, when she got back.

"Have you managed to get there, as well?," she asked.

"Not recently, I replied. "But the memory of Rwanda — like Nigeria — can stay with one for a lifetime." She laughed and I could not have been more pleased at the prospect of being back in touch with her.

In the meantime, Los Angeles took over. Two projects combined to dominate my working days and nights. The most immediate was launching a new VOA West Coast Bureau in time for the opening of the Olympic Games. The second was my old friend from the Seychelles, the Space Shuttle. The new bureau involved hiring and training additional staff, as well as building new facilities. The staffing part was easier, since I could largely control it myself. There was no shortage of talented and experienced people in the Los Angeles area. There was also no shortage of stories to be covered.

The facilities part of the project consisted of a new studio and office space, both of which were mostly out of my hands. Engineers and technical experts came out from Washington to do the design and order the equipment. All I could do was offer the occasional suggestion and help negotiate our way around any problem areas with the federal build-ing agency — our landlord — which had its own sometimes distinct and often unpredictable way of managing its properties.

As for the Space Shuttle, it was like greeting an old friend. There had been several years of flights since the first mission I covered from the Seychelles. Landing the spacecraft still presented problems, how-ever. Under the best of circumstances, the Shuttle would have been launched and recovered at Cape Canaveral. But local weather conditions at the Cape were rarely ideal for landing and the Space Shuttle often ended up at Edwards Air Force Base where an adjacent dry lake and California desert weather of-fered better conditions for bringing the spacecraft back to earth. This did not stop the national space agency — NASA — from trying repeatedly, and failing, to land the Shuttle at Cape Canaveral.

On more than one occasion in the small hours of the morning, I would answer a call from the VOA Newsroom in Washington to be told that a scheduled landing at the Cape had been cancelled by bad Florida weather.

"Get on up to Edwards as fast as you can," VOA would demand. "The Shuttle is now expected to land there at 0600 hours!"

Driving up to Edwards Air Force base from Los Angeles normally took an hour and a half, but on these occasions — in the middle of the night — I could cut the time down considerably. When Space Shuttle landings were rescheduled at the last minute from Cape Canaveral, there would be no possibility for the usual live broadcast from the Edwards runway. I would be lucky enough to verify to the Newsroom that the spacecraft and its crew were safely on the ground. I would then grab breakfast and get set to cover the crew's news conference that followed an hour or so later.

Normal — scheduled —- landings of the Space Shuttle and Edwards were much more easily handled. VOA engineers flew out from Washington and did most of the hard work. They would arrive at Los Angeles airport with several hundred pounds of equipment, rent a station wagon to haul it and themselves into the city, and then hire a Winnebago-type recreation vehicle to be converted into a broadcast studio.

Both vehicles would then be driven to Edwards Air Force Base — near Palmdale, an hour or so north of LA — where the Winnebago would be set up near the end of the long Edwards runway.

The VOA engineers would create a sound studio and control room inside the Winnebago which would be used for interviews and editing. But the live broadcast would be done from up on top of the vehicle where I had a clear view of the spacecraft's approach and landing. This could get a bit chilly on the high desert during a winter's pre-dawn darkness and thermal underwear was sometime required to guard against shivering and teeth-chattering while I was on the air. I would climb up to the Winnebago's roof and position myself, microphone in hand, so that I could hear the sonic boom of the spacecraft passing overhead. Listeners usually could hear it as well, even over my talking. I would describe the spacecraft's slow approach to the runway, noting that its rocket engines were shut down and that it was being flown to its landing without power — as a sort of space glider. Often the Shuttle itself could be heard as it approached the Edwards dry lake runway. Moving through the air with no engine noise, it made a strange, almost unearthly moaning sound — often loud enough to be picked up by my microphone and, like its sonic boom on arrival, passed on to listeners as part of the broadcast.

I covered both the Challenger and Columbia

shuttle landings at Edwards over a period of nearly two years. These two spacecraft would later be completely destroyed in flight and all of the astronauts on board would be killed. I count myself very lucky to have missed those stories. All my shuttle missions came home safely — for which I was personally very grateful.

One flight I covered at Edwards had nothing to do with the Space Shuttle. NASA wanted to test a new additive it hoped might make aviation fuel less inflammatory than the petroleum product currently in use by commercial airliners. The national space agency also had a new type of seat fabric theoretically less likely to catch fire in case of an airliner crash. In addition, there was an improved passenger seat belt designed to work better in a crash. NASA proposed deliberately crashing a remotely-controlled jet airliner at Edwards to test all three products simultaneously.

The test aircraft would be flown full speed into a controlled crash. Special steel barriers would rip the wings off to assure that the fuel tanks would be ruptured at the moment of impact, thus putting the new fuel additive to a realistic challenge. Cameras inside the aircraft would record the event up to the last mini-second before the crash and life-size human dummies would be positioned so that the new seat belts could be tested. The dummies, dressed realistically as airline passengers, would also be wired for telemetry to record the temperatures reached in the cabin, as well as the shock effects of the crash itself.

In advance of the test, NASA released photographs of the airliner's interior showing the dummies dressed up for the crash and seated in rows of typical economy class seats. They looked very realistic. Some were even smiling. A Los Angeles civil rights group then noticed that the dummies all appeared to be Caucasian. Pointing out that non-white people also travel on airliners, the group insisted that at least some of the dummies be made to represent people of color.

NASA agreed to look into the situation, but then reported back that all of the dummies in the front of the airliner were hard-wired into their seats for telemetry purposes and there was not enough time to replace them before the test. New dummies that appeared to be non-white could be added, NASA said, but they would have to be seated to the rear of the airliner.

I can't recall how this particular dilemma was resolved. It was clear, however, that NASA's new fuel additive did not prove to be a success. The airliner crashed as intended, but there was a huge fireball that virtually destroyed the test aircraft and practically everything in it. I never learned how much scientific data NASA salvaged from the scorched wreckage, but the racial diversity of the dummy passengers did not become an issue again.

The second of my principal tasks — the new VOA West Coast Bureau — was reaching completion, well before the deadline of the Los Angeles Olympics and it was time to begin thinking of an opening celebration. VOA Washington had kindly offered to help with some of the expenses. Tom Bradley, then Mayor of Los Angeles, had agreed to do a welcoming broadcast to athletes around the world from our new studios. I decided to put the two events together by having him officially declare the new VOA West Coast Bureau open. He said yes and I immediately asked Washington for additional funds to help turn the event into a suitably festive occasion.

Politics then raised its head. 1984 was an election year and Ronald Reagan was running for a second term as U.S. President. Mayor Tom Bradley, a prominent Democrat who had lost the race for California governor two years earlier, began being mentioned as a possible Vice Presidential candidate — against Reagan. My VOA Washington boss, a Reagan appointee, promptly withdrew his offer of support for the opening ceremony. When I mentioned this sad turn of events to several local merchants, who happened to be Democrats, I had no trouble obtaining substantial contributions of good California wine and cheese. The opening ceremony — and Bradley's pre-Olympic broadcast — were a considerable success, the Reagan administration notwithstanding.

Helen Picard returned from Central America not

long after this and we resumed our long distance telephone communication. She was interested in my recollections of Rwanda and I was interested in her recollections of the year we spent together in Nigeria. We agreed that it would be good to meet one more time, however briefly, before she left for Africa. I gallantly proposed a rendezvous halfway across the United States at some mutually agreeable midway point. For no particular reason except that it sounded nice, we chose Louisville, Kentucky — where neither of us had ever been before.

I offered to wear a red necktie so that she would be certain to recognize me. She allowed that this probably would not be necessary. As it turned out, she was right: we had no difficulty picking up where Nigeria had left off — 18 years before. I returned to Los Angeles after the Louisville week-end determined that I was not going to let Helen out of my life again.

My marriage to Anne had not benefited from the empty-nest syndrome, once both our sons had left for college. There seemed to be no end to the bickering back and forth, mostly over minor issues. Worse yet, there was little left by way of a genuine community of interests between us. It was as though Anne had her world and I had mine. Our sons were virtually on their own. My career as a broadcast journalist had already reached the point where I could see a succession of managerial-type assignments leading to an eventual retirement. At fifty-two years of age, the spark seemed gone out of practically everything in my life, except the possibility of being once again with Helen.

I told her I wanted to come to Washington and see her again before she left. She bought tickets to a National Symphony concert at Wolf Trap Farm and halfway through Beethoven's Ninth, I proposed marriage. To my great joy, she accepted. The next day, I met most of her immediate family for lunch at a Greek restaurant not far from where she had been living in Old Town Alexandria. There were the three older children Helen had adopted from Fritz Picard's first marriage. In addition, there was Catherine, Helen's eleven-year-old daughter from her own marriage to Fritz. We announced our engagement over humus and babaganouch. That night, close VOA friends held a highly impromptu engagement party at a farm in the Maryland countryside.

Early the next morning, I went into VOA headquarters in Washington, having phoned ahead to request an urgent appointment with my boss. He greeted me with some surprise, clearly wondering why I was not in Los Angeles and why I had requested a meeting on such short notice.

"Is this about a raise, or some new assignment?," he asked.

"Neither," I replied. "It is about the fact that I am quitting my job, divorcing my wife, and going to Africa to be with the woman I love."

"Under the circumstances," he said, "I think that probably qualifies as a genuine mid-life crisis."

"Quite so," I replied, "which is why I felt it was important that you should learn about it directly from me." I then told him I was giving him three months notice and I suggested that he have his administrative people send the necessary papers to Los Angeles as soon as possible.

I said good bye to Helen the next day, promising to write and phone much more often that I did in Nigeria.

As might be expected, Anne did not take the news lightly in Los Angeles. Her reaction to my request for a divorce to marry Helen traced an emotional trajectory that ran from outright denial and rejection over a period of months, during which I moved out of the house, to a gradual acceptance of what must have seemed to her as an inevitability. We finally agreed to an uncontested divorce based on irreconcilable differences. A financial agreement was reached between us that would make it possible for her to live fairly comfortably in California for the rest of her life, without having to seek employment.

The divorce would take six months to come into effect. I went ahead and bought a one-way ticket to Kigali, anyway.

For once, it was not chaos that I was chasing.

16.

Ending with Mandela, Mostly

Helen and I were married by the Mayor of Kigali in 1985. Our good friend John Blane, U.S. Ambassador to Rwanda, gave the bride away and also served as an official witness. We had asked that the ceremony take place in the garden at his residence, but the Mayor feared that his municipal writ might not extend to what was nominally U.S. territory. So we settled for the Mayor's parlor, which had formerly been his garage.

It was one of those rare good times to be in Rwanda. Peace had broken out across the land. The frequently warring Hutu and Tutsi tribes had settled down to a period of relative tranquility. The government of President Juvenal Habyarimana, a Hutu, seemed to be enjoying the support of the Rwandan people. At least it looked that way to most outsiders.

I began writing a book about chaos in the Congo.

Then came the shocking murder in 1985 of Dian Fossey, a 54 year old American zoologist who had been studying gorillas in the mountains along the Congolese border north of Kigali. She was found slashed to death with a *panga*, an African bush axe. Her research papers were scattered around her mountain cabin. Someone had apparently broken in by prying open one of its corrugated tin panels. The noise of the night time intrusion must have warned her since she was killed as she tried to stuff the wrong-sized bullets into her pistol.

Word of her death reached Helen and me on the shores of Lake Kivu where we were enjoying a New Year's holiday with Helen's 12-year-old daughter Catherine, and my son Brenton, a talented young photographer who was spending his college graduation present visiting Africa. When the Associated Press Bureau in Nairobi reached me by phone to ask that I start covering the Fossey story, they also requested photos. I offered Brenton's services as my AP photographer and they gratefully accepted.

Dian's body was wrapped in a sleeping bag and carried by hand from the Karisoke Research Station she had established on the 10,000 foot slopes of Mt. Visoke. It was there that she had written her best-selling book Gorillas in the Mist, which brought the plight of the endangered Mountain Gorilla species to world attention. The trail down from the mountainside was steep and slippery, but several teams of porters managed the descent successfully to the Kinigi trail head where trucks were waiting for the three hour journey by road to Kigali.

The American Embassy had in the meantime sent a telegram to Dian's parents in California, notifying them of her death. They cabled back that they wanted the body flown to the United States. This raised several immediate complications.

There was no commercial airline scheduled to fly out of Kigali for several days. Rwanda — which lies just south of the Equator — had, at that time, no mortuary facilities. Since the 1994 genocide, the situation may well have changed, but in 1985 when someone died, they were either promptly buried, or cremated, usually within 24 hours.

Kigali's Belgian-run hospital refused to accept Dian's body, but the American Embassy had better luck at the local brewery. Its manager agreed to keep her body in a cold storage room — providing the arrangement could be kept a secret. If word got around that the brewery was being used as a morgue, the manager feared that Rwandans — who are inclined to be superstitious anyway — might not buy as much beer on New Year's Eve, which was when the brewery normally made its biggest profits.

Rosamond Carr, who had helped Dian Fossey get established on Mt. Visoke in 1967, had since become her oldest and closest friend in Rwanda. She recalled Dian once told her she wanted to be buried in the forest graveyard she had created near her research station for the Mountain Gorillas killed over the years by poachers. The American Embassy passed this wish along by telegram to Dian's parents, pointing out that it would also cost them several thousand dollars to fly her body back to California. They quickly agreed to her burial in Rwanda.

The Embassy carpentry shop had built her a pine coffin — two of them in fact, the first having proved to be much too short. Four teams of six porters each were hired to carry Dian back up to her research station on Tuesday, December 31, 1985. It had been raining hard during the week-end and the trail was even more treacherous. I remember climbing hand over hand up the muddy slope — wondering how the porters behind me were dealing with the heavy casket. But not so seriously concerned that I was willing to slide back down the path to find out. Brenton, having just climbed Mt. Kilimanjaro in Tanzania, scampered up and down the mountainside showing no strain whatsoever.

Leading the mourners was 73-year-old Rosamond Carr who had begun the climb earlier in the day, knowing that it might take her longer than the others. She was accompanied by her friend Reverend Elton Wallace, an American missionary who would conduct Dian Fossey's brief graveside ceremony. Wayne

McGuire, a University of Oklahoma reseacher and the last person to see Dian alive, stood slightly in the background during the service. Karl Hofmann, a newly assigned Vice Consul at the American Embassy in Kigali was in the front row, facing Reverend Wallace. Hofmann had another reason for being there. Washington had assigned him to track the progress of the Rwandan police investigation into Fossey's murder. Brenton quickly shot the pictures he needed and we hurried back down the trail to report the story by telephone to the AP bureau in Nairobi.

It was not easy to raise anyone at Rwanda's international phone service on New Year's Eve. When I finally got through to an operator, she told me she had no lines open to Nairobi. I should try later. I did. Many times throughout the evening. Finally, in exasperation, I said to her, "Listen, if my country can put a *mzungu* on the moon, you can surely get me through to Nairobi." *Mzungu* is the kiSwahili word for white man. My remark made little actual sense, but she saw the weird humor of it, giggled, and finally found me a line to Nairobi.

I dictated a quick story to the AP and made arrangements for someone from the bureau to meet our daughter Catherine's plane as it transited Nairobi airport the following day. In the great foreign correspondent's tradition of pigeoning film and text, she carried Brenton's film out with her on her way to her

school in Switzerland. My story on Dian's funeral
featured the first of what would be many AP by-lines
over the years to come. Brenton's photos appeared
in newspapers around the world and were eventually bought by Life Magazine and published in
Farley Mowat's excellent 1987 book Woman In the
Mists — The Story of Dian Fossey and the Mountain
Gorillas of Africa. His credit line would make any
photographer envious: "Photo by Brenton Kelly/*Life*
Magazine".

Wayne McGuire stayed on at the research station after Dian's funeral. He tried to continue with
his doctoral thesis, manage the center, and keep up
Dian's anti-poaching patrols, but he was soon faced
with limited resources and a diminishing staff. The
Rwandan police had begun taking his trackers away,
and holding them indefinitely in jail for questioning.

Eventually he got some help from Ian Redmond,
who headed the London foundation established
earlier by Dian to raise funds for gorilla research.
Redmond visited Rwanda in early January to inventory Dian's possessions, and help decide the Karisoke
Research Station's future. He was joined on the trip
up the mountain by Vice Consul Hofmann, who was
also interested in completing an inventory of Dian's
effects.

Later in Kigali, Redmond met with reporters and
announced that Dian might have been the victim of
hired assassins. He said he had discovered a copy of

a letter among her effects in which she told of having seized a witchcraft amulet from a poacher brought to Karisoke by her trackers in November. She described the man as becoming violently upset when she took the amulet from him. She wrote that he tried desperately to get it back before she had him taken away by police.

Redmond suggested that Dian may have been killed when the poacher arranged from prison to have someone break into her cabin and try to recover the amulet. Although her bedroom had been thoroughly ransacked by her attackers, he said he found many valuables left behind, including more than 2,000 dollars in cash and travelers checks. "All the evidence," he said, "suggests a very professional killing, perhaps by hired assassins…".

Redmond turned his findings over to the Rwandan police, but they seemed to have their own notion who killed Dian, and it was not a Rwandan poacher. On February 8, 1986, they brought Wayne McGuire to Kigali for questioning. He stayed with Karl Hofmann, who by now had become a fairly close acquaintance.

McGuire later said Hofmann told him he should leave Karisoke and get out of Rwanda altogether. He would have been perfectly free to do so, since he was not under any arrest or restraining order. McGuire could tell from the questions asked by the police that he was now being considered a prime suspect by the

Rwandan government. Curiously, he did not take Hofmann's advice.

Instead, he went back up the mountain to try and complete his research. As he later put it, "There's an old saying that the line between dedication and stupidity is a thin one. Maybe I crossed that line, I don't think I truly realized what was happening. Or maybe I denied it to myself."

World interest in the story was growing. I got a call from the NBC bureau in Nairobi asking if I would help in the arrangements for a television crew to visit the research station and film Wayne McGuire and the gorillas for the "Today Show." I got them all accredited with the Rwandan Information Ministry and hired two Land Rovers and drivers to meet them at the airport. We then drove to the Kinigi trail head where Wayne was waiting to take them up the mountain.

I had agreed to meet them at the trail head with the Land Rovers in two days. It had rained during most of their stay and the trip up and down the mountain was not easy, particularly with all their equipment. Mud-spattered and hungry, they had were nonetheless delighted with the results of the trip and we stopped off at a hotel on the way to Kigali to celebrate the outcome with beer and pizza. While we there, members of the televison crew left their shoes and boots on the terrace to have the mud cleaned off by the hotel staff. They did such a superb job of cleaning and polishing, the crew decided to present the staff with the shoes as a gift, especially after I pointed out that there was a good Bata shoe store in Kigali. Unfortunately, Bata was closed by the time we reached town. Several of the crewmembers had dinner that night at a posh Kigali restaurant in their stocking feet, but no one seemed to mind terribly.

The NBC "Today" sequence on the Fossey gorillas proved a big success. So much so, I got a call from a Hollywood producer asking if I could help with a film version of Dian's book Gorillas in the Mist. He was interested in hiring me to assist his screenwriter. I quickly agreed to do so. The salary and expenses were generous and I was finding reporting assignments becoming rather few and far between, once the excitement of Dian's funeral subsided. Not even the investigation into her murder continued to arouse much interest among news editors. So I was happy to meet Anna Hamilton Phalen and her husband at the Kigali airport in May and begin drawing my first paycheck as a very minor Hollywood mogul.

The Phelans spent ten days in Rwanda. I introduced them to Karl Hofmann in Kigali, and then I dropped them off on the trail to the research station where they visited Dian's cabin and spoke at length with Wayne McGuire and others who had worked with her. I also took them to Gisenye on Lake Kivu near the Congo border where they met with Dian's friend Rosamond Carr.

Anna Phelan was interested in visiting the space that Dian had occupied while she was in Rwanda, as well as sharing the memories that people retained of their relationships with Dian. She had already come to the conclusion that Gorillas in the Mist, would take up a very small part of the film's story, perhaps little more than the title itself. What intrigued Phalen was Dian's motivation. Why did she abandon the comforts of a sheltered life in California to come to Africa and devote her life to the study and conservation of the Mountain Gorilla? This seemed to Phalen to be where the real Dian Fossey story was to be found.

After returning to California, Phelan happened to see a space adventure film starring Sigourney Weaver. She told me she was immediately struck by the apparent physical resemblance between Weaver and the photographs taken of Dian Fossey at the same age. She also felt that the sense of Dian's determination to protect the Mountain Gorillas came through in Weaver's screen portrayal of a woman defending a young child from attack. Phalen was convinced she had found the only actress who could truly play Dian Fossey. She hung a large photograph of Sigourney Weaver over her desk as she completed the script for Gorillas in the Mist.

As it turned out, Anna Hamilton Phelan of Universal International Studios and I were not the only people working on a Dian Fossey film project. At least two other Hollywood studios were sending writers to Rwanda. Warner Brothers had already commissioned Farley Mowat to do a book as well as a film based on Dian's life. Rosamond Carr told me she was interviewed by so many writers, she lost count. "I only wish," she said, " someone would finally say something nice about Dian."

On behalf of Universal International, I met with officials from the Rwandan government and tried to obtain an exclusive agreement to film a story in Rwanda based on Dian Fossey's life. This could be accomplished, I was advised, but it would probably require a profit-sharing arrangement with the Rwandan government, or at least some other "significant financial contribution".

Rwanda, one of the poorest nations in the world, clearly viewed Hollywood's gorilla wars as a new and totally unexpected source of foreign aid from America. But Universal International, having announced that it had already committed 17 million dollars to the Fossey film, was not interested in sharing unmade profits in Rwanda — to its later regret.

Meanwhile, Wayne McGuire was quietly informed through Karl Hofmann that Rwanda intended to arrest him for the murder of Dian Fossey. The advance notice was intended to give McGuire the option of leaving the country quickly, thus avoiding a public trial which could prove difficult for all concerned, particularly McGuire if he were to be found guilty.

Karl Hofmann later told me he was convinced

the Rwandans had no real evidence against McGuire, but were perfectly capable of finding him guilty, anyway — in which case he could face execution by a firing squad. Nobody really wanted that to happen, least of all the Rwandans which is why they had tipped off the Americans in the first place. There being no extradition treaty between Rwanda and the United States, all McGuire had to do was go back to Oklahoma and forget about ever returning to Rwanda.

Oddly, McGuire seemed in no hurry to leave. He did go to Kigali where he made several calls to the United States, seeking advice over an open phone line as to whether or not he should flee Rwanda. His mother sent him a first class ticket to Paris on Air France which may have helped him decide to leave. But after clearing Kigali airport customs and immigration, he learned that his flight had mechanical problems and would not leave as scheduled. Air France was going to put him up in Kigali's best hotel. He stayed there for two days, and finally left for Paris — after once again dutifully clearing Rwandan customs and immigration. His Kigali departure was thus well advertised to the Rwandan authorities — who made no effort to interfere with it.

The Rwandans waited several weeks — possibly to give McGuire sufficient time to get all the way back to Oklahoma — and then they issued an international warrant for his arrest which they admitted had no validity in the United States. McGuire was strongly advised by his American attorney not to go back to Rwanda and face trial. It was advice, for once, that he followed.

Meanwhile, Universal International and Warner Brothers studios decided between themselves that there was no point trying to outbid each other while the Rwandan government watched greedily from the sidelines. They cut a deal in Hollywood and jointly produced Dian Fossey's Gorillas in the Mist, starring, as it turned out, Sigourney Weaver — with a script by Anna Hamilton Phalen.

As for Wayne McGuire, he was convicted of Dian's murder December 11, 1986 during a 25-minute trial in Rwanda which he wisely did not attend. A week later, he was sentenced to death by firing squad — an event in which he also declined to participate.

I went back to writing my book about the Congo.

Rwanda had settled down, but both NBC and the AP continued to call on my services from time to time, as did the Christian Science Monitor radio news program and the Voice of America. The USIA speaker's bureau also kept me traveling throughout Africa on journalism lecture and work shop assignments. Later on, I ran voter education radio and television projects for the National Democratic Institute in Namibia and Mozambique. Altogether, it was a fairly active retirement. In my spare moments, I would return to the Congo book project.

Helen pursued her rediscovered diplomatic career in Africa, which had been interrupted during the years she had been married to Fritz Picard. After Rwanda, we moved together to Senegal and then Swaziland which gave us a vantage point on the rapidly changing events in neighboring South Africa. It also put me in much closer touch with the AP and NBC bureaus in Johannesburg. The State Department facilitated our travel by giving us extra passports — one of which was always kept "sanitized" from any South African immigration stamps. Many African nations would, at that time, routinely deny entry to any traveler whose passport contained evidence of having visited South Africa.

In July 1987, NBC asked me to report on what turned out to be a historical milestone of major political importance for South Africa. It was a meeting in Dakar, Senegal between exiled leaders of the African National Congress, which was banned at the time in South Africa, and a group of influential white, mostly Afrikaans-speaking South Africans. Organized by IDASA, the Institute for a Democratic Alternative in South Africa, the conference explored various strategies for bringing about fundamental change in South Africa. It looked, as well, at the possible structure the government of a free South Africa might take. Additional topics included the building of national unity and South Africa's future economy under a democratically-elected government. Altogether, it was a very ambitious and highly controversial agenda, particularly when viewed in Johannesburg or Pretoria.

The apartheid regime actively discouraged contacts of this sort, but was unable to stop them from taking place outside South Africa. The fact that the Dakar meeting occurred under the personal sponsorship of Senegalese President Abdou Diouf and Madame Danielle Mitterand, wife of the President of France, made it all the more of an irritant to the South African government.

I interviewed Thabo Mbeki in Dakar, as well as several other ANC representatives who would later serve as government ministers in Nelson Mandela's first cabinet. Mandela himself was still in prison. I would very much like to have interviewed him, but Pretoria had managed to keep him hidden from the international press for years. He had not, in fact, been seen in public since being sentenced to life imprisonment on Robben Island in 1964. Those who had seen him in prison described him as being in reasonably good health, despite his age and the long years of imprisonment. But few people had any clear idea of what he actually looked like. It was against the law to publish his picture in South Africa, even if you could manage to obtain a recent one.

Among his few outside visitors in 1986 was a

special delegation picked by Commonwealth Prime Ministers to call on Mandela in prison, ascertain the state of his health, and seek his views on the future of South Africa. By that time, he had been transferred to a prison on the mainland, but he was still being kept in isolation.

In his autobiography, Mandela describes the preparations for his meeting with the Commonwealth delegation. "The government regarded my session with the group as something extraordinary." The prison commander told him, 'Mandela, we want you to see these people on an equal footing. We don't want you to wear those old prison clothes, so this tailor will take your measurements and outfit you with a proper suit.'

Mandela recalled, "The tailor must have been some kind of wizard, for the very next day I tried on a pinstriped suit that fitted me like a glove. I was also given a shirt, tie, shoes, socks and underwear. The commander admired my new attire. 'Mandela, you look like a prime minister now, not a prisoner,' he said and smiled."

As the meeting with the Commonwealth delegation got underway, Mandela noted, "We were joined by two significant observers: Kobie Coetsee (South African Minister of Justice) and Lieutenant General W. H. Willemse, the commissioner of prisons. Like the tailor, these two men were there to take my measure."

The delegates were impressed with the 67-year-old prisoner. As they later reported to the Commonwealth Secretariat, "We were first struck by his physical authority—by his immaculate appearance, his apparent good health and his commanding presence. In his manner, he exuded authority and received the respect of all around him, including his jailors. Mr. Mandela, according to all the evidence, is a unifying, commanding and popular leader, Recent opinion polls, as well as our personal observations, revealed that blacks, Indians and coloreds look overwhelmingly to Nelson Mandela as the leader of a non-racial South Africa."

I had been intrigued by Mandela since first reading about him in the South African press during the early 1960s. Reporters marveled at his ability to keep out of the clutches of the South African security services. He always seemed to be one step ahead of them. He would be seen publicly in South Africa and then suddenly vanish, only to reappear at an international conference in Ghana, or Ethiopia. When he was finally trapped in a South African police roadblock, I immediately suspected my own government had a hand in his capture. As an American diplomat posted in Southern Africa at the time, I was fully aware of the close cooperation that existed between our own security agencies and those of the South African police and military.

It turned out that I was not alone in my suspicions.

There are many versions of the events leading

up to Mandela's arrest near Howick, South Africa on August 5, 1962. Here are three of the most authoritative, beginning with Mandela's own account: "The most oft-cited story was that an American consular official with connections to the CIA had tipped off the authorities. This story has never been confirmed and I have never seen any reliable evidence as to the truth of it. Although the CIA has been responsible for many contemptible activities in its support for American imperialism, I cannot lay my capture at its door. In truth, I had been imprudent about maintaining the secrecy of my movements. In retrospect, I realized that the authorities could have had a myriad of ways of locating me on my trip to Durban. It was a wonder in fact that I wasn't captured sooner." .

Perhaps the best researched version of the Mandela capture was written by James Sanders who did much of the fact-checking for Mandela: The Authorized Biography by Anthony Sampson which was published in 1999. Sanders went on to write his own book in 2006 and investigated all of the known accounts of the Mandela arrest. He even went so far as to interview Donald Rickard, the alleged CIA officer involved, who told him he would be "making a mistake" in citing Rickard as the man who turned Mandela over to the South African police.

My own suspicions have been somewhat eased by one of Mandela's closest ANC associates, Ahmed Kathrada, who had been imprisoned with him on

Robben Island. Years after the arrest, Kathrada wrote: "Mandela is a proud man and not without a touch of vanity. By the time he went underground in 1961, his most recognizable feature was his beard. Photos of the bearded Mandela had appeared in newspapers and leaflets. I was among the small group who had been charged with organizing every aspect of his underground life."

Kathrada located the safe houses and the venues for secret meetings. He provided for Mandela's transport and set up contacts with selected media people. To make all of this possible, he said Mandela had to be "disguised and transformed into a 'new man'. Among other things he had to forsake his stylish and expensive clothing. But above all, he had to shave his beard."

Mandela stubbornly refused to shave, according to Kathrada. "We regarded this de-bearding as absolutely essential. but couldn't persuade him. It must be remembered that the security forces had launched a countrywide hunt for him, setting up roadblocks, stopping vehicles at random, searching houses, questioning people. But the beard remained. It was there when photos taken in an Algerian army camp appeared in the press. And it was still there when he was eventually arrested in Howick on August 5, 1962."

Kathrada's account of the failed de-bearding campaign and Mandela's own admission of imprudence tend to take the CIA off the hook, as far as I am concerned — particularly since no one has been able to prove otherwise over the past half century. However, this didn't make me feel any easier the first time I encountered Mandela. As an American, I expected my questions might receive a somewhat frosty reply.

It was at a news conference in Namibia, shortly before the elections that brought Mandela to office as the first democratically-elected President of South Africa. I had asked him one or two questions during the conference and, since he seemed friendly, I ventured over afterwards to shake his hand. He looked up at me and, smiling broadly, said: "You know, you intimidate me with your height."

I searched my mind for a good answer and remembered the photos of him wearing boxing gloves in a ring, looking very much like Joe Louis, the world champion prize fighter.

"Ah, Mister President," I replied, "I'm certain you are the better boxer."

He threw his head back and laughed. "In my youth, " he said, "in my youth."

I covered his election campaign in South Africa and his presidential inauguration for the Associated Press. I could not have asked for a better story to cap my career as a reporter. Years later, when Helen and I were living in Cape Town and Mandela was no longer president, he and his wife acquired a house near us in the suburb of Bishopscourt — not far from the university where she had recently been named Chancellor. A reporter from one of the Afrikaans newspapers asked me what I thought about having the Mandelas living next door. "Well," I said, "this neighborhood has needed some racial diversity for years. Now it is getting it from the top down."

The same could have been said for all of South Africa — and none too soon.

Notes

Chapter 5:

Page 64 "Moroccans and Algerians were among..."
Bernard Fall, <u>Hell In A Very Small Place</u>, J.P.
Lippincott, New York 1967 page 439.

Page 65 "I learned much later..." State Department
telegram: CONFIDENTIAL AMCONSUL RABAT
TO DEPT DECEMBER 31, 1954, <u>Foreign
Relations of the United States</u> 1952-54 Volume XI
AFRICA AND SOUTH ASIA part 1.

Chapter 7:

Page 109 "As Hoyt later..." <u>Captive in the Congo</u>,
by Michael P. E. Hoyt, Naval Institute Press,
Annapolis, MD 2000, page 65.

Page 110 "David Halberstam…" <u>The Making of a Quagmire</u>, by David Halberstam, Random House, New York 1965, page 10.

Page 173 "Having assessed the Congolese…" <u>The African Dream: the Diaries of the Revolutionary War in the Congo</u>, by Ernesto "Che" Guevara, Grove Press, New York, 2000, page 26.

Page 124 "Rogers suggested…" <u>Mercenary</u>, by Mike Hoare, Corgi Books 1968, page 261.

<u>Chapter 9:</u>

Page 162 "Seizing the moment…" <u>The International Politics of the Nigerian Civil War</u>, by John Stremlau, Princeton University Press, Princeton, New Jersey 1977, pages 121-127.

Page 175 "The final act…" <u>The Brother's War</u>, by John de St. Jorre, Houghton Mifflin Company, Boston 1972, page 401.

<u>Chapter 11:</u>

Page 195 "The signs were all … " <u>Trial By Fire: the 1972 Easter Offensive, America's Last Vietnam Battle</u>, by Dale Andrade, Hippocrene Books, Inc. New York, 1995, page 28.

Page 198: "Painful as these…" <u>The Rescue of BAT 21</u>, by Darrel D. Whitcomb, Naval Institute Press, Annapolis, MD, 1998, page 112.

<u>Chapter 12:</u>

Page 232 "The answer, as it…" <u>The War of Atonement</u>, by Chaim Herzog, Little, Brown and Company, Boston 1975, pages 33-35.

Page 233, "Clearly, he later…" <u>Years of Upheaval</u> by Henry Kissinger, Little, Brown and Company, Boston, 1982, page 463.

Page 233, "Kissinger's remarkable ability…" <u>The Road to Ramadan</u> by Mohamed Heikal, Quadrangle/The New York Times Book Co., New York 1975, page 205.

Pages 234-240, Kissinger quotes all drawn from <u>Years of Upheaval.</u>

Page 240, "Transcripts of the … " <u>Nixon and Kissinger,</u> by Robert Dallek, HarperCollins, New York 2007, page 616.

Page 242, "Israeli journalist Matti…" <u>The Secret Conversations of Henry Kissinger,</u> by Matti Golam, Quadrangle/The New York Times Book Co., New York 1976, page 62.

Page 243, "Initially, Kissinger saw..." <u>Crisis: The Anatomy of Two Major Foreign Policy Crises</u>, by Henry Kissinger, Simon & Schuster, New York, 2004, page 293.

Chapter 13:

Page 252, "The internal pressures..." <u>A Basement Seat to History</u>, by Philomena Jurey, Linus Press, Washington DC 1995, page 61.

Page 258, "Fortunately, not everyone..." <u>To Set the Record Straight</u>, by John Sirica, W.W. Norton & Company, New York 1979, pages 203-205, 222.

Page 262, "The fact that..." <u>Nixon and Kissinger</u>, by Robert Dallek, HarperCollins Publishers, New York 2007, page 310.

Page 262, "I shared Nixon's views..." <u>Years of Upheaval</u>, by Henry Kissinger, Little, Brown and Company, Boston 1982, pages 116-117.

Page 263, "Another White House..." <u>Kissinger: A Biography</u>, by Walter Isaacson, Simon & Schuster, New York 1992, pages 330.

Page 269, "On August 1..." <u>Palace Politics</u>, by Robert Hartmann, McGraw-Hill, New York 1980, pages 125-137, see also <u>Thirty-One Days</u>, by Barry

Wirth, Random House, New York 2006, pages 19
and 204-205.

Page 270, "Judge Sirica was..." <u>To Set the Record</u>
<u>Straight</u>, by John Sirica, W.W. Norton & Company,
New York 1979, pages 232-235.

<u>Chapter 14:</u>

Page 283, "On April 14..." <u>Voice of America — A</u>
<u>History</u>, by Alan L. Heil, Jr., Columbia University
Press, New York 2003, page 476.

Page 284, "We have got a..." <u>A Basement Seat</u>
<u>to History</u>, by Philomena Jurey, Linus Press,
Washington DC 1995, pages 88-89.

Page 288, "When reporters on..." <u>Palace Politics</u>,
by Robert Hartmann, McGraw-Hill, New York
1980, pages 321-323.

<u>Chapter 16:</u>

Page 340, "In his autobiography..." <u>Long Walk to</u>
<u>Freedom</u>, by Nelson Mandela, Back Bay Books/
Little, Brown and Company, New York 1994, page
528.

Page 342, "Perhaps the best..." <u>Apartheid's Friends</u>
<u>— The Rise and Fall of South Africa's Secret</u>

Service, by James Sanders, John Murray, London 2006, page 17.

Page 343, "Mandela stubbornly refused..."
Mandela —The Authorized Portrait, Andrews McMeel Publishing, Kansas City, Missouri 2006, page 103.

Acknowledgements

Many people have helped me in the process of writing this memoir. Those I would particularly like to thank include Philomena Jurey; Anne, Jim and Lloyd Gould; Amy Bell Mulaudzi; Paul Rifkin; Catherine Picard and Eric Bercovici who got me started in the first place. Anna Ely of Outskirts Press kindly saw the project through — as did my agent, Alison Picard.

Index

CPSIA information can be obtained at www.ICGtesting.com
Printed in the USA
LVOW080821070612

285055LV00001B/9/P

9 781432 7455